MW01223773

NO ROADS LEAD TO ROME

R.S. GOMPERTZ

VIA DEL PRAT

No Roads Lead to Rome

ISBN: 978-0-9825829-0-9

Second Edition
LSI 011010

Library of Congress Control Number: 2009940539

www.noroadsleadtorome.com

Vía del Prat

Prologue

When it comes to assassination, execution is everything.

With no witnesses to testify otherwise, and no documents to the contrary, Hadrian seized the reins of the Roman Empire. His claim to the imperial purple, a last minute writ of adoption, was as thin as the vellum it was scribbled on. To avoid civil war, the legions rallied behind him. After the deaths of four opposing senators, the surviving majority gave their unanimous consent.

On the site of the Golden Milestone, the geographic center of the world from which all distance was measured, Hadrian built a column commemorating the former Emperor's conquests and with great ceremony, buried Trajan's ashes at the foot of the monument.

Then, reversing everything Trajan had fought for, Hadrian issued a confounding decree. Status quo might be Latin, but it was not his credo. The empire, he said, was swollen to the point of bursting. Rome was overextended, her borders too vast to maintain. Where Trajan had spent his lifetime burning the benefits of civilization across the sacred groves of ungrateful barbarians, the new ruler would shrink the empire. He would set free those who could never be governed, and build a wall around those who could.

One
I

123 AD.

Centurion Marcus Valerius, a veteran from North Africa, struck fast. He knocked the suspicious conscript to the ground and planted a wet sandal squarely on his chest. The quarry foreman where Valerius had spent the night insisted that the young man called Gaius Severus had been drafted, but Valerius took nothing for granted. Too seasoned to accept anything or anyone at face value, the sharp tip of his short *gladius* was the perfect instrument to probe for truth.

"What's the best stone for building an aqueduct?" Valerius snarled. A military levy in a peaceful province was not without precedent as soldiers were always needed elsewhere in the empire. Severus looked harmless enough, but before delivering him to the local garrison, Valerius wanted to double check the kid's *bona fides.*

Severus tried to speak, but the sharp sword point pressing into his throat made it difficult to do more than gurgle. He looked up the length of the blade at the short, bronze-skinned centurion and realized that the masquerade was over.

Severus' recently cropped hair—the only disguise he could muster in the day since the security sweeps—slouched backwards in stiff brown clumps. Following his father's instruction, he had fled to the quarry, only to be snared in a trap and marched back towards Tarraco, the provincial capital. Now he was flat on his spine with steel at his throat and mud wicking up his backside. Alive or dead, he would soon join his unfortunate kin.

"You don't fool me, kid," Valerius said. "You're as phony as the rest of this province."

Centurion Valerius had been in Hispania for a week and already hated her rutted roads and cold, gray skies. Somewhere along his journey from Mauritania, the sun had disappeared, confirming to him that the upper reaches of the world were bathed in darkness. Valerius did not know why Governor Biberious had summoned him, but he hoped to leave as soon as he secured his pension and honorable discharge from the emperor's service.

A murder of crows cawed loudly as they passed overhead; there was no mistaking the omen. Something was amiss. Silently cursing the brown hills and northern chill, Valerius choked down a shiver, ran a chapped hand over his close-cut hair, and scanned for more portents.

"A real stone mason would know the answer," Valerius said. His small muscular frame tightened. "Assume your life depends on it."

"There's an aqueduct just outside of Tarraco, sir," Severus said cautiously. He paused to think about the question, but instead wondered if Valerius was also masquerading. What kind of legionary would get so worked up about an aqueduct? Severus tried to twist out from underneath the knife, but Valerius gave him no quarter. "Some say it was built by Pompey the Great, sir."

"I didn't ask for a history lesson, schoolboy." Valerius tightened his grip on the *gladius,* the perfect tool for justice at arm's length. It would be sad to kill a boy, but sadder yet to be killed by one. A worthless conscript would not be missed, a missing spy wouldn't be sought after, and either way, the rain would wash away his forgotten blood. "The aqueduct—what's it made of?"

"The columns and arches are made from blocks of travertine, from the quarry where you found me." Severus stuttered at first, but then spoke more rapidly. "Tufa stone would work better, but we don't have any here. The coliseum at Rome is made of both. I'm told that my grandfather helped to build it. It probably won't last long though, because—"

"Enough." Enough to suspect, but not enough to strike. Valerius withdrew his blade an inch.

"Did you know, sir, the columns are hollow and filled with concrete?" Severus shifted away from the blade and kept talking, shrill and rapid. "Quicklime and a mineral powder; you mix it dry so it sets hard especially when you're sealing a watertight pipeline or rendering an open channel. Underground conduits and lead pipes are better for long hauls—more difficult for sneaky farmers to tap. I'd wager that half the piss in Hispania started as stolen water."

"Stop!" Valerius shouted. "You talk too much for a quarry boy."

Valerius sheathed his *gladius*, but kept a watchful eye on Severus. That the kid had answered the question proved nothing; any half-trained spy would have thought through the basic details of his cover story. Valerius had not spent the last twenty years outwitting Hades himself just to be entrapped by a stool pigeon like Severus.

"Get up. Start marching unless you want to feed the jackals."

Gaius Severus stood up slowly and kept a respectful distance from the cranky old veteran. Valerius looked to be in his mid thirties—a relic in tarnished armor. "Are you really a centurion?" Severus asked. "You're not a slaver, are you?"

Valerius indicated their new direction with a rough sweep of his hand. "March in front of me and stop talking."

The sky darkened a second before a bolt of stiff lightning crackled over the damp chaparral. The air smelled of goats and smoke and these omens were not lost on Marcus Valerius. When the thunder shook overhead, he stumbled over a weed-infested pothole.

"Curse this stupid province!" Valerius shouted. "Of all the vexed places to be in November."

November was generally a lucky month, but Valerius knew that certain days required special vigilance. Soon, on the dreadful eighth day of November, the gates to the underworld would open and no mortal soul would be safe until they slammed shut again.

Valerius fought another shiver and tightened the belts of his weathered cuirass. Instead of spending his last two months of service patrolling a warm border on the southern edge of the empire, he was now wandering half-frozen in the crumbling province of Hispania. "Why weren't those ruts filled?" he asked.

"The worst road in Egypt is better than this goat trail. Where are the vexed road crews and engineers, anyway?"

"They've all gone north to build Hadrian's Wall," Severus answered. "Surely you know about the wall, Centurion? That must be why I was conscripted. Rome needs stonemasons and quarrymen like me to build a great wall across Britannia."

"The wall? That vexed wall. So that's your story, is it? You're a wall builder?" Valerius found that shouting made his frustration more bearable, so he shouted louder. "Why is our glorious emperor building a wall across some moldy island? Enemies are defeated with swords, not bricks."

"But sir," Severus said, "Hadrian's Wall will prevent barbarians from destroying civilization."

Valerius laughed. "Is that what your mother taught you?"

"Please don't mention my mother, sir."

Valerius did not see the sadness on Severus' face. Instead, he lost himself in a chance to rail against a fraction of all that had been bothering him lately. "Since when do warriors build walls? When did Rome go soft? All barbarians understand is force. Force is the only thing they respect."

"Perhaps in the long run respect is better than force," Severus said. "Maybe if we treat people with respect, they'll be more loyal. They might steal less, pay their taxes, and stop rebelling."

"Now you're talking like one of those vexed Christians," Valerius said, lowering his voice to a growl.

Before Severus could respond, the dark sky unleashed an angry hailstorm. The frozen pellets bouncing off Valerius' armor rattled like a drum roll. The men ran and took refuge under an olive tree until the assault subsided.

"Frozen stones!" Valerius said. "What in Jove's name was that?" He shook a few cold granules from his sandals and wondered how to interpret this latest dark omen.

"Hail, sir," Severus said. He looked over Valerius' dull and dented gear. Something about the gruff old geezer did not add up. A real centurion would never look so ragged. Had he plucked the uniform off a dead man? Even taking his story at face value, why would a North African soldier be banging around in Hispania?

There was more than one reason to harbor suspicion. "After such a long trip, you'll need to polish your armor."

"Polish my own armor?" Valerius grabbed the scruff of Severus' tunic and jerked him forward. Normally, he would have given the impudent conscript a good drubbing; instead, he just sent him spinning. "In the old days," he said, "we had a team of slaves ready to polish armor, sharpen swords, and maintain our gear in fighting condition. It all worked just fine until some Roman numeral cruncher decided slaves were too expensive. Can you believe it, *slaves* too expensive?"

"Sorry," Severus said, once he recovered his balance. "Who polishes the armor now, sir?"

"You." Valerius gave his charge a quick once-over and saw that the kid might be useful for something. "My sword needs to look sharp when I meet Governor Biberious. As soon as we get to Tarraco, you'll have it shining like the sun."

"Governor Biberious is dead, sir," Severus said, but Valerius had already charged ahead to investigate something rustling in the nearby shrubs.

Valerius threw a sharp stone into the underbrush and an offended jackal—another ruinous portent—scurried away. "Four-legged jackals are nothing to worry about," Valerius said. "In Rome, they walk upright."

A light rain began to fall and soon the drizzle turned into a merciless downpour.

Valerius was on edge: cold, wet, and fed up with being lost on the west side of nowhere. "It's all part of Hadrian's vexed *Imperial Transformation*," he muttered. He stopped a hair's breadth short of blasphemy after realizing that the bony scorpion Severus might be eager to witness a treasonous outburst. The kid, a mere sapling of sixteen, was clever beyond his days but Valerius hadn't spent twenty years outwitting Rome's southernmost enemies only to be taken off-guard by a young spy in a backwards province.

Trust no one. Say nothing. Watch your back. Those were words to live by.

"*Transformation?*" Severus said. "Is that Latin?"

"It is now," Valerius said. He quickened the pace and tried to ignore the rain and whatever Gaius Severus was now jabbering on about. There was something unsettling about the kid's smart talk and smooth hands. In which nursery had they found this one?

"There must be some logic to this *transformation*," Severus continued. He was a head taller than the sun-baked foreigner in front of him and couldn't quite adjust his swinging gait to match the centurion's short stride.

"Since when do quarry boys use words like *logic*?" Valerius shook another stone loose from his muddy sandal. "You don't get it, do you? It's not about saving money. Rome is loaded. You're just too green to see the real agenda."

"What agenda?" Seeing the veteran stiffen, Severus stepped back to avoid another blow.

Valerius tried to keep his temper in check on the off chance the kid—an informer, no doubt—had a concealed weapon and actually knew how to use it. "Fewer citizens," he said once his anger subsided.

Severus perked up. Military life was turning out to be much more interesting than spalling quarry stones. "What's wrong with fewer citizens?" he asked.

"I'll tell you what's wrong!" Valerius shouted. He glared as if the Fates had chosen Severus as their agent of mockery. "If our leaders take away the dream of dying a Roman, what's left to live for?"

Valerius started marching fast, hoping to force the cheeky conscript to gasp for breath and choke on his next inane question. Tarraco could not be too far away. Retirement was so close he could feel the weight of his armor lifting.

"But Roman citizens have over one hundred and fifty paid holidays a year," Severus said, following in lockstep. "All those triumphs, games, and week-long celebrations must cost us a fortune."

Valerius whipped around and raised his dark eyes to confront the phony quarry boy who dared to torment a veteran. "I've defended civilization from Egypt to Mauritania. I rose from nothing, fought hard, and became a citizen. Listen to me, milk-pup:

The dream of Rome is a beacon in the darkness for the conscripts, the slaves, and the subject peoples. It was for me, and it better be for you."

"Yes, sir!" Severus said. He saluted first with his left arm and then, unsure of the protocol, followed with his right. Eventually such procedures would become second nature; for now, he thought it better to overcompensate with good intentions.

Valerius paused and considered recounting his life's story but then thought the better of it. There was no point in admitting his ignoble birth and unlikely ascent. Even if Severus were a real conscript, he would never survive a day on the battlefield. Why lecture him about the dream of citizenship? Citizenship for provincials was probably just another benefit that the paunchy visionaries in Rome would soon slash to divert more gold into their own purses. "Vesuvius!" he muttered. "When did saving money become the over-arching purpose of the Roman Empire? And since when did whelps like you think about more than wine, war, and wenches?"

Having no such thoughts, Severus took two precautionary steps sideways. "I think I understand," he said. "Most slaves and subjects never become citizens, but they die trying and that's good for Rome."

Valerius looked up and saw a new cluster of clouds bearing down like a colony of gray vultures. The smell of recent lightning—clean and threatening, lingered like smoke on the sage.

"Citizenship is our greatest reward and now it's dead," Valerius said. "In the old days you could just capture a barbarian, dangle the promise of citizenship in front of his big nose, and he'd follow you around like a whipped dog."

"You mean the legion isn't allowed to capture people and put them to work anymore?" Severus said. "So what am I—"

"Enough talk," Valerius said. "You're too sticky with mother's milk to understand anything."

"Please don't mention my mother, sir." Severus said, unable to mask his sadness. Could she see him from heaven? He hoped not—not in this state. Severus followed in silence, torn with guilt over having abandoned his kin. He had run away from the *vigiles*, leaving his brother to be beaten and his father dragged off to jail. He had fled like a coward, taking refuge in a granite quarry, with no better plan than to bide his time until the proscription passed. But someone had betrayed him for a few coins or promise of favor and now he was marching off to the unknown depths of the Roman Empire.

"Is this really the Roman Legion?" Severus asked. "It occurs to me that—say, how long have you served, Centurion?"

"Almost twenty years," Valerius answered proudly. "I've got the scars to prove it."

"Jove, twenty years is longer than I've been alive. What will you do next?"

"Don't ask," Valerius said. "Just talking about it could hex my plans." He picked another stone out of his sandal and threw it at a crow that only grew bolder with the provocation. The signs were unmistakable. Something had changed for the worse and, as usual, Valerius was the last to know.

Severus stumbled over a pothole that the centurion had just sidestepped. "Only five more years till your retirement," he said, recovering his stride. "It's not that far away."

"Five years?" Valerius said, shaking his head. "I'm under the old plan, kid. I've got two months to go, and one night until I'm rid of you."

"As I understand it, sir, after twenty-five years in the legion— assuming I survive, of course—I'll be entitled to ten years' pay, a bronze plaque, and a parcel of land in a veteran's colony."

"Is that what they're promising these days?" Valerius asked. Severus' feigned innocence was depressing. The milkweed conscript had no idea how badly the odds were stacked against making it to day three. "No empire ever went broke paying pensions to old soldiers."

"So, what I'm wondering, sir—in your case, for instance—will you take the money as a lump sum or a series of annual payments?"

Valerius scanned the darkening sky and cursed the approaching wall of black clouds. Tarraco had to be nearby, hopefully just beyond the next hill. He reckoned that they would arrive by nightfall. Shuddering at the prospect of bivouacking in unfamiliar territory with the suspicious conscript, Valerius drew his cloak tight across his shoulders and walked faster. The temperature dropped as the wind picked up.

Severus had nothing to protect him from the elements. After a few thoughtful paces, he shivered and tried to continue the conversation. "I think the lump sum is the way to go, sir. That way you have control over your money. You can invest it and get rich."

"Get rich?" Valerius had heard it all before, usually on the eve of a battle before the conversation turned to lies about women. "If I knew how to invest, I wouldn't be a soldier. Now stop talking."

"I never asked to be a soldier, sir," Severus said, ignoring the order. "Anyway, investing isn't as noble as defending the empire. I mean, what's so honorable about 'buy low, sell high?'"

Valerius wheeled around with a warrior's glare that stopped the boy in mid-speech.

"Since when do quarry boys have so many opinions?" Valerius searched his memory for any reason the gods might be punishing him but came up clean. He took solace in knowing that he would soon dump the nattering conscript at the garrison. Once rid of Severus, he planned to spend the night drinking honeyed wine and swapping soldiers' stories with Fidelis Magnus, an old comrade who had moved north a year ago.

They crested a small hill and saw the dusk-covered city before them and the gray Mediterranean beyond. At the city's edge, dockhands were unloading a small cargo ship. Firetrap tenements slouched towards the port and eventually gave way to busy plazas near the center of town. Above the circus and the forum, a stone palace watched over the day's fading commotion.

"Tarraco, sir," Severus said, trying to steady his voice, "the capital of Hispania."

For a brief moment, the dank air bore the sweet scent of freedom. Gods' willing, tomorrow Valerius would meet with Governor Biberious, a former legate under whom he had once served. He would settle the confusion over his pension, and retire in peace, far away from the fools, thieves, and opportunists who had taken over the empire.

Two
II

No crowds welcomed him to Tarraco and for once Festus Rufius was content to be anonymous. The prospect of getting off the miserable little boat and becoming the new Governor of Hispania was all that moved his weary corpse forward.

Searching for a silver lining among the black clouds, Rufius found comfort in knowing that history would never remember the grimy vessel and the barefoot mariners that had delivered him. He alone among the unsavory crew was unstoppable, destined to rise. So, unfortunately, was everything he had eaten during the past week.

Sailors pushed past him, jostling to reach the dockside chop shops and cut-rate depravities that overflowed the port of Tarraco. Rufius tried in vain to ignore their crude sniggers and look regal in case anyone saw him descend weak-legged and weary down the gangplank.

He stepped onto the dock and lost his balance, barely catching himself by hugging a rough-hewn pylon. A seagull hovered overhead, behaving rudely.

Rufius, a senator's son, had been told to travel *in cognito* for reasons that the relocations bureaucrats assured him would be obvious upon arrival. Now, after four miserable days at sea, he had arrived and nothing was obvious except that he smelled worse than the two motley German slaves waiting to unload the boat.

Disguised in a commoner's rough cotton tunic, now soiled beyond salvation, he had traveled with little more than a jealously guarded strongbox. Carefully wrapped in an elegant toga that he had forgotten to don before disembarking, he had hidden a priceless document—evidence that would soon pay an imperial dividend.

Rufius steadied his well-bred bulk, ran a pair of pudgy fingers through his wavy black hair, and tightened his cherubic face to hide his disappointment. Beyond the port, the capital town of Tarraco could have hidden in the noon shadow of one of Rome's seven hills. Above the skewed rooflines of sagging tenements, the setting sun broke through a cloud to shed a last ray of light on a terraced hillside covered with olive trees. Atop the hill stood a hulking granite mansion, the Governor's Villa, Festus Rufius' new home. It was small by Roman standards, but it was his.

Rufius turned his salt-caked face towards the last shaft of sunlight but before Apollo could herald his arrival, he was betrayed by the Earth spinning beneath him. Struggling to maintain balance, he plodded towards solid ground until he realized that he had forgotten his precious strongbox. He stiffened his aching abdomen and trudged back towards the boat. The trunk, the contents of which would soon bring down more than a few powerful rivals, was too important to entrust to the ragged slaves now unloading the ship's cargo.

The boat, a squat, square-sailed vessel called the *Goddess Livia* was named after the deified wife of the Divine Augustus, Father of the Empire. Enthusiastically boarding the *Livia* earlier in the week, Rufius had mused that Augustus would have gladly returned from the afterlife to watch his bride's wooden torso slapping across the water. But after four queasy days of watching Livia's venerable breasts cut through the frothy Mediterranean, the allure of heaving cleavage was forever ruined.

Like her namesake, the *Livia* had been full to the point of bursting. She was transporting thousands of gallons of garum, the pungent fish sauce favored by civilized people across the empire. Prior to this voyage, Rufius had loved garum. The sharp sauce, one of Rome's many contributions to human progress, was as delightful on a crust of bread as it was an otherwise dubious cut of meat. The best garum, made from fermented fish and salt brine, was reserved for Rome. The low-grade export, the variety the *Livia* carried in her hold, was concocted from whatever could be scraped from the moldy bowels of fishing boats.

The breeze shifted and a familiar stench assaulted Rufius' chapped and protesting nostrils. He turned his back to the foul smell, but could not escape it. During his voyage the swelling sea had tossed the *Livia* and smashed her slurry-filled amphorae together. Cheap garum had spilled into the bowels of the rocking vessel, releasing a cloud of rank, acidic vapor that soon permeated every strained sail and creaking timber. The stench still filled his pores, clung to his stained tunic, and burned his lungs. Rufius' stomach clenched, reminding him of the hours spent leaning over the *Livia's* gunwales, offering up the remains of his swallowed pride to Neptune's hungry minions.

Before Rufius reached the vessel, he realized that he was being followed. A small, wiry, mouse-faced man and a large red-haired slave were heading straight towards him. Worried about recovering his strongbox, Rufius stumbled back towards the *Goddess Livia*, but the tiny man maneuvered in front of him and blocked his way. The muscular slave, looking short on brains and long on menace, obstructed any possibility of escape in the other direction. The mismatched strangers sandwiched Rufius and edged him away from the boat.

"Good job with the disguise, Governor," the little man said. "I almost didn't recognize you."

"Out of my way," Rufius said. "I've already got two of whatever you're selling."

"Welcome to Tarraco, Excellency," the small fellow insisted. "I've got a litter waiting to take you to the Villa."

Excellency! The word rang pure and true. It was the first time Festus Rufius had ever been called "Excellency" and while he was far from feeling excellent, he already loved the sound of it.

Governorships rarely opened up, and when they did, it was usually a foregone conclusion which son of which powerful family would win the lucrative post. But Hadrian's wanted to ring in a new era and wring out the old guard. His approach to developing Rome's next generation of leaders was a radical departure from past practice. Nepotism and bribery were no longer enough. Talent and promise were now essential considerations in the imperial calculus.

Hadrian had a nose for potential. He had plucked Festus Rufius from a dull destiny and named him Governor of Hispania. Never again would Rufius suffer the slanderous whispers and salacious gossip under Rome's colonnades. Success would be his salty revenge upon those who had insisted that he would never live up to his father's legacy or his brother's achievements. His moment to shine had finally come.

"Your orders, Governor?" the little man asked.

"Who are you?" Rufius asked.

"I'm called Minem, Excellency. Winus Minem." The tiny man bowed so low that his beige toga fell from his shoulder. In contrast to the stern goliath towering behind him, Minem looked clever as a jackal. He rearranged the fabric and bounced forward to continue his introduction in near-perfect Latin. "I'm with IA, Imperial Associates. Your father hired me as your temporary chief of staff."

"Hired you? With whose money?"

"Your father, the Senator, thought—"

"Thought that he'd spend my inheritance on Greek philosophers?"

"Not at all, sir—I'm Macedonian."

"Worse." Rufius felt dizzy and drained. He struggled to remain regal. "What's with the big nightmare behind you?"

Minem looked back with disapproval at the muscular slave. "This is Vindex. He's a murderer masquerading as a bodyguard."

"Welcome, My Lord," Vindex said. His voice had the dull ring of a lingering hangover.

Exhausted, Rufius staggered forward and wondered if being Governor of Hispania was a reward or a curse. He had barely arrived and hustlers were already dogging him. "I don't need you and I don't need a bodyguard," he said.

"I'm afraid you do, sir. All is not well in Tarraco," Minem said. "Fortunately, I'm an ex-administrator and Vindex is an ex-gladiator. Fascinating story, really. His entire tribe was captured along the Danube and enslaved by our former emperor. Vindex was just a boy when Trajan put most of his kin to death in—"

Rufius waved his hand to silence the small fellow. Whatever this little man claimed to be, at least he appeared harmless, unlike his lumbering sidekick. Since no one else had stepped forth to offer assistance, they would have to do for now. Not wanting to address the slave directly, Rufius looked at Minem and said, "Fetch my trunk then, won't you?"

Minem passed along the order. Vindex grumbled and trotted down the dock to board the vessel that was now being loaded with amphorae of olive oil bound for the bathhouses of Rome. A few minutes later, he returned with the strongbox, proceeded to the quay, and tossed it into the waiting litter.

At the end of the rocking quay, Rufius pulled himself up the ramp to stand on *terra firma*. Solid ground should have been a relief, but his sense of equilibrium was still at sea. It was probably customary for a new governor to kiss the provincial earth, but nobody was watching, and the ground was muddy. He worried that if he knelt down, he would never have the strength to get back up.

Rufius climbed into the unadorned litter and pulled the door shut. The bench was hard, but it felt good to sit down on a still surface. "Why haven't my subjects come to greet me?" Rufius asked,

"You've arrived on the eve of the funeral," Minem said. He threw open the door, slid in beside Rufius, and craned his short neck to look through the tiny window. He scanned cautiously along the docks and, seemingly satisfied, drew the curtain. "Good," he said, "nothing too out of the ordinary."

Rufius cringed as four slaves hoisted the litter onto their shoulders and lurched forward with Vindex stalking alongside. It was clear that the indifferent slaves had no experience transporting noble passengers. The litter rocked worse than the cheapest ride in Rome.

Rome. It seemed like long ago, but less than a week earlier Rufius had received the unexpected promotion along with orders to report to Hispania immediately. So sudden was the news that he had barely found enough time to call in a few favors, say good-bye to his mother, and shutter his luxurious *domus* in Rome.

Instructed to travel light, he happily ditched the pouting wife his father had recently arranged for him to marry. Her dowry already spent, she could come later, if at all. His administrator—the type of spiteful bureaucrat who loved to make suffer the more fortunate—had assured him that his household goods, slaves, and most importantly, his extensive collection of fine wines dating from the time of the late Republic would soon follow.

As the litter pitched and tossed, Rufius fought to maintain his dignity, but every gasping lungful of dank air seemed like his last. He felt like his body was turning inside out, his aching stomach emptier than a taxman's conscience. Hoping to calm his rebellious intestines, he leaned forward and gulped a mouthful of sea air.

"No promotion merits this much suffering," Rufius whispered. "I think I'd prefer to walk."

"Good idea, sir," Minem said. "I'll send the litter ahead to create a diversion."

"Fine," Rufius said, "but the box stays near me."

Rufius willed himself forward with dreams of a warm bath, a hearty massage, and the feeling of freshly oiled skin. It seemed like a century since he'd felt the reassurance of cobblestone under his feet.

Minem led him through a narrow alley and into the slums that crowded the docklands. It was quiet, dark, and—quiet? Since when was a portside village quiet? In sleepless Ostia, the great port where the River Tiber met the sea, Rufius had barely been able to push his way through the throngs of enterprising slave girls. At Ostia, the revelry did not wind down until the sobering light of dawn. In comparison, the port at Tarraco was as silent as a snake.

"Where are the people?" Rufius asked, now feeling too exhausted to die.

"They're at the ceremony, I suppose. The former governor's corpse is lying in state at the Temple of Augustus. If we hurry, you can deliver the eulogy."

Festus Rufius, the new Governor of Hispania, slumped down onto a stoop. "Just get my corpse home or the only eulogy I deliver will be yours."

Three
III

Two nights earlier, a bleak wind blew through the tenement canyons of Tarraco. Smoke from illegal braziers smoldering in firetrap apartments drifted out across the harbor and guided the last ship into port as darkness reached across the slums.

Twilight gave way to evening as Gaius Severus and his older brother Marius watched their father attempt to conjure flame from a dry lamp. Their father, a pious, part-time butcher known as "The Rabbi" to the town's tiny diaspora, had no money left for oil.

"The lamp of the Maccabees burned for seven nights," the old man said. He glanced up at the ceiling sagging under the weight of heaven. "Can't mine burn for just one night?"

"Miracles are in short supply these days." Gaius, the taller and darker of the two brothers, sat against the cold wall of their tiny apartment. His back hurt from a hard week at the quarry, cutting granite into blocks for villas in whose courtyards he would never be welcomed. Calluses from where his sandal straps had chaffed his ankles bore witness to the five-mile trek home through the foothills to reach his kin before sundown.

It was the first day of November and tonight there would be no dinner beyond a thin, lukewarm broth. In addition to Gaius' meager stipend as a quarry boy, Marius had earned a few coins by scraping mold from the walls of the plebian bathhouse. The brothers had brought in just enough during the week to keep the landlord at bay. With any luck, next week's Sabbath would offer more bounty.

"Bless the bread," Marius said, impatient as always. "We need the crumbs more than God needs us." Marius was nineteen, one head shorter but, by his own ledger, two heads smarter than his bird-faced brother. He had his mother's deep-set eyes and his father's wiry black hair. His thin lips barely hid his anger at God for having scattered the Jews like sand across the Roman Empire.

At an age when most young men had already wed and started families, Marius' sharp tongue and lack of a steady trade had soured the only two families whose daughters were still available for a reasonable dowry. While Gaius toiled as an apprentice stonemason, Marius, older and wider than his more dependable brother, worked odd jobs, charmed widows, and plotted the downfall of the Roman Empire.

"Sabbath, the bride of twilight," their father said as the sliver of sky above the alley surrendered its hue. Faint light feathered into the room from the rising moon. Abandoning the lamp, Rabbi Severus said the blessing over a small piece of flat bread that remained from the morning. He thanked God for having brought forth grain from the earth, and broke off a fragment of stale bread for each of his sons. The darkness rendered his face more gaunt than usual.

"Perhaps next week the Lord will bring forth a bit more," Marius said. He cracked through the crust with his front teeth. "Freshly baked, if it's not too much bother."

"Perhaps you'll get a real job and stop blaming God for our troubles," Gaius said, before his father waved a hand to silence them both.

While the two young men partook of the dry sacrament, their father blessed them as he had at the start of every Sabbath since they were born. A tear welled in his better eye at the mention of their departed mother whom he blessed *in absentia*.

"May the Lord bless you and keep you," he said. The old man extended his arms and moved his open hands in a slow circular motion. His wrinkled face folded into a loving smile and the tufts of his gray eyebrows floated like rain clouds over his dark eyes. "May God shine His face unto you and show you favor. May the Lord protect you and grant you peace."

But peace was in short supply as shouting in the street below interrupted the brief promise of Sabbath calm. The sound of hob-nailed sandals pounding across the cobblestones and the drunken laughter of ruffians storming up rickety stairways heralded the arrival of darkness.

"*Vigiles*," Marius said, parting the torn curtain to look four storeys down into the street. "God has truly forgotten us."

There was no longer any reason to wonder when the flood of official vengeance would arrive. In the shops, baths, and forum people had talked of nothing else for the past two days. The murder of Sextus Biberious, Governor of Hispania, would not go unpunished.

The security sweep was as predictable as the foregone conclusion that whoever had actually assassinated the corrupt old governor would never see justice. While those who might directly benefit from the governor's demise slept in comfort, an irregular cohort of dockhands and sailors had been incited to deliver a taste of Roman justice to those who needed no reminding of their station.

The promise of violence rattled through the lower corridors of the building. The banal sounds of terror—unhinged doors and smashing plates—punctuated the cold November night. In the name of justice and the absence of reason, the *vigiles* ransacked households too poor to pay for protection. What the vulnerable citizens, slaves, and freedmen of Tarraco did not render unto Caesar in taxes and tribute, they would now pay his henchmen in bribes, bruises, and futile supplications.

Alerted by the shouting in the corridor, Gaius Severus hid the family's few belongings in the space between two floor joists while his brother attempted to bar the entrance.

The door—nothing more than a few pockmarked planks lashed to a leather hinge—gave way with barely a whimper. When two rough sailors charged into the one-room residence, Marius stumbled backwards and tried to draw them into the room so his kin could slip away to the relative safety of the darkened streets.

"Long live Hadrian!" Marius shouted on the off chance that invoking the emperor's name would dissuade the thugs from their devilry.

But the invaders patriotism did not extend beyond plunder. One of the dockhands, a bald, dog-faced northerner, carried a canvas sack that was already half-filled with stolen goods. He shoved Marius aside and stormed into the room. To buy time for his family, Marius lunged for the other man's leg and brought him tumbling down.

While Marius wrestled with the smaller man, the larger fellow looked around for something worth stealing but found nothing of value beyond a small charcoal stove, a bowl of apples, and a pile of scrolls. He slit their only mattress with a knife and rifled through the straw. Coming up empty handed, he turned in frustration towards Rabbi Severus. In the darkness, his bald head and hollow eyes gave his canine face the dull sheen of a funeral mask.

"They're not as poor as they look," said the other man, still struggling with Marius. His accent was Corsican and his unshaven face was as rough and ruddy as a vein of pink granite. He shook Marius loose, grabbed one of the Hebrew scrolls from the table, and tore it to pieces. "Papyrus," he said, and shredded another.

"Stop!" shouted Rabbi Severus. He threw himself against the invader and tried to save the remaining scrolls.

The Corsican knocked the old man to the floor like a toppled statue and threw the unlit oil lamp against the wall, smashing it to pieces. He looked around the tiny room and cursed in a dialect that needed no translation while the fearsome northerner pounded on the thinly plastered wall and stomped around on the floor in search of hiding places.

"Aha!" the northerner said, finding a hollow spot. He bent down to pull up a loose floorboard.

"No!" Gaius shouted. He grabbed the nearby stool and broke it over the northerner's head, surprising both of them with his audacity.

The northerner wavered for a second and then fell hard enough to shake the entire fourth floor of the apartment complex. In the corridor, neighbors ran for the stairway, children in tow.

The Corsican laughed. Keeping the family at bay with a drawn blade, he removed a small silver menorah from the compartment, examined it in the thin moonlight that filtered through the window, and stuffed it in his partner's sack. "What else have you got?"

The brothers planted themselves between the ruddy Corsican and their frail father. The old candelabrum was the family's only heirloom, a link to a past that would soon fade to legend. They could not allow the ancient menorah to fall into profane hands. They lunged at the Corsican, but were easily rebuffed.

In the few seconds it took the Corsican to finish searching the tiny apartment, Rabbi Severus had crawled over to the window and shoved a discarded plank into the open window across the narrow alley. He gestured for his younger son to escape. "Run to the quarry and don't look back," he whispered. The wan light made his thin, curly hair look like a crown of smoke.

"What about you and Marius?" Gaius protested.

"We'll be right behind you," his father insisted. "Now go!"

Four storeys had never seemed so high. "*Tempus moriendi,*" Gaius muttered, quoting one of his father's old scrolls. "Time to die."

While Marius delayed the Corsican, Gaius Severus climbed over the windowsill and scrambled onto the makeshift bridge. The young man of sixteen brief years tried to maintain his balance high above the cobblestone, but he had never felt comfortable looking down from the windowsill. The fear that had been welling, now churned like sea foam in his stomach. His pounding heart threatened to throw him off balance with each beat.

Gaius Severus willed himself forward, inching along the wobbling plank, until he finally pulled across the chasm. He slipped under the threadbare drapes that provided their neighbor a shred of privacy and somersaulted onto her floor. Wiping the cold sweat from his brows, he looked up slowly and found himself eye-to-eye with two crying children. Their widowed mother cowered in the corner.

Hearing shouts from his home, Gaius sprang back towards the neighbor's window in order to steady the plank for his father to come across, but the old man was no longer at the sill. The taste of panic welled in Gaius' throat and a scuffle in the street below attracted his attention. He glanced down the length of the uneven façade where a struggling neighbor was being dragged away by an enterprising dockhand, an amateur mercenary hoping to receive a few coins for filing the prison.

Peering back into his father's apartment, Gaius heard the northerner laugh and strike his elder brother. Marius' shadow fell below the windowsill. Their father lunged for the window, but the gruff Corsican pulled him back into the apartment.

"Vesuvius," Gaius cursed. He froze in place; too stunned to move, but not too proud to pray. "Save them, Lord," he whispered, "Is that too much to ask or do you thrive on tormenting us?

The Corsican lifted one leg over the window sill, squeezed through the opening, and planted a wide knee firmly on the makeshift bridge. He flashed a malicious grin that needed no explanation. For the squat and muscle bound sailor, a scrawny wishbone like Gaius Severus was easy prey.

Shoving his bulk forward, the vigilante managed to slide halfway across the narrow bridge between the buildings. The weak moonlight illuminated the folded dome of his fleshy head. Midway across the chasm, with no possible way to turn back, he could not move without causing the sagging bridge to vibrate.

With the Corsican stuck on the straining plank Gaius Severus helped the terrified neighbor woman scoop up her crying children. They ran into the corridor, bolted down four loose flights of stairs, and stumbled into the street below.

The commotion in the other tenements had flushed many residents into the alley.

Severus handed back the child and shoved through the crowd that had gathered to jeer at the vigilante, treed like a cat high above the street. Gaius pushed towards the entrance to his father's building, but the street was too thick with spectators to reach the door.

"Jump!" an elderly woman shouted up to the frustrated Corsican.

Stuck and steaming, the bald aggressor tried to steady the rocking bridge, but every breath put him in greater peril. On the cold street below, poor citizens and freedmen savored the mercenary's predicament.

An old man whose hair was still full of straw from a shredded mattress, pried loose a cobblestone and broke it against another. Neighbors rushed in to grab the fragments and throw them at the brute teetering high above them. Seeing the big man fall would be small compensation for the night's terror, but the downtrodden denizens of Hispania's capital had long ago learned to collect payment in whatever form it took.

"Stop!" the Corsican shouted from his perch after a stone hit his broad forehead. Hoping to lower his profile and slide to safety, he tried to lie down along the splintering plank.

"If he falls, I'm not cleaning up the mess," announced a street-level resident known to everyone for having tapped illegally into a water main. "The end of civilization starts with people not tidying up after themselves."

Overwhelmed by all that had just happened, Gaius Severus wiped a sudden well of tears from his eyes just in time to see his father and brother dragged away by the dog-faced northerner. Marius' glare was defiant, but his hands were bound like a condemned slave.

"Father," Gaius whispered as the men passed.

"Save yourself," was all the old man had time to say.

Four
IV

Festus Rufius slept for two fitful days, plagued by a recurring nightmare of fleeing from a giant. Still aching from the rude trip to Hispania, he awoke to hear heavy breathing on the other side of the bedroom door. Vindex, the fearsome ex-gladiator was either standing guard or posed to attack. Parting the dark curtain to look through the thick and pitted window, Rufius noticed two kitchen slaves with butcher knives patrolling the garden.

The smell of a fresh food tray on his nightstand drew him back from the window. He inspected the fare for something edible, but found little to his liking. When Winus Minem entered the room, Rufius was back in bed, studying a bowl of honeyed wheat porridge.

"Did one of the slaves sample your porridge, sir?" Minem asked.

Rufius gave the porridge a sniff.

"Not to worry, sir," Minem said. He pulled open the curtain to let gray light into the room. "If it was tainted, we'd know by now."

"This lousy bowl is ceramic." Rufius smashed the bowl down on the nightstand loud enough to register his dissatisfaction and hard enough to dent the wood. "I prefer lead. Ceramic is too earthy, especially in the morning."

"Duly noted," Minem said.

Rufius shifted out of bed, cracking his knees and knuckles loudly. He gestured indifferently towards a tray piled high with delicacies. "Have a stuffed dormouse. My appetite's still out at sea."

The platter was laden with cheese basted in honey, hermit crab shells stuffed with pickled sardines, and every internal organ a roasted pig could spare. A brown jug decorated with a terra-cotta relief of a snake wrapping itself lasciviously around a dancing wood nymph hinted of fine drink and sultry venom.

Minem nibbled an olive and began the morning briefing. "Hispania's broke," he began, but Rufius shushed him with a wagging finger.

"I'd fire you now, but Father's already paid in advance." Rufius arched his back and cracked a few vertebrae. Twisting from side to side, he noticed damp spots dappling the coved ceiling. Dissatisfied with how the day had started, he drew a deep breath and sank back onto the bed. The hope that Winus Minem, Hispania, and the dull yellow room were all part of someone else's dream vaporized the instant he lifted his eyelids to the daylight again. "If you want to be useful, you can plan my inaugural celebration," he mumbled. "How's this province stacked for female gladiators?"

"Let's ask the expert." Minem opened the door and as Vindex advanced, Minem retreated. In distancing himself from the green-eyed gladiator ducking through the doorway, Minem backed into a corner table. Pretending his intention all along had been to fill a goblet, he smiled and caught the pitcher before it wobbled off the edge. "You remember Vindex, Excellency?"

"Like a beating," Rufius said. He sniffed at the wine in his goblet, grimaced, and handed it back to Minem.

Vindex shuffled into the room and knelt so low that his coarse brown tunic crept up his backside. He bowed until his muscular folds doubled upon themselves, preventing him from going lower. His long red hair fell forward like a flaming waterfall, almost touching the tile. "My Lord," he said dramatically, "On behalf of the Villa's dedicated staff—"

"Fine." Rufius wavied him away. "Now scram."

Knowing his place and occupying more of it than others, Vindex backed into the doorway. He sneered at Minem before disappearing down the hall, the sounds of his footsteps echoing like funeral drums.

Noticing that Minem was now inspecting the strongbox, Rufius ambled over and nudged him away from the heavy, metal-clad case. Rufius ran his hand over the hinge, discreetly feeling for the hidden lock mechanism. He had a sudden impulse to tell

Minem that the box contained something so important it could bring down the gods themselves, but decided against it. Minem, the self-proclaimed advisor, had done nothing to earn his trust, or for that matter, a salary.

"For security reasons, we'll call Vindex your valet," Minem said. "That thick-headed thug was an early suspect but, after a thorough interrogation, they determined his alibi was mostly sound."

"Alibi … suspects … you sound like a Greek tragedy." Rufius walked barefoot across the warm floor tiles, grateful that someone had thought to fire up the furnace. After looking over the austere bedroom, he contemplated his watery reflection in the warped mirror hanging on the bare yellow wall. "Let's have a tour of this dump, shall we? Maybe we'll find some decent wine." Slipping into a pair of oversized sandals, he shuffled towards the door and waved for Minem to follow. "While we poke around, I'll dictate ideas for my inaugural celebration. Bring a stylus, Minem. Take notes as we walk. Always do two things at once; that's the secret to success."

"Duly noted." Minem ran out the door, wax tablet and bronze stylus in hand. Still determined to delve into detail, he continued his briefing as he followed behind the governor. "Let's start with the first-and-foremost and work down to the last-and-aft-most, shall we? We've got a dozen or so suspects rounded up, three of whom have already confessed to the murder even though they weren't anywhere near the crime scene."

"Torture can be so unreliable," Rufius sighed. Trying to pull ahead of the awkward little advisor, he forged down the corridor, his sandals slapping the tile.

"On the night of the murder, two slaves found Vindex bound, gagged, and unconscious outside the bedroom door," Minem continued. He jogged to keep pace with the governor. "Frankly, sir, I'm still suspicious of him, but either way, I'm sure the killer will eventually make a mistake and—"

"The killer?" Minem was so small it strained Rufius' fleshy neck to turn back and look down at him. "Will you stop talking about killers? I didn't come all the way here to worry about someone else's misfortune."

"Sir?" Minem said cautiously, "Have you been fully briefed about the situation? Has no one informed you that your predecessor was murdered in bed?"

"Enough theater!" Rufius said. "It's all I can do to maintain my pluck in this disappointing Villa. This so-called palace has nothing palatial about it."

Minem followed Rufius into a small adjacent dining room.

"Where are the woven curtains, the ivory faucet handles, the intricate designs on gleaming tiled floors?" Rufius continued. "There's no harmony, no style, no elegance. Look at that fresco. Landscapes are such pap! No wonder Biberious died. Who could live in this hovel? And what's that awful smell? I can barely breathe in such a lifeless place."

Exiting the room and continuing down the next corridor, they found Vindex burning a pile of stale bread in a futile attempt to freshen up the dank hallway.

As he entered the banquet room, Rufius glanced at a low serving table made of knotty pine. "Pine ... how painfully rustic. I can't wait to see my cypress dining table in here. It's trimmed in cedar and inlaid with gold. Pine is for burning." He kicked the small table over onto its side. "Vindex, use this to heat the bath house."

"My Lord?" Vindex was clearly conflicted by the order. "This table belonged to the Divine Augustus himself."

"Poppycock! Let it join him in the afterlife."

"As you wish." Vindex could barely hide his delight. Such a relic would bring a windfall on the black market. He hoisted the table and left the room at once.

"The emperor will be expecting an update on how you intend to pay off the deficit." Minem said, after Vindex had left. "Perhaps you can dictate your report."

"Tell him Hispania is hopeless." Rufius said. "End of report." Finished with the update, he took notice of three simple couches and found them unworthy of the elegant and erudite guests he would soon entertain if the province boasted anyone of distinction.

His fine lemonwood sofas with the tortoise-shell inlays would restore some much needed decorum.

"Look at these sofas," Rufius said dejectedly. "The fabric is threadbare, wine-stained; at least, I hope that's only a wine stain. In any case, they're not worth fixing. Have Vindex burn them, too."

"They look solid enough," Minem protested. Forgetting his open-toed sandals, he kicked a stout leg of the nearest couch to prove his point. "Perhaps you should wait for your shipment to arrive before burning all the furniture. Those relocation agents often relocate things indefinitely, and we're not exactly flush with cash around here."

"Nonsense, Minem. My shipments will be at the docks tomorrow. Judging from what I've seen so far, I'll need to request a larger furniture allowance."

"Please, sir. I must advise restraint. Hadrian, may his coffers be flush, wants you to save money, not spend it." Seeing that his attempts to counsel caution had fallen on deaf ears, Minem looked down to see if any of his throbbing toes were bleeding. "The emperor is quite impatient with Hispania."

Rufius smiled as if enjoying a private secret, his rosy, dimpled face free of the worry lines that often accompany great responsibility. "Hadrian may be tightfisted, but I'm sure we'll come to an arrangement."

After selling Augustus' table to one of the enterprising petitioners who gathered daily at the gates, Vindex rejoined the entourage. The three men proceeded to the outdoor kitchen, a large covered patio with multiple ovens for baking and roasting. Earthenware bowls and plates were stacked unevenly on shelves alongside a pile of blackened oil lamps. Two fat kitchen slaves were busy playing knuckle bones on a chopping board.

"Let's put the kitchen to the test, shall we?" Rufius ran his finger along the edge of a large bowl and sniffed at the residue it produced. "Though they look incapable of boiling an egg, let's see if these sporting cooks can prepare a decent plate of bull stones for my luncheon today."

"It was clearly a murder, sir," Minem whispered. He glanced nervously at Vindex and the array of carving knives hanging on the wall. "The last governor was poisoned and then stabbed."

"Consider it a small victory for good taste." Rufius looked over a worn set of household gods perched in a dusty niche and did not recognize any of the small, charred ceramic figures. "Vindex," he called over his shoulder, "find another home for these dated little deities."

"With all due respect, sir," Vindex protested, "that would bring bad luck."

"If they're truly gods, they'll understand that antiquity ended long ago," Rufius said. He stepped into an adjoining salon that gave access to an enclosed courtyard. While scowling at the fading paint on the columns, he accidently kicked over an abandoned jug.

A familiar smelling liquid leaked out across the floor tiles, wicking along the grout lines.

"Don't step in the urine, my Lord." Vindex warned.

Rufius jumped back before the puddle reached his exposed toes.

"Urine is used to clean the linens, Excellency," Vindex explained. He wandered off towards the kitchen in search of a cleaning crew.

"Governor Biberious encouraged the staff to donate their— uh, fluids to help keep costs down," Minem said, shrugging his shoulders.

Rufius tugged at an earlobe and exhaled loudly. "As Governor of Hispania I hereby forbid the use of urine in any of my laundries."

"Duly noted." Minem pulled the bronze stylus from behind his ear and opened a small, hinged wooden booklet containing a wax tablet upon which he quickly scratched the new ordinance. "Shall I have this decree posted in the forum immediately, sir, or will there be more?"

Rufius had already crossed the courtyard and entered the atrium, where he stood shaking his head at the lack of opulence.

"The atrium should be the living soul of the *domus*." Rufius sniffed at the green water in the rain basin at the center of the room. "It is here that first impressions will be dispensed. My atrium needs to be a great room, an intimidating room."

The new governor turned his attention to a nearby fresco, a floor-to-ceiling image of naked women dancing ecstatically in a forest while winged cupids scattered armfuls of spring flowers in all directions. The image caught Rufius off-guard and he flushed with sudden nostalgia. The scene reminded him of his mother who had been a Vestal Virgin before leaving the fold.

"Nice painting," he said, proceeding to the far side of the atrium. "On the other hand, this mosaic over here is quite possibly the most artless creation I've ever seen. Look, the colors are faded, the curves are, why they're as rough as jagged little stair steps. This dreadful Greek eyesore simply won't do, Minem."

Minem shrugged and followed dutifully as the governor quickly moved to the other side of the room. "Sir ... on a limited budget—"

"Look at this statue." Rufius ran a hand down the bronze torso of Galba, the obscure emperor and former Governor of Hispania who had managed to seize the throne and hold it for a few deadly months during the chaos following Nero's demise. "This statue is a fraud, an imitation, probably a copy of a copy." His narrow eyes darted around quickly, his plucked brow increasingly exasperated. "I don't even see a bust of our current emperor, may his frigid wife bear a hundred sons. He may not last long but, long as he lives, he must never know of this impudence."

Not waiting for Minem's reply, Rufius stormed towards the main entrance. His loose sandals shuffled across the tiled floor beneath his crimson-trimmed toga.

"What's this tasteless fresco?" Rufius asked. He rubbed his forehead and stepped back to take in the faded painting of the Athenian skyline. "A jumble of columns and temples cowering at the foot of the Acropolis. Hoary faces of forgotten Greeks scowling around the edges. Honestly! Why are Romans so obsessed with Greeks?"

"The Greeks are the fathers of—"

"We need to fix this mess immediately." Rufius grabbed a bronze candelabrum and brandished it like an axe. ""I've got a much better design in mind."

"But sir, the emperor is—"

"The emperor will thank me for this." Rufius smashed the base of the candleholder into the fresco, wedging it deep behind the lath, and painted plaster. He tried to wrestle it loose, but the candelabrum was stuck.

"Perhaps we should focus on the bigger picture." Worried that Rufius might break something else, Minem tried to distract the governor with work. "You'll need a strategy for turning this province around. Taxes haven't been collected and tribute hasn't been paid for months. Unless you move fast, Hadrian will have your hide."

Leaving the candelabrum protruding from the wall, Rufius stepped back and brushed the dust and broken plaster from his silk-trimmed neckline. "Honestly, Minem I'm beginning to see why I was so urgently needed. Good taste is dead in this Gods' forsaken province."

"So is the last governor," Minem replied. "Murdered in the very bed you slept in."

"Vindex," Rufius ordered, "go get a wrecking crew."

The delighted giant pounded away like redheaded thunder

Using an abandoned silver platter as a mirror, Rufius picked faun colored flecks of fresco out of his dark hair. Behind him, in the wavy reflection, Minem looked more and more like a mouse in sandals.

"A governor—your predecessor, the emperor's representative—was killed. His ashes have yet to take wind." Minem watched the governor preen in the makeshift mirror and wondered if Rufius was blissfully ignorant or just blissful. As a member of Imperial Associates, he knew that the Biberious and Rufius clans were rivals in Rome's biggest game. After generations of machinations, both families had finally landed a favorite son on either side of the emperor. "The murder of an enemy doesn't imply that Tarraco's crawling with friends."

"Biberious was an idiot," Rufius said. "Now, if you want to be useful, send an inquiry to find out where my furniture and clothing shipments are."

Disoriented by the governor's odd priorities, Minem nodded and backed away slowly just as Vindex returned with a ragtag crew of kitchen slaves and gardeners clutching picks, hammers, and shovels. With uncharacteristic enthusiasm, they tore into the faded fresco of a pastoral picnic scene before Rufius intervened to send them to the correct target. Swinging their tools with abandon, the slaves made it apparent just how much they enjoyed the chance to unleash a loud and dusty ruckus.

Instead of leaving, Minem led the governor into the courtyard, away from the debris and clamor. When he was sure that nobody was listening, Minem continued to brief his indifferent client. "The words 'Avenge the Republic' were found on the wall, sir, written in blood."

"Enough!" Rufius walked across the garden and reached for a lone orange hanging from a sickly branch. He picked at it carefully, lest the hard, shriveled peel damage his manicured fingernails.

Minem watched two magpies fight over the a garter snake and wondered if Rufius was simply testing his trustworthiness. As a senior Imperial Associates operative, he had to be careful. Revealing his familiarity with the empire's secrets, even to a senator's son, could be dangerous. Throughout IA's long, shadowy history, there had been more than one backlash against their access to information and power. IA's business depended on knowing too much and selling it to those who knew too little. The *consultorium* had flourished for longer than anyone could account for, thriving through times both flush and fallow until Hadrian changed the game. Now the empire was clamping down on the high cost and excessive influence of the many advisors accused of suckling the treasury like Romulus did the she-wolf.

"With all respect, sir, the murder of a Roman governor must be treated with great *gravitas*," Minem insisted, shouting above the demolition din. "Tarraco is watching to see your reaction. This is an excellent opportunity to set a tone for your administration."

"I suppose you're right." Rufius threw the sour orange at the magpies and turned his attention to a patinaed fountain drooling brackish water into a tiled basin. "Justice must be served so put all the house slaves to death."

"Execute all the slaves, sir?" Minem choked down a wayward gasp. "Is that sort of thing still legal?"

"Have Vindex tear them apart in the arena with his bare hands. That would make for a fairly memorable inaugural celebration, no?" Rufius' puffy brown eyes grew wistful as he recalled the splendor of spilled blood and severed limbs in the great coliseum at Rome. "Better yet, we could lash them all together and let loose a team of starving tigers. I saw that once in Rome. It went over pretty well with the mob, though a couple of the tigers weren't hungry enough; a bit fickle, tigers."

"If all the slaves are dead, who will make supper?"

The noise in the nearby atrium died abruptly. Thick, colorful dust blew out through the open door, and the eight slaves' fifteen collective ears—one had been severed as punishment for eavesdropping last year—pretended not to be listening.

"Condemning the slaves is a bit hasty, no?" Minem whispered. "The murder investigation hasn't reached a final conclusion."

"I see you're a bit of an idealist, but trust me, I know how these things work. It's always some servant, all worked-up about some pish-posh. But the law is clear: When a slave murders the master, the whole kit and caboodle must pay with their hides."

Minem was at a rare loss for words.

"The house staff needs pruning, just like this tree." Rufius reached up and grabbed the branch of a fig tree growing near the central fountain. The branch cracked, and Rufius left it hanging by a fiber. "I'm not an unreasonable ruler. Let's give these sods the benefit of the doubt. Twenty-five souls, assuming slaves have souls, will be enough for my celebration. To show my benevolence, I'll commute the sentences of the others."

"What you perceive as mercy, the people of Tarraco might not appreciate as such."

"Iberians must live by the same laws as the rest of the empire and I need bodies for my inaugural games," Rufius said, wagging a finger at the advisor. "Believe me, no one will mourn for a few missing slaves and these corpses are *gratis*. The price couldn't be lower if they were dead already."

The slaves who had finished the demolition just in time to overhear the details of their death sentence dispersed to spread the dust and devastating news.

"Don't you realize that the empire contains more slaves than citizens?" Rufius lowered his voice. "As governor, I need to stand firm. Relax your guard for a second, Minem, and you've got Spartacus reaching right up your toga."

Five

V

Centurion Marcus Valerius had remained alert as an eagle. Vigilant the entire night, he waited for the suspicious conscript to make a move, but the attack never came. By mid-morning, his taut bronzed face barely hid his exhaustion as he and Severus finally wandered out of the muddy hills above Tarraco, the capital of Hispania

Not realizing that the man who had summoned him was well beyond the day of reckoning, Valerius reviewed his case for retirement: In twenty years of fighting, he'd never been routed, and never had to decimate his troops for cowardice. The men of *Legion III Africanus* had shown bravery suppressing the riots at Alexandria. His troops had outwitted raiders along the Libyan frontier, and shed blood to secure the trade routes between Mauritania and the African heartland. Valerius had no family connections, no great patrons. He rose in the ranks by grit and valor, earning distinction for banishing pirates from the strategic outpost on Purpua, the Moroccan island whose mollusks, the murex, produced the imperial purple dyes. He found it strange that this last task, defending shellfish, had won him the most merit, but purple togas spoke louder than blood stained tunics.

With the sea now in sight, retirement to a small soldier's colony on the fertile coastline of Africa, was so close he could smell it. Scanning the clear sky for crows, the portent he had learned to respect over all others, he saw none. Instead, a hare—an excellent sign—darted across the road. All would be well if only he could finish his business quickly and leave Hispania before the gates to the underworld cracked open on the eighth day of November.

Valerius surveyed the town, now in full view. At the far southern end beyond the tenements, the port pulsed with merchant ships. Slaves busied themselves on the docks removing cargo and charging the holds of square-sailed vessels with amphorae bound for Rome.

"Tarraco." Severus' gaze rested on where the half-finished arena sat like a giant bird's nest near the water. Knowing that his might be locked in one of the damp cells underneath the edifice, he tried not to imagine the horrors that had entertained the populace there. He wondered if his father was still alive.

The prospect of returning to town was unsettling, but Severus tried not to reveal his anxiety. He pointed to where the governor's mansion hulked atop an olive-terraced hillside. The Villa looked out over the teeming forum, the empty circus, and the Temple of Jupiter.

"Have you ever seen such a grand building, sir?"

Valerius nodded. The governor's mansion hardly compared with what he had seen in Alexandria. Compared to the capital of Egypt, Tarraco was no better than any other coastal village with a ragged hemline of docks and slums.

"It's big enough for an emperor." Severus had seen the site from many angles but he had never noticed the alabaster skylights dotting the rooftop like the whitecaps on the sea beyond the town. "I wonder what he did to deserve such a place."

"Nothing. Just born right." Valerius, born wrong, swallowed his disdain. Powerful fathers, influential brothers—he had no such blood ties. Valerius had never known his father. His mother, shamed, shunned, and impoverished by her unwed status, would have been within her rights to sell him into slavery or simply leave him to die of exposure. Instead, she'd saved her child's life and apprenticed him to a metal smith when he was barely seven. At the age of twelve, Valerius ran away to clean pots, sharpen knives, and once old enough, join the Roman Legion.

The soldiers entered the *Campus Martius*, the Field of Mars, the military parade and training grounds on the west side of the town wall. Two boys brandishing sticks ran across the field, chasing behind a lopsided iron hoop, taking turns whacking it and each other. Their torn, mud-stained tunics offered little protection against the cold, but their faces were flushed with play. A leather charm, a sign of consecration, dangled from the neck of the smaller boy and provided the older one with a leash to pull on.

The lack of soldiers in the garrison did not bode well. Valerius looked up at the three fortified towers watching over the western edge of the unguarded capital. The tower nearest to the barracks was dedicated to the Divine Augustus, the adopted son who fathered the empire.

"Augustus lived here once," Severus said. He looked around nervously for signs of the Corsican or his dog-faced partner. With any luck, the two might have already shipped out. "Augustus was only eighteen when Julius Caesar was murdered. He spent the next twenty years avenging his father and consolidating the empire."

"I didn't ask for a history lesson." For Valerius, the statue was a stark reminder that the empire's footprint was permanent. He found it strange that Caesar and Augustus, the two men who had raped the republic, had become Gods. After destroying democracy, they sailed into immortality and left a trail of mad dictators in their wake. If tyrants such as the deified Nero now walked the streets of the afterlife with impunity, one could only wonder who was left in hell.

"Augustus started this province," Severus said. "Tarraco was once the center of the empire."

"Now it's the center of nowhere. Where is everyone?"

Valerius looked around for signs of life. Normally, soldiers would be training, but today the garrison stood nearby, eerily silent for midday. Was it already the eighth of November? Perhaps the grounds had been abandoned as a precaution. Seeing no one to whom he could hand over the questionable conscript, Valerius instructed Severus to wait by an old olive tree. After the governor granted his pension, Valerius would beg passage on a southbound freighter and never see this irritating kid again.

Valerius walked off towards the guard tower dedicated to Mars, the God of War, and passed through the unmanned gates. Once inside the town walls, he walked uphill towards the Villa, stopping only to clean the mud off his sandals in a small puddle.

At the gated entrance to the Villa, Valerius was delighted to find his old comrade-in-arms, Fidelis Magnus, standing guard over a potted palm. The centurion's relief at seeing a familiar face was short-lived. Like the empire itself, his once valiant second-in-command had transformed beyond recognition.

"I'm sorry, old crow, but the new governor isn't seeing anyone this morning." Magnus' well-fed face was no longer hungry for adventure. A glint in his good eye suggested that he enjoyed having a bit of authority over his old commander.

"New governor?" Valerius rattled the gate, but it was locked. "What happened to Biberious?"

"Haven't you heard?" Magnus leaned into the ironwork, reveling in his comrade's confusion. "He joined the majority. His funeral's today."

"He's dead?" The news dropped like a stunned bird. Valerius had served in Egypt under Biberious. He had been counting on their former acquaintance to help secure his pension and a decent tract of land. Yesterday's dark omens now made sense. "He just summoned me a week ago. How can he be dead?"

"Governor—a job to die for!" Magnus seemed positively gleeful. "I shouldn't tell you this, but Biberious was murdered. Poisoned and then stabbed like a steak. That's why they called on me, old chum. I'm in the security business now. Easy work, though not without risk."

"Smart move taking a security job." Valerius muttered. "Smarter than any move I've ever made."

"Not so sure. The last security chief died under torture. Poor sod. They say he died right on the verge of confessing."

Valerius stared at Magnus but did not recognize him. While Valerius had risked the last year patrolling the fringes of the empire, Magnus had maneuvered his way into an easy job that required nothing more than staying awake and, judging from his paunch, slurping up scraps from overflowing tables. Could his old confidant still be trusted, or had Magnus sold his dreams to the lowest bidder?

The sharp sounds of ceramic smashing against stone, muffled as the noise traversed the rooms and corridors, leaked out the front door of the compound. Valerius perked up and listened for hints of malice or mishap while his indifferent friend gobbled an apple, stem, seeds, and core.

Previously a straight talking soldier, Magnus now rambled on in perfect riddles, saying and apparently believing things like, "After an exhaustive self-assessment, I determined that my skills weren't well aligned with the mission of the greater empire. When a lateral opportunity came my way, I jumped at the chance to deepen my commitment."

As Magnus droned on about "imperializing possibilities" and "crystallizing visions for the next Roman century," Valerius listened in disbelief, eventually concluding that Magnus' brain had gone softer than his gut. The way Magnus had changed from a solid sub-centurion who lived on the balls of his feet to a security guard with no balls at all made Valerius' skin crawled under his armor. He felt like sneezing—allergic to Hispania, allergic to the whole vexed century. Had hard work and merit suddenly gone out of fashion, or had they never been valued in the first place? Did Magnus actually believe any of the nonsense he was spouting and, more importantly, could he still be trusted? Magnus had clearly joined the other side, the easy side, the only side left. Valerius' lower intestine rumbled with the sinking realization that his twenty years of hard-fought achievement was now worth less than half a bladder of sour wine.

"While you've been guarding these high-born bandits, I've been fighting for their right to plunder." Valerius said. "Who's the new governor, anyway?"

"Festus Rufius," Magnus chuckled with schoolboy delight. "Rushed here on the hush-hush. They say he was chosen by Hadrian himself."

"Rufius?" Valerius chewed on the family name for a minute. "The senator's son, the consul's brother? That party boy is governor?"

"None other." Fidelis Magnus yawned proudly and opened the wrought iron gate for his stunned friend. "Go see for yourself."

Six
VI

Festus Rufius' dream of an easy year in a sun-drenched, beachfront palace faded when another cloudburst darkened the day. He worried that there might not be enough olive oil in the empire to light the Villa's damp, dull interior. The leaky mansion's tacky decor and weathered furniture was almost as unbearable as Winus Minem's apparent obsession with missing taxes and murdered governors.

In spite of Minem's insistence, Rufius did not feel personally threatened by the murder of the previous governor. The demise of Biberious had conveniently eliminated one of the Rufius family's direct political rivals. Between his new position as governor, the powers vested in his senator father and consul brother, and the inflammatory contents of his strongbox, Festus Rufius hoped to get within striking distance of the imperial purple.

But in the Villa's musty library, purple was indistinguishable from the darkness where piles of scrolls lay undisturbed by dust and disinterest. Rufius was about to resume touring the site when he noticed an empty shelf, recently cleared of cobwebs.

"Shine your lamp over here, Vindex," Rufius ordered. Having Vindex as a bodyguard made him uneasy, but Rufius had always felt inadequate around gladiators. "Not that your opinion matters, but should my inaugural games begin with a triumphant march through town?"

Vindex entered the room and nearly filled it. "Your brother had a triumph?"

The lamp light flickered and Rufius avoided the former barbarian's eerie gaze. "I'm only proposing a small triumph, Vindex, a governor's triumph," he said.

"Your father—he's had a triumph?"

Vindex pulled the door shut, cutting them off from the corridor and the world beyond.

Rufius stiffened. There was rancor in the slave's voice that needed to be set straight. "It's not your station to question my desires."

"My father had a triumph." Vindex's words hung like cobwebs in the corners of the small, damp library.

"Your father had a triumph?" Rufius laughed. There was no domesticating a barbarian—one might as well trust a wolf. Why hadn't Trajan finished this one off? "Who do you take me for?" he said.

Vindex snuffed the flame with his fingers and the room went dark. He spoke in a low, resonant voice, evoking menace and melancholy. "My father marched behind your Emperor Trajan. He marched through the streets of Rome."

"Poppycock!" Rufius cursed himself for getting trapped in a lost corner of the Villa with a moss-eating murderer whose former specialty was tearing victims limb-from-limb with his bare hands. Whoever had hired this feral giant would have hell to pay.

"My father marched through the streets behind the emperor's chariot," Vindex said. A slow crescendo rose from deep within his vaulted chest. "He marched with my uncles, my brothers, and the other warriors. They dragged their chains all the way to the coliseum. Romans cheered when my kin were tied to posts, covered with pitch and straw, and set on fire to light the games. I saw everything."

Rufius retreated into the darkness, feeling along the moldy shelves to find the door. Clearly, Minem was right: There was a murderous conspiracy in Tarraco, no doubt run by whoever controlled this morose monster. Security guard, indeed! Every small town jailor knew that security guards commit more crimes than they prevent. What numbskull would believe Vindex's cheap alibi about Biberious' murder?

"Vindex," Rufius said with all the authority he could muster, "I order you to—"

But Vindex had vanished, leaving Rufius to ruminate in the dark.

"Minem!" Rufius threw the door open and ran shouting into the dim corridor. "Minem!"

By the time Winus Minem found Rufius wandering lost in the corridors, the governor had made up his mind and regained his tenuous composure. "Gather the slaves. It's time to weed their little garden of conspiracies."

Rufius' fleshy face was folded into deep wrinkles. The laugh lines bordering his brown eyes showed no signs of amusement.

"Whatever you're thinking," Minem said, "I advise against it."

"All slaves, including Vindex, will serve in my inaugural games." Disoriented by the maze of corridors, Rufius waited by a doorway that had been nailed shut. A drop of water, dirty from having seeped through the ceiling, broke loose and hit him on the head. "We can't let one bad grape spoil the wine. Go make the announcement and earn your commission."

"In a case like this, it would be better to communicate via rumor," Minem said. "We can let slip some chatter about how slaves have become too expensive and drop a few hints about getting costs under control."

"No." Rufius started walking again, watching the ceiling to avoid leaks. "As true as whatever you just said might be, I can't afford to have fifty slaves slinking around like sun-starved vipers."

Hearing the approach of heavy footsteps, Rufius turned abruptly down an adjacent corridor, which like many in the Villa, brought him back to the same place he had been standing a moment earlier. He realized that he would need a map, a trained ferret, or a native guide to navigate this labyrinth. Alternatively, since half of the corridors led nowhere, he considered knocking a few holes in the walls so he could get lost faster.

"We strike them before they strike us," Rufius explained to Minem who, knowing the corridors, had not followed. There was something devious about the advisor, something Rufius would have to worry about once he had expelled the thieving slaves and their thick-skulled ringleader, Vindex.

Rufius took off down a perpendicular corridor, one with dim light at the end of the passage.

To keep up with the agitated governor, Minem doubled his pace and lengthened his stride to the point where he was almost jumping from tile to tile. "It would be better if you deliver the message personally," he said. "The rank and file will appreciate hearing that you share their pain and that you too are making sacrifices. Besides, legally speaking, I'm not sure an advisor can authorize the summary execution of four dozen slaves."

"Is that why my father hired you?" Rufius bolted down another corridor, resigned to the possibility that it, too, would lead nowhere. "To dodge responsibility?"

"My responsibility is to help you become an effective leader, sir." Minem said. He needed to catch his breath, but could not afford to miss an obvious opportunity to grow his influence. "You do want to rise in the hierarchy, don't you? Consider this your first opportunity to make a name for yourself."

"I have a name," Rufius said, "and my name has a date with destiny."

The corridor emptied into a small banquet room that stunk like something long dead. Not sure where he was relative to anywhere he had been before, Rufius peered into the dark corners but could not find the exit or the source of the smell, until Carbo the kitchen slave entered the room with a plate of grilled wolf's livers.

"There's a centurion here to see you, my Lord. He's waiting in the atrium," Carbo announced.

"How did you know where to find us?" Rufius asked. He inspected the fare and scowled. His disappointment with the Villa now included everything and everyone in it. "These aren't the lark's tongues I ordered."

"Fresh out of lark's tongues, my Lord," Carbo said. It was his first encounter with his new master and, having heard that many slaves would be fed to lions, the small, ageless servant was desperate to make a good impression. He hunched his narrow shoulders and looked down with deference. "Wolf liver is said to be an excellent tonic against gout and lechery."

"Wouldn't want gout." Rufius' sudden hunger outweighed his general reticence to eating predators. After a few mouthfuls, he waved Carbo away. "Go. Gather everyone in the garden."

The worried slave disappeared and Minem led Rufius back through the confusing hallways, taking extra time to ply his trade as they proceeded towards the atrium. "Now in a case like this, sir, the staff may exhibit some misdirected anger upon learning that they are to be executed. That's why you must speak in a soothing, neutral tone. If they still froth up over the prospect of an early afterlife, tell them that you share their disappointment."

Seven
VII

Centurion Marcus Valerius entered the atrium and gasped as if gutted by a gladiator. He clenched down on a rotting molar until the pain reminded him to loosen his bite and breathe again. Looking around the room, he saw enough wealth casually displayed to feed a legion for a year. Gilded statues, fine furniture, vases and goblets—by anyone's estimate, half the tax money in the province never left the Villa.

"Mother of Bacchus," he mumbled.

Two whispering slaves were polishing marble pillars; another appeared to be scraping mildew off the tiles with a meat cleaver. The new governor, his status obvious from the crimson trim of his toga, was waving his hands at two artisans hunched beside an elaborate mosaic. When a pillar polisher alerted Rufius that yet another petitioner had entered the room, the governor turned and beckoned theatrically.

"*Avé.*" Valerius returned the greeting and sized up his superior. The governor looked personable but avoided eye contact. He bore his paunch regally, and his face rippled like a dollop of half-risen dough. The first impression confirmed Valerius' hunch that Rufius had not ascended by merit alone.

"I hope I haven't kept you waiting," Rufius said. "I'm trying to get this province back on its feet, but people keep interrupting trying to gain some shred of favor."

"I understand perfectly, Excellency." The governor's thin geniality made Valerius feel immediately unwelcome. He looked around the room again, trying again to take it all in without choking on the ostentation. The conclusion was unavoidable: for the last twenty years, while he supped on gruel and bivouacked under more than a few hostile stars, the privileged sons of senators had been getting fat and living large.

Rufius let himself get distracted by a shadow passing over the skylight. Once satisfied that nothing was amiss, he dropped into a plush sofa, and left the dumbfounded soldier standing at attention. "Our beloved Hadrian, may he outlive the moon, says we mustn't get complacent. The empire is stable, but he says rot comes from within."

"And above," Valerius added, but Rufius was not listening. Valerius had seen his type before. The sons of wealthy patricians passed through the legion camps during times of peace in order to play soldier just long enough to claim they had served the empire before serving themselves. They were harmless until they returned home and voted to send the troops off into deserts and bogs in pursuit of territory, tribute, and exaggerated threats.

"The entire empire is in such an exciting state of flux," Rufius said, waving his arms limply.

"Flux and reflux," Valerius said. He now understood from whom his old friend Fidelis Magnus, the jargon-slinging security guard, had taken inspiration. Feeling out of his element, Valerius elected to do as the Romans. "In actual fact, I'm here to discuss my own flux," he said, the last word buzzing slightly on his tongue. "I was summoned by the former governor, may he rest in peace."

"Unlikely." Rufius yawned. "Murdered men never rest in peace."

"I've been a loyal servant of our Emperor Hadrian and Trajan before him, may the gods favor them both. I've served Rome for twenty years. And now—"

"And now for some grapes," Rufius interrupted, clapping his hands.

Carbo appeared from behind a shadow looking slight and ancient. The tiny servant deposited a gilded bowl in front of his master and scurried away faster than a drenched cat.

Rufius picked at the grapes, looking for one to his liking and not offering any to his visitor. After losing interest in the imperfect fruit, he focused his attention on the distant wall of the great room, squinting until his cheeks folded over. As if remembering something urgent, he kicked off his oversized sandals

•

and shuffled across the heated floor towards the unfinished mosaic.

"Come see this new mosaic," he said to Valerius. "The tile work is so fine that it seems like a painting. Look carefully! I'll bet even an eagle-eyed sentry like you can't see the individual tiles. Admit it, soldier, you can't see them, can you?"

Valerius considered the emerging mosaic, and concluded that the labor and materials were easily worth twice the pension he had come to claim. He suspected that the imported fragments of red, yellow, and azure organized by color across the floor had travelled farther than he had. Not sure what to say, Valerius pretended to admire the tile work and wondered why the governor seemed indifferent to the sounds of bare feet stomping.

"Governor Biberious summoned me here to discuss my pension."

Rufius continued to examine the detailed mosaic, squinting and eying it with disappointment. "There's something about this design that's really nagging at me," he said. "The transitions between colors still look too abrupt. No doubt about it, Centurion. These tiles aren't small enough. It will just have to be redone."

Valerius suppressed an urge to grab the governor's shoulders and shake the frivolity from his flaccid face. Instead, he held his breath to keep from shouting and tried not to let his exasperation show. Marcus Valerius knew how the world worked: being born right set the stars in motion. From the moment Festus Rufius slid down the birth canal, his path had been well greased. The governor's soft gut and tousled black hair bore witness to a lazy lifetime of pork, pleasure, and pampered living. With men like this in charge, Valerius saw little hope for the empire.

He watched Rufius run his smooth hands over the tiles and step back to examine the mosaic from a new angle. The governor muttered something under his breath about the difficulty of finding good help in the hinterlands and shook his head with disapproval.

"If I'm not needed here—," Valerius said.

"It's not that we don't need you, Centurion." The governor accepted a glass of wine from Carbo, who, again, appeared as if from nowhere. Rufius leaned against a freshly polished pillar and ran his stubby fingers over the cold pink marble. "We just don't need you here."

"Then my retirement is granted?"

While Rufius sipped his wine, Valerius noted that the three slaves were now exchanging conspiratorial glances instead of pretending to clean. Carbo looked nervous enough to dissolve into a corner. Valerius' senses perked up; even a conscript could see something was amiss. The commotion that had been growing in the hallways suddenly went silent.

The sound of a man grunting broke the silence. Valerius turned in time to see Fidelis Magnus, the security chief, fall into the room and land bound and gagged on his backside.

Valerius sprang forward with his *gladius*, but before he could cut his old comrade's hands free, six knife-wielding slaves burst into the atrium. The three pillar polishers joined the mob, adding to the odd lot of angry slaves.

Working quickly, Valerius ripped the swatch of material from Magnus' mouth. Looking up from the floor, Magnus winked at Valerius with the delight of someone unaffected by the bad news he was about to deliver. "Bit of a problem," he said. "The slaves are revolting—"

"When slaves aren't revolting, they're just plain disgusting," Rufius turned and was surprised to see the mob facing him. He stepped behind the centurion for safety. "What's the meaning of this?"

Nervous, but determined, the slaves shifted about and looked at each other, but none had the audacity to speak. More footsteps and shouting rumbled in the corridor and, within seconds, another wave of slaves crowded through the door and shoved their uneasy comrades forward.

"I've got a legion at the entrance," Valerius said, *gladius* in hand, "but I don't think they'll be needed."

Surprised to see a centurion, a few slaves turned to leave, only to be blocked by the more militant among them. The mob shifted in place, waiting for a leader to emerge, but no one stuck his neck out.

"We're not guilty," said someone deep in the crowd and others mumbled in rough agreement.

"We'll die to prove our innocence!"

"Dying proves nothing but stupidity." Valerius maintained the calm, measured tone of one who had outsmarted more than a few armed rebels.

"Now, now, Centurion," Rufius said, from his new vantage point behind a pillar. "Don't provoke these misguided slaves. They mean no harm; do you, my good fellows?"

Valerius kept his eyes on the mob, but realized that he was stuck. As long as he was in Hispania, he was under the questionable command of Festus Rufius, a man who had just proven himself quick to coddle mutiny. How had someone so thick survived his own childhood?

The slaves prodded each other forward; digging their heels into Fidelis Magnus as they stepped on and over him. Valerius drew a mental line on the floor beyond which any advancing slave would die but, before he could muster a defense, Carbo materialized into the narrowing breach and leapt into his arms.

"I'm a hostage!" Carbo shouted.

The kitchen slave's popularity was enough to halt the mob's advance. The lull suggested that Carbo's predicament had not been foreseen.

"One more step and the soldier will kill Carbo!" Rufius shouted. He took advantage of the confusion to jump out from behind the column, run out a nearby door, and slam it shut.

"Slip out the door, we'll lose them in the corridors." Carbo whispered to Valerius. He then began squirming in the centurion's arms and shouting, "Back off! He'll kill me if you make another move!"

Valerius edged backwards and the barefoot crowd crept towards him. When he tried to open the door that Rufius was holding shut from the other side, the angry slaves surged forward and pounded on his back.

"Open the door," Valerius shouted.

After a plate crashed into the door above him, Valerius dropped Carbo and wrenched the door open. He squeezed into the corridor and tried to drag Carbo from the scrabble, but Rufius managed to pull the door shut before the little slave could escape to safety.

"These bleeders need to learn who's in charge!" Rufius' panic filled the hallway. Trembling, he steadied his nerves by pressing all his weight against the door and secured the lock with his trembling hands.

The scrum raged on the other side of the heavy door, throwing furniture, breaking statues, and pummeling Fidelis Magnus with blind and random fury.

"I'm going to rescue your kitchen slave," Valerius said, struggling with Rufius to get control of the door handle. "He saved your life."

"No!" Rufius laced his fingers through the handle and held on with the full weight of his aristocracy. "Tough times require sacrifices. Get me to safety and I'll overlook how you provoked the rebellion."

Valerius eyed the governor. In the thin yellow light, Rufius looked weak and pallid but his vested authority was as unquestionable as his false testimony would be at a court martial. Some commanders' glory came from valor; others from vanity, but in either case, rank was sacrosanct. Valerius had no choice but to obey.

Valerius saw a wall sconce and a series of doors down the long corridor, but as the men proceeded down the hallway, the exits seemed to dissolve. Tendrils of smoke from the guttering lamps beckoned them forward, but each new portal proved false as the men lurched from door to disappearing door.

One corridor gave way to other inky hallways, snaking and knotting upon themselves like the Medusa's hair. Valerius smudged his finger on the wall every few paces, leaving a trace to follow in case they got lost, but his strategy failed when a burst of cold wind extinguished the remaining lamps.

The sudden darkness was so disorienting that Rufius lost his balance and fell to the ground. Valerius helped the governor up, and tried to make sense of the chimeras floating like shadows in the night. He wondered if the earth and sky had changed places. It was as if the Villa were perched atop the maw of Hades. Echoes washed through the hallways and swirled around him like a pack of jays.

"A Minotaur!" Rufius shouted. "Half man, half bull!" He jumped up and disappeared down the hallway, only to return a second later. "We're lost, doomed," he whimpered. "There's no escaping the monster."

Valerius took a deep breath and steadied his nerves. Though the eighth of November was still a few days away, there was no denying that the air was alive with phantoms. The odds of a Minotaur escaping from the depths were slim, but in such a winding, fetid womb anything was possible.

His eyes adjusted to the darkness as followed Rufius through the hallways, turning this way and that until he recognized his own finger marks in the charred plaster above an extinguished lamp. "We've been here before," he said.

"No, we haven't," Rufius insisted, beset with fear. "These corridors are endless."

Approaching footsteps drummed against the floor tiles and bounced off the coved plaster. Slamming doors and the chanting of angry slaves throbbed in the thick air. Valerius felt the blood surge of approaching battle, though he was uncertain as to the nature of his enemies. If the corridors truly issued forth from the gates of Hades, the arrival of a few armed slaves would be the least of his problems.

"Forward!" Rufius shouted, announcing their position to anyone who might be interested. "Attack!"

Valerius hushed the governor. "Are you trying to get us killed?"

Rufius smashed the wine glass he still carried against the wall and waved it wildly in the darkness. "Kill them all. Spare no one!"

"Quiet," Valerius whispered. "Unless we're attacked from both directions, this corridor will be easy to defend."

"Our foe isn't human!" Rufius shouted.

"Follow me." Valerius drew his *gladius*. His first obligation was to defend the governor even if Rufius seemed determined to make it impossible. Valerius nudged the trembling governor forward. "We'll turn right at every corner until we're out of here."

"You can't fool me," Rufius said, trailing closely behind Valerius. "This uprising was your idea. My slaves were happy until you showed up. You're in league with those who want to reverse our Roman way of life."

Valerius tightened his jaw and ignored the provocation. He fought back the growing suspicion that someone—his ex-friend Magnus or the odd conscript Severus—had impugned his patriotism to the governor. If, in fact, Rufius was trying to ferret out Valerius' old republican leanings, he had chosen a dark and narrow corridor to confront an armed man with little left to lose. He hoped that the entire episode would prove to have been a final test of his mettle and that he might still emerge from the labyrinth with his pension in hand.

"Turn left," Rufius insisted.

For the first time in his life, Valerius ignored the order of a superior. He turned right and the barefoot governor shuffled behind reluctantly. After two more right turns, they saw a dim oil lamp glowing at the end of a short corridor.

"My bedroom!" Rufius tried shoving past Valerius, but the centurion blocked the passage.

"About my pension," Valerius said.

"Sorry," Rufius said. "Hispania's broke." He tried to reach past Valerius, but he was unable to reach the door handle.

The menace of marching feet grew louder. Trembling like a pot of fresh porridge, Rufius found himself caught between the hardened centurion and a rising rebellion. "Let me through or we'll both be killed," he insisted.

"Have you never faced death?" Valerius looked past the shaking governor to the stubborn column of slaves now edging towards them with lamps, shovels, and knives. He smiled for the first time since entering Hispania.

"You can't blackmail a man with no money," Rufius said. "Alive or dead, I can't pay your pension."

The eyes of a dozen slaves seemed to hover and draw closer, glowing yellow in the wan light. Their murmurs dropped to the low droning menace of shuffling feet and strained breathing.

"I've got an idea," Rufius whispered. "Let's discuss this in my bedroom."

Valerius cracked open the heavy door and the men slipped through to safety before the wave of angry servants could crest and break upon them.

Eight
VIII

As soon as the grumpy commander was out of view, Gaius Severus disregarded his orders. Seeing no sign of *vigiles* or the Corsican, he stole across the empty parade grounds.

Tufts of thorny weeds and pristine puddles bore evidence that no training had taken place for days. Perhaps, finding no enemy, the cohort had finally disbanded. Besides enforcing tax collection, legionaries had little else to do in Tarraco and the greater province hadn't seen military action since the *Pax Romana*—the *"Pox" Romana* as his father used to call it—had taken root.

Proceeding cautiously, Severus could hear the markets, *fora*, and streets of Tarraco vibrating on the other side of the stone ramparts. Smoke wafting from illegal braziers drifted above the rooftops of firetrap tenements like the one he had lived in just a few days prior.

He walked towards the southwestern watchtower, the one dedicated to Minerva, Goddess of Wisdom. Severus considered the wisdom of plunging back into the thick of the town where he might still be a wanted man. Minerva had wisely seen fit to abandon humanity, but Severus had no choice but to return.

Passing under Minerva's gate, Severus noticed a small, bird-pecked pile of congealed entrails left as an offering to a small statue gracing a worn granite altar. Severus considered offering a prayer, but the impulse passed quickly. His father had never embraced the Roman gods, so they could not be expected to intervene now on his behalf. If Minerva truly watched over Tarraco, she had turned a blind eye to his kin.

Severus wondered if his father was still alive, cowering in a dark cell under the arena, waiting for the games to start and his life to end. What if he was suffering? A poor man's testimony was not valid unless extracted by torture, which meant that, at best, one's innocence could only be proven posthumously.

Mid-day shadows fell from the ramparts whose stones came from the same quarry where Severus had worked and taken refuge. Unsure if the terror had subsided, or if he was he about to spring a trap of his own making, Severus entered the city.

The smells of frugal midday meals—salted fish balls, boiled sausages and egg yolks being prepared in wine bars, flats, and snack shops—reminded Severus of his hunger. He zigzagged through the narrow streets of shops, stalls, and squalid, fire-prone flats, changing direction often to avoid being followed, trying to blend in, though he was a head taller than most of his countrymen.

He hugged the walls to avoid the slop that people routinely threw from the top floors. A slurry of waste water ran down an open channel in the middle of the street. The richer neighborhoods enjoyed underground sewers, but here the smell of sausage, smoke, and sewage swirled and flowed with the raw pulse of the plebian slum. By day, the streets bustled with petty crime and commerce. By night, the alleys hosted lascivious larcenies and cheap pleasures. If a sailor could not find what he needed in the docklands and slums of Tarraco, he simply was not trying.

"Fresh water!" called a boy pushing a wheelbarrow loaded with sloshing, upright amphorae. The city plumbing barely extended to the edge of this neighborhood, and only the wealthier homes, those on ground level, were tapped into the water mains, legally or not. "Free delivery!" he cried.

A girl Severus recognized called down from her perch three floors above street level. From atop a tattered cascade of drying laundry, she indicated which rickety stairway the water boy should climb to reach her warren. Severus looked up towards her balcony and felt a sudden urge to deliver the water himself until her mother, a flabby-armed *domina* he had no desire to tangle with, came out to monitor her daughter's modesty. The sagging matron with hair like the Medusa leaned over the railing with a scowl that purged Severus' heart of past, present, and future flirtation. Quickly metering out a frayed rope, the glaring woman lowered a slop bucket that Severus barely had time to sidestep.

The boy ladled water into a small urn and wrestled it up the crooked stairs. As soon as he disappeared into the dark beehive of apartments, a moneylender clutching a well-used abacus darted over to the cart and filled his cup. A nearby dentist watched disapprovingly from behind a table laden with pulled teeth from satisfied customers.

Severus continued down the street, slowly navigating the flowing canal of carts, commerce, and commotion. Faded graffiti from a recent wave of protests had been covered with an advertisement for the services of a professional calling herself "The Exotic Zina." The greasy odors of the cook-shops mingled with the rising stench of urine from a basement wool fuller. Above, a layer of smoke seemed to brace the buildings from slouching into each other and crumbling onto the street below. It was in tenements like these, blocks of lice-infested *insulae*, that the forgotten citizens of the wide empire turned flour and flax into bread and linen and offered daily thanks to their household gods.

Severus looked up cautiously and saw from an unfamiliar blanket airing on the windowsill that his former flat had already been occupied. Saddened, he proceeded cautiously towards the *Via Sacra*, at the end of which stood the great temple where long ago a palm tree, the symbol of Augustus and Apollo, had sprouted miraculously out of solid rock.

Unlike the vibrant popular district he had just left, the fine shops and establishments along the *Via Sacra* were shuttered. A long funeral procession was snaking towards the marble columned temple, preventing Severus from crossing the street. The swelling crowd behind him made it impossible to turn back.

"Dead nobleman?" asked a fisherman who smelled like he had just gutted a large tuna. He and Severus watched the procession approach from behind the swarm of well-dressed citizens. "A magistrate, perhaps?"

"The governor," Severus replied and turned away from the parade. He knew that of all the bad places for a wanted man to surface, a noble funeral, thick with security, was the worst. Finding himself hemmed in by the crowd, he bent his knees to lower his profile, and came eye-to-eye with the angler. "Biberious was murdered, or so they say."

"And I say the bastard deserved it." The fisherman spat on the ground in disgust.

"The old goat turned off the grain dole," said an elderly woman standing next to them. She pulled a faded green *stola* around her shoulders. Her hair smelled of old rose water, evidence that she had passed the morning at the public bathhouse. "Without that grain the whole town will starve."

The woman's comments attracted agreement and unwanted attention. Severus' bent knees began to tremble, but he could not escape from the packed crowd, nor could he stand up straight and risk being seen.

"Money, child, it's all about money, isn't it?" The woman said, louder and more seditious. A few people nodded in agreement; others stared in disbelief that she was expressing publically what many dared not say in private. She clenched her teeth and glared at the funeral procession. "Biberious didn't care a rat's tail if we starved. Good riddance, I say."

"Don't get so worked up, Ma'am," Severus whispered. He stared down at the ground so as not to be recognized. "I'm sure the new governor will get the dole started again."

The outspoken woman, looked up at him with suspicion, and considered her response carefully. "Where is our new governor? Why isn't he paying his respects? If he doesn't bring back the bread dole…" she slashed two crooked fingers across her wrinkled throat.

Blaring trumpeters announced a line of solemn men in stiff-pleated, crimson-trimmed togas. They wore the plaster death masks of the deceased's ancestors. Clearly, the ex-governor was someone who would not have to haggle with Charon, Hade's boatman, over the price of passage to the afterlife.

Severus pulled the folds of his cloak over his head, as both a sign of respect and a convenient way to shroud his face should the watchful eyes of the secret police chance upon him. He straightened his knees slowly, and looked over the heads of the crowd.

Severus strained to see if a bite or two of fresh meat or, better, a pitcher of warm, honeyed wine might be found at the end of the parade route. His stomach grumbled loud enough to wake the dead.

Gripping his gut and turning back towards the upstream procession, he saw eight men approaching. They carried a bier upon which the dead governor lay lifelike on his side, arm bent at the elbow, head propped against his hand. He stared sternly at Severus as he passed by. *You'll soon share my fate*, he seemed to say, *but not my comfort*.

Behind the dead man's bier, Biberious' stern wife followed in a sedan chair carried by eight slaves. She sat behind translucent silk curtains, her bracelets jingling rhythmically. Professional mourners wailed, trailing the family, friends, and former clients of the mysteriously departed.

Severus watched the parade pass and estimated how long he had been away from his post. In addition to the danger of being caught by the *vigiles*, the old centurion might send out an unforgiving search party. Absent without leave would not be a favorable start to his military career, but depending on the next few minutes, his career as a soldier might never start.

Nine
IX

Valerius barred the bedroom door against the onrush of angry slaves and Rufius tapped his way along the wall, hoping to find a hollow spot where he could break through to the outside.

"I'm not going back in the corridors ever." Rufius grabbed a wooden stool and smashed it against the wall between his bedchamber and the garden. After crashing through the lathwork, the stool hit stone and was reduced to splinters.

"Stop," Valerius shouted. He steadied Rufius by the shoulders and took the remains of the stool from his hand. "The window is hinged."

"Your hand is on my person." Rufius brushed Valerius away like one might a gnat.

While Rufius fumbled with the window latch, the slaves shouted in the corridor and pounded on the oak door. Their persistent drumming echoed back and forth through the bedroom until the air seemed to shake.

"Uppity slaves! Free food ... a roof overhead ... why are some people never satisfied?" Rufius turned to Valerius; his scowl made it clear that were it not for the present menace, their meeting would have long been over.

Valerius regarded the governor from across the distance that brought them together and still left them so far apart. He had spent twenty years fighting and winning lesser battles but had nothing in his arsenal for a foe such as Rufius. He drew his *gladius* and stepped forward with grim determination.

"The emperor needs generals in Germania," Rufius said, his voice quivering. "If you can stop this rebellion, I could arrange for a promotion." He edged backwards until he realized that Valerius had only drawn the long knife to chip the thick paint off the window hinges.

"Germania?" The slaves redoubled their efforts to pulverize the heavy door and Valerius considered throwing it open. A phalanx of angry slaves was preferable to a capricious governor, a pampered pillow pusher who intended to ship him off to die in the wet forests of Germania. Though history might never miss or make note of Festus Rufius, the temptation to remove him from its rolls passed quickly. Rufius was slippery as snake snot, but Valerius knew he was honor-bound to obey a superior.

Refusing to admit defeat, Valerius established a fallback position while wrestling with the stuck window. "What about staying here to improve the roads, build aqueducts and triumphant arches? Surely you still need legionaries in this province?"

"Yes, yes, but alas, Centurion, we need to prioritize." Rufius sighed loudly, wagging a finger as if chastising a child. "We can do anything, but we can't do everything. Arches, aqueducts, and all that whatnot are all well and good, but they don't kill barbarians, and that's what the emperor needs you to do."

The pounding grew louder. The door bent and swelled like a drum skin. Impatient with Valerius' slow progress, Rufius grabbed another stool and hurled it towards the window, but it hit Valerius in the back of the shoulder instead.

"It seems you still need a few legionaries in Hispania." Valerius ignored the flung stool.

"You're needed in Germania," Rufius insisted.

Valerius could think of no greater ignominy than dying in Germania, the wolf infested bane of the empire. *Germania!* It was just as Severus had said. Where did that kid get his information? Valerius saw he had been right to suspect that Severus was a spy, wrong to think that Magnus was an ally, and foolish to assume one governor would honor another's commitment to a loyal soldier.

"What possible good can a southern soldier do in a place where babies cry poison tears, women have three breasts, men mate with mountain lions, and—"

"Break open that vexed window before I have you arrested."

Ignoring the panicky, chair-throwing governor, Valerius climbed atop the stool and calmly chipped at the old paint between the casement and the lintel. He worked at the window while

Rufius paced like a pigeon. After a few more minutes of ramming the door, the slaves abandoned the task, leaving the two men awash in thick and sudden silence.

Creaking window hinges and a timid knocking at the door soon replaced the noisy rebellion. Someone tapped a distinct rhythm, drumming a pattern that offered a welcome counterpoint to the hammering of fists moments earlier. Recognizing the secret pattern, Rufius wrestled with the door as Valerius wrenched open the window.

"Carbo," Rufius said, quickly swallowing any relief he let slip. "You survived?"

Carbo the kitchen slave entered with a fresh pitcher of red wine, locked the door behind him, and poured a glass for his master. After handing the drink to Rufius, the tiny, timeless servant waited by the open window, withdrawn to the point where light seemed to pass right through the gray folds of his tunic.

After wiping his knife clean along the hem of his tunic, Valerius rubbed his eyes and tried to focus on Carbo, but the loyal slave appeared to flicker in and out of existence. A sudden ray of sunlight split and bent around his body, giving the impression that he might dissolve into the slightest wind. Valerius had heard talk of phantoms whose spirits inhabited canyons, shrines, and dwellings where they had unfinished business. If Carbo was such a sprite, why was he acting so helpful?

Rufius stopped pacing long enough to sip wine from his goblet. "Enough small talk," he said after a second's consideration. "Forget Germania. Instead, I'm assigning you to lead *Scipio IV Hispania*. They left a few days ago, marching north across Gaul. Under your able leadership, they'll help build a great wall across Britannia."

"The *Scipio*? The empire's most, er, challenged cohort?" Valerius stiffened his upper lip and lower intestines. "Am I being punished, sir? If there's something I've—"

Chanting slaves, more militant than musical, could be heard through the open window. Both men looked to Carbo for an explanation as to why all of Hades seemed to be rising..

61

Looking rejuvenated for having soaked in the passing sunlight, Carbo stepped away from the window and refilled Rufius' goblet. "Vindex has gathered the slaves in the garden," he said.

"That muscle-bound moron! He was supposed to gather them in the arena." Rufius accepted and drained another glass of wine in one fluid gesture. "Haven't I had enough excitement for one day?"

"Vindex has them contained for the moment," said Carbo, his pitcher poised to intervene if needed. "They're ready to talk with you."

Rufius bristled at the notion of jawboning with the same rabble that had just tried to break his skull. Between Minem's constant talk of assassins, Vindex's hubris, and the petulant slaves, Hispania seemed more and more like a stepping stone to nowhere. Tarraco was an unlikely haven from which to spring the contents of his strongbox on the empire. Fortunately, the timely appearance of the desperate centurion suggested a change in strategy. Valerius was stoic, idealistic, and dull enough to be considered trustworthy.

"If you're too old to fight in Germania, and too stiff to build walls across Britannia, there is one other possibility …" Rufius dragged his strongbox from the corner and turned to Valerius. "I've got important cargo that needs to be escorted out of here."

"In other words," Valerius said, "You're trying to fob me off without a pension."

"My predecessor drained the treasury," Rufius said firmly. "In appreciation of your service to the empire, I'm awarding you a top-secret mission for which you are uniquely qualified. You will transport a package to my brother, Consul Rufius, who will meet you in one month's time at Londinium. The coast road is probably swimming in spies, so take the mountain route to avoid detection."

Valerius tugged at a fold in his tunic and tried not to look as discouraged as he felt. "Any chance of staying in this province, Excellency?" he asked. "You're aware that I was scheduled to retire in two months?"

"Believe me, we are all making sacrifices for the cause," Rufius reassured him.

Valerius stood ashen-faced trying to imagine what sacrifices Festus Rufius might be making.

"You have your orders, Centurion." Rufius' stomach rumbled loud enough to startle himself. "If you can complete your task before the Ides of December, I'll move Olympus and Earth to secure your pension."

Valerius considered the offer and weighed it against the fat man it came from. There was no reason to believe anything Rufius said, but as long as Valerius wore the uniform, he had no better option than to follow orders. As setbacks went, a six week mission through peaceful territory could be considered tolerable, even lucky given the alternatives. How far away could Londinium be? "Consider it done, Governor."

"Excellent. You are dismissed, Centurion." Rufius climbed out the window. As an afterthought, he peered back into the bedroom. "Enjoy the food in Britannia. I hear it's excellent."

Ten
X

Gaius Severus snuck away from the funeral procession and walked down a trash strewn side street towards the plebian baths. The slums hid so many secrets that it would be a simple matter to disappear into the grime and never return to the garrison. Why should a cynical old centurion care if some scrawny conscript of questionable military value went missing?

The smells of sustenance drifting over the open-air market reminded Severus that he was as hungry as a beggar. He could barely remember his last bowl of thin porridge. Late autumn was supposed to be a time for eating salt fish, citrus, and roasted nuts; a time for savoring the last apples before winter. He dug into a hidden pocket inside his tunic, but could not find one sorry *sesterce* to spend. Poorer than the lowliest house slave, he realized that the garrison was the only place he might find a free crust of bread.

He stopped in front of a table laden with dried fruit where a young woman with wide hips attended to an old slave with an empty basket. She was the same girl Severus had seen looking down from a balcony and he stopped to find out if her fetching smile had been directed at him or the water boy. Pretending to inspect the fruit, Severus popped a prune in his mouth, smiled at her, and nearly choked with surprise to see the stubble-faced Corsican coming towards him. The same man who days earlier had beaten his brother and dragged off his father was pushing through the crowd with lawless determination.

Severus retreated slowly so as not to attract the man's attention. Perhaps the brute had just been a hired hand; a momentary mercenary paid a coin or two to lend his muscle to the understaffed *vigiles*. Maybe the Corsican had already forgotten the blur of terrified faces he had seen that night.

Maybe cats would bark.

Severus turned slightly and saw that the man was following so he dashed into the market street and tried to disappear into the crowd. The thug's persistence meant revenge, a reward, or both. As he weaved in between the shoe peddlers, fishmongers, food carts and shoppers, Severus recalled his last encounter with the Corsican. If the man's dog-faced counterpart had plummeted four floors to the cobblestone, Gaius Severus might be wanted for murder.

A boy pushing a cart full of red apples rounded the corner, swerved to avoid the oncoming wave of funeral spectators, and lost control. The cart capsized and toppled into the street, forcing the Corsican to dodge the sudden obstacle and the anonymous forest of hands stealing the runaway fruit. Hunger trumping terror, Severus grabbed an apple as he sped past.

"Sorry," Severus called back to the boy who would undoubtedly receive a sound beating when he returned empty-handed to his master.

Taking advantage of the confusion, Severus slipped around the corner, knocked down a rubbish heap, leaving a slippery mess behind. He ran towards the entrance to the commoners' baths and before entering through the whitewashed door, looked back to verify that he had escaped. He felt as if the entire town could hear his heart pounding. No doubt, they would cheer to see it ripped out on the arena floor by an unshaved Corsican.

Panting, he ducked into the steamy entrance. The bath attendant was snoring on his stool. His eyelids were swollen and purple, his face puffed with bruises.

"My master lost his loin cloth here last week," Severus said, shaking the attendant's shoulder. "I've come to recover it and re-cover him, if you please."

Marius Severus gasped at the sight of his younger brother. "Come with me," he said, jerking the front of his brother's tunic. He dragged Gaius down a narrow hallway, yanked open a door, and the two stumbled into the dank storage room, darkened from years in the humid air. "Idiot! Coming here? Are you crazy?"

It was not the welcome Gaius had been expecting from his older brother. "I'm in trouble, Marius," Gaius said, "and I'm being followed."

"So you came to me? Are you trying to get us both killed?" Marius Severus let go of his younger brother's tunic, but not before shaking him in frustration. "Do you think proscription is a game?"

"I don't think the police saw me come in here." In spite of his hobnailed sandals, the tile covering the brick plenum leading to the *tepidarium*, was warm underfoot.

"Don't think? You never think. Informers are everywhere—it's the most profitable job in the whole bloody empire and these baths are swimming with them."

"So what are you doing here?" Gaius squinted to see his brother through the shadows and steam. Marius had their father's long nose and their mother's dark, narrow-set eyes. His hair tended to curl when he let it grow, but a bounty hunter looking for one brother might easily collect a reward for the other. His face still bore the bruises from the Corsican's beating.

They heard someone barge through the main door and slam it shut. Marius peeked down the corridor. "It's him," he whispered. "The Corsican."

Trouble's heavy footsteps pounded down the hallway towards the small room where the brothers were hiding. Marius dropped to his knees and struggled with a swollen wooden plank that opened into the heating channel. Gaius lodged his fingers into the warped grillwork and the two managed to pry the panel open.

"Down there," Marius whispered. He pushed Gaius into the narrow plenum, and, not waiting, squeezed in behind.

By lying sideways on their shoulders, they managed to fit into the tight channel. Marius reached up with difficulty and slid the access panel askew across the gap just before the door burst open. The brothers could hear the angry Corsican's heavy breath above the hissing of the hot air through the gaps between the bricks and their bodies. Seeing no one in the room, the thug slammed the door and stomped back down the corridor.

Marius nudged the panel forward, tugged on its underside, and snapped it back into place.

"Shhh," Gaius whispered.

The door flew open and the Corsican charged back into the storage room. While he struggled to wedge his fat fingers into the grating, the brothers inched down the warm plenum like fat, frightened snakes.

"Go!" Marius pushed at his brother's legs, almost squirming over him.

The Corsican reached down and grabbed Marius by the heel.. Before Marius could wriggle free, the bounty hunter lowered his head into the passage, extended a hairy arm, and managed to capture an ankle. He held tight and pulled Marius backwards.

"Fifty *sesterces* and you're free," he said in a raspy voice, but the brothers were in no position to negotiate. They had no coins, no credit, and nowhere to go but forward into the hot breeze rising from the furnace.

Marius reached ahead and dug his fingernails into the brick. He managed to pull forward just enough to unbalance the Corsican and drag his dry elbows across the bottom of the rough plenum. After a brief struggle and a shallow kick, Marius jerked free of the man's grip and slithered away. For every inch that Gaius advanced, Marius progressed two and was soon doubled up over his brother's calves.

The Corsican struggled, but he was unable to advance or retreat. Too wide to extract himself from the shallow tunnel, his grunted and shouts echoed down the ductwork. The brothers slithered forward, knowing it would only be a matter of seconds before someone came to pull the overheated henchman from his predicament.

"It's getting hotter," Gaius said, squeezing along the brick-lined plenum. The hot air blowing towards him made his face feel cool as the dripping sweat evaporated.

The temperature rose as they shimmied towards the central furnace. At a junction where the channels split and widened, Gaius noticed a bit of dim light streaming through grillwork off to one side. He wiggled into the secondary channel, and was relieved to sense the hot air blowing from behind. He felt a blister forming where his shoulder had been rubbing the rough channel.

Through the brick and tile floor above them, they could hear the muffled chatter of voices in a steam room.

"Father told you to hide at the quarry," Marius growled. He found it easier to pull forward by tugging at his brother's feet then by snaking along the channel, but this had the undesired effect of dragging his brother backwards.

"I did," Gaius said, "but the legion nabbed me." He dug his fingers into the space between the bricks to prevent his brother from negating his progress.

Heavy footsteps pounding above them suggesting new pursuers had joined the hunt. The Corsican had offered others a cut of the reward and Gaius Severus was saddened to see how little his life was worth.

The brothers lay still and silent until the commotion passed. Both were parched from the heat, exertion, and inhaling the brick dust they had kicked into the hot wind.

Gaius' shoulder was bleeding, his legs were cramped, and his eyes stung with dripping sweat. The narrow plenum, the whistling sound of the hot tailwind blowing up the back of his tunic, and the thought that a gruff Corsican wanted to sell his skin for the price of a drink drained his will to go forward. Breathing heavily, he stopped and voiced the unspeakable. "Is Father dead?"

"We're dead if you don't keep moving," Marius said.

Gaius snaked towards the vent, listened for a second, and then rolled his shoulder upward into the woodwork, popping it loose. Reaching up with one arm, he grunted, twisted, and lifted himself into the room above. From the steamy air and the wet floor, he could tell that he had surfaced into one of the many bath chambers.

A trio of elderly, naked women stood up in the sunken bath, revealing their immodest surprise. They stared at Gaius as if he had just risen from Hades.

"Good day, ladies." He greeted them as best he could before choking on a lung full of brick dust. Gasping for air, Gaius crawled to the tub and drank directly from their bathwater.

Two shrieking matrons clambered out of the bath and ran naked into the corridor.

"Don't panic," Marius said, emerging red-faced from the ductwork. "We work here."

When Marius buried his face in the bath, the third woman tried to run but instead slipped and fell. Gaius helped her to her knees and was rewarded with a hearty slap in the face before she ran shouting into the hallway and crashed into someone who had come to investigate heard the commotion.

The old woman and unseen newcomer fell with a wet thud in the corridor. The brothers did not wait to see if the sound of familiar grunts from the bottom of the wrinkled pile came from the bounty hunter. They sprinted away in the opposite direction before the collision of flesh and fury had time to untangle.

"Follow me!" Marius pulled his brother into a nearby laundry room. "Here's an opening to the outside," he said before diving into a pile of moist and threadbare towels.

Gaius followed, swimming through the dirty linens until he found the narrow doorway to daylight. The laundry chute was too small for the Corsican to fit through; he would lose valuable time finding another way out of the bathhouse.

Once outside, the brothers ran into the alley and sprinted uphill, away from the harbor. Remaining outdoors rendered them easy prey so the brothers took refuge in the second tenement on the block. They bolted up the dark stairway, stumbled out onto the roof, and doubled over, wheezing in the cold November air.

"It's not safe to stay in Tarraco." Marius looked over the roof's edge into the street below but did not see the Corsican.

Gaius joined him at the edge and looked up towards the governor's villa rising on the pruned hillside above the town. The noble stone edifice was close as the crow flies, but otherwise miles away from his station in life. "I'm so hungry I could eat my hand," he muttered. "A day's scraps from that mansion could feed half the families in town."

Beyond the Temple of Saturn, they could see the harbor and the gray Mediterranean that their father and grandfather had once crossed, fleeing persecution in Rome. Once generation later, it was time to flee again.

"Assassination demands justice," Marius said, peeking over the far edge of the building. The streets were busy, but appeared free of threats for the moment. "An insult to the empire will be repaid a hundred times over. A murdered governor gives the new man an excuse to round up an arena full of rivals and riffraff."

"Father was neither."

"Jews are both." Marius crawled along the perimeter. He scanned the street below but saw nothing more than the humdrum of daily life.

"I know how it works." Gaius mimicked his brother with an air of sarcasm. "Rome's justice is brutal; her celebrations are worse." He peeked into the six-foot gap where the roofs of two leaning tenements came closest to each other. "Bread and circuses … spare me the lecture."

Ignoring the admonishment, Marius continued speaking as if an older brother had a birthright to state the obvious. "For a new governor, crucifying a few unlucky sods sends a clear message to his enemies. Feeding some victims to the mob helps them forget their hunger. It's not about guilt or innocence; it's about controlling the plebes. Father would be better off dead."

"Father isn't dead," Gaius insisted. He knelt by the edge of the roof and watched people scurrying about their daily business like ants on a dunghill. Looking upon humanity from on high, he felt as if the earth was spinning away from him. The chasm below brought back the night he escaped on a plank wobbling above the street. Had his pursuer fallen four floors to the cobblestone? He dared not ask. Dazed by the memory and the altitude, he backed away from the roofline. "If Father's alive, there's still hope."

"Hope isn't enough." A momentary trace of sadness showed beneath Marius' bruised eyes. He looked aside to avoid his brother's gaze. "Hope is what Father preached despite overwhelming evidence to the contrary. It's lucky that Mother isn't alive to see this."

"Mother said we must believe in the sun, even when it isn't shining."

"It isn't." Marius brushed his ripped tunic, but seeing the red dust rise, he stopped rather than signal their location. He walked to the center of the slate covered roof and let out a sigh of frustration. "Is this why you came back—to badger me with cheap philosophy? It served Father well, didn't it? His stupid dreams may have cost him his life."

"I thought you said he was alive."

"So much for being one of the chosen people." Anger flared in Marius' eyes. Frustrated with heaven and earth, he shook his fist at the sky. "Next time, choose someone else, damn you!"

Not wanting to provoke his brother or the Lord further, Gaius said nothing. Marius' conclusions were hard to deny. Those who risked their lives to follow the God of Justice seemed doomed to suffer from his indifference. The Romans, on the other hand, who kept adding new gods to their collection, were squarely on top of this world and the next.

The sound of footsteps welling up from the stairwell attracted their attention. Gaius wiped his dirty face with his sleeve and crept over to investigate.

"Someone's coming," Gaius whispered.

"Assume the worst." Marius gestured towards the building on the other side of the street. "We can jump."

Gaius blanched. "It's six feet across and four storeys down at the closest point."

The footsteps stopped at the top of the stairway.

"Do you believe in God?"

Gaius nodded.

"Then you've managed a bigger leap than this!" Marius ran across the slate roof and leapt across the divide.

The door flew open and the Corsican burst out onto the roof.

In an instant, Gaius followed his brother across the breach. He jumped the six feet and fell forward onto the flat roof with inches to spare. Marius pulled him up and pointed to the next building, a lesser leap across an equally deep chasm. Without waiting for the Corsican to choose a course, Marius ran and cleared the next gap.

"Hurry." He beckoned to his brother. "Jump!"

Stunned by his own audacity, Gaius hesitated and looked back at the Corsican. The man looked like a bull, red-faced and ready to charge. Seeing the bounty hunter crouch and then run across the opposing rooftop, Gaius quickly weighed the risk of waiting to see the outcome versus putting more distance between them. Hearing Marius call out and realizing that if the Corsican succeeded, there would be no time to recover, he sprinted over the slate tiles and tried to imagine himself as a bird. Ignoring everything except the need to land on the far side, he gathered speed and let fly. As he landed and rolled forward, Gaius heard the Corsican's shouts fade and fall into the gap.

From atop the third building, there was no way to verify what had happened to their pursuer, but the shouting of passersby echoing up from the street below suggested that the Corsican's future was not promising.

"I've got to escape," Gaius said, panting. Nausea and tears welled up as it dawned on him what he had just done. "I seem to have been conscripted, and—"

"Conscripted? You're in the legion?" Marius laughed recklessly.

The door to the stairwell was locked, but only nominally. With combined effort, the brothers pulled it open and descended the stairs to street level.

"I need to hide. I can't go to Britannia with the legion."

"Britannia?" Marius started to laugh again but suddenly turned serious. Realizing that the ground level hallway was no place to share secrets, he stepped into the street and, seeing no danger, beckoned his brother to follow. "If the Romans want to teach you how to fight, it's a skill that will come in handy."

They proceeded down the street in the opposite direction to the commotion they had caused. At best, the bounty hunter would be nursing a few broken bones. At worst, a crowd of morbid onlookers would be speculating about his death and searching his tunic for coins. The noise subsided as the brothers ran down the side streets towards the western gate and the garrison beyond.

"You're saying I should go to Britannia?" Gaius recognized the look on his brother's battered, dirty face. A plan was emerging in Marius' mind—the sort of farfetched, foolhardy plan that had kept Marius in trouble's corner for his entire life. "I'm afraid to ask what you're thinking."

"Do you remember the name of grandfather's birthplace?" Marius asked.

"Of course, it's in Judea."

Marius touched a finger to his lips and looked up as if paid informants might be hiding in the clouds above them. "After your basic training, find a way to escape and meet me there. Meanwhile, I'll find a way to free Father and the others."

"Grandfather's birthplace?—it's across the sea. Are you crazy?"

"These are crazy times." Marius smiled and looked around the corner and down one of the many poor streets where they had spent their meager childhood. Passing an unattended fruit stand, he grabbed a handful of roasted almonds and shared them with his brother. "There's something you need to understand. Father taught more than just Jewish history, he taught resistance. Our people have been beaten, but not broken. A rebellion is coming and we'll need men like the one you are about to become—trained soldiers who understand the enemy from the inside out. Now promise me you'll do as I've asked."

Confused and far from comforted by the thought of marching off with the Roman Legion, Gaius Severus nodded half-heartedly. He knew better than to start a debate when his brother caught such a notion. Marius had always suffered from an infectious grandiosity that usually faded after a night's rest.

The danger had diminished, but they knew the lull was temporary at best. The brothers stood in silence, each contemplating the difficulties ahead, neither willing to bid the first farewell.

"Good luck." Marius hugged Gaius good-bye at the western gate. "We'll meet again in Judea."

"Be careful." Gaius choked back a tear. "Try to have faith. Remember, God works in mysterious ways."

Marius laughed. "That's why it's best not to count on Him for anything."

Eleven
XI

Rufius slipped out his bedroom window, snuck into the garden, and planted himself behind a dying Arbor Vitae to avoid detection. He watched and listened as fifty agitated slaves pounded along the portico and uprooted what was left of the garden. Some exchanged angry rumors and outdid each other with conspiracy theories. Others peeled up paving stones and threw them into the mouth of a cistern.

Rufius was surprised when Vindex rose before them, cleared his throat like a thunderclap, and blamed Winus Minem for everything wrong in Hispania.

"He murdered Biberious!" Vindex shouted. His commanding voice bounced off the walls and echoed through the colonnade. He lifted the wriggling, wiry advisor and held him up for derision. "Now he wants to murder you."

Minem squirmed and protested, but his resistance was overwhelmed by Vindex's iron grip and the shrill cheers of the shouting slaves. Vindex tossed him flailing into the air, caught him by the ankles, and dangled him over a stagnant fountain.

"Dunk him!" shouted a slave.

Rufius emerged from the edge of the crowd. "Stop," he commanded.

Surprised at seeing that his new master was still alive, Vindex dropped Minem headfirst onto the flagstone and parted the crowd.

Rufius squeezed through the mob unmolested, but they quickly closed around him, blocking any hope of a graceful exit. He tried to rise above the impending fray by climbing onto a stone bench near the brackish fountain.

"It's not fair to kill us for a crime we didn't commit," an anonymous voice in the crowd called out.

Flush with a sense of mission, and motivated to survive past sunset, Festus Rufius, Governor of Hispania, faced down his rowdy house staff with a tentative smile. He signaled for the crowd to settle, caught his breath, and bought a little more time for Valerius and Carbo to escape with the precious strongbox.

"Long live Governor Biberious!" shouted a misinformed angry slave.

"Ignore the heckler, sir, there's one in every mob." Minem sneered at Vindex and jumped onto the bench next to Rufius. He shook the dust out of his hair, buried his trembling hands in the loose folds of his torn toga, and plied his trade. "If the slaves froth up over the prospect of an early afterlife, tell them that you share their disappointment."

A flash of ear-to-ear bonhomie broke unevenly across Rufius' flushed, round face. He raised his hands in the air in a gesture no one confused for a benediction. "If everyone could form one big circle around the fountain, please—let's arrange ourselves from smallest to tallest."

Nobody moved. Rufius turned to Minem. "They understand Latin, don't they?" he asked.

"Why can't we go to Master Biberious' funeral?" someone shouted and others chimed in their agreement.

"Why are we locked inside the Villa?"

"I see," Rufius said. "You want me to reward your crimes with a day's vacation?"

"We're innocent," a slave shouted. Others began yelling and pushing towards the governor. Pressed shoulder to shoulder, there was simply not enough room for the uncoordinated mob to maneuver or gather speed.

A stone landed in the murky fountain and another sailed over Minem's head before Vindex stopped the impending tempest by shouting something in his native tongue. The threat needed no translation.

Hoping that a positive first impression was still possible, Rufius did his best to establish trust. "Now that we've all had a little chance to become acquainted, let's play a game. I need you to divide into two teams. Why don't we split right down the middle?"

He waved his arm to indicate the parting line down which he intended to escape as soon as a gap formed.

Again, nobody moved.

"You can't execute us. You need the magistrate's permission, and besides, we don't even belong to you," on slave pointed out to general agreement of the others.

"A lawyer in the house?" Rufius grew angry. "Listen to me, Mister Smarty-tunic: you belong to Rome and the law is crystal clear in a case like this."

"He's going to kill us!" a washerwoman shouted, feeding the rising panic.

The crowd tensed like a coiled snake and, before it could strike, Minem jumped up onto the bench with Rufius. "No one is being executed," he announced. "It's true we may need to shrink a bit, but the governor intends to provide a fair and equitable severance."

"Severance our heads!" a kitchen slave yelled.

Minem tried to appeal to the mob's diminishing sense of reason. "The governor's hands are tied, you see. Circumstances beyond his control—"

Rufius took the cue, but not very far. "What we're doing now is simply identifying a pool of eligible workers who ..."

The crowd resumed shoving and Minem teetered on the edge of the narrow bench, waving his arms to maintain balance. "That is to say—after giving great thought to the skills needed in our new administration—quite frankly, some of you simply don't figure into it. We'd like to move you into a more permanent position—"

"Dead, you mean?" shouted the washerwoman.

Minem's attempt to keep the mood cheerful provoked the opposite result. "You'll be retrained for an exciting new role," he said.

"Rolling in the arena!" another laundry slave yelled. She picked up a loose garden tile and threw it. Others tore up the course mosaic underfoot and threw fragments at their leaders.

The slaves pushed past Vindex and rushed the bench. The washerwoman pushed Minem into the dirty fountain.

"I can't swim," he shouted before realizing that the dark water was only six inches deep. He stood up and scraped the pond scum off his forearms.

Vindex waded over as if swimming through the throng. He scooped Minem under one arm, tucked Rufius under the other, and floated them to safety through the irate crowd.

"Sell us!" a scribe shouted.

Others took up the chant. "Sell us, sell us, sell us!"

The slaves pounded their feet on the patio, their defiant cries rising into the sky above the capitol.

"Down with Vindex!" they shouted once it was clear on that the mighty champion was on the wrong side of their rebellion. "Gladiators go home."

A small, sharp tile hit Vindex in the forehead. Nearby slaves grabbed his legs and tried to pull him down, but he shook them loose and sailed forward.

Rufius, his paunch pinched as he dangled beneath Vindex's armpit, gasped for breath. Being carried away by his rough bodyguard was not the most regal of exits but, seeing that Hispania's slaves were not as reasonable as their Roman counterparts, it was not a bad coda to his first public address. "Rome thanks you for your understanding and obedience," he muttered as Vindex stuffed him back through the bedroom window. Waving magnanimously and twisting to avoid Minem who had just been tossed into the opening, he whispered a final order to Vindex: "Round up these ingrates and take them to the arena."

Twelve
XII

Gaius Severus ran along the outer ramparts, following the rough curve of the city wall to the Field of Mars. He hurried to the parade grounds, propelled in part by his brother's rebel dreams, but mostly by the realization that the legion was safer than the streets. Returning to the large oak tree where he had been ordered to wait, he was relieved to see that his commander had yet to return.

Thin November light offered a mild respite after the recent storms; a sliver of afternoon sun barely warmed the ground. Severus found a dry spot under the old oak tree and nestled into a comfortable niche among the exposed roots. He pondered his brother's grandiose vision of cleaving Judea from the empire but after a moment, nodded off to sleep. Just short of dreaming, his commander's boot brought him back to daylight.

"Attention!"

"Huh?" Seeing the centurion scowling above him Severus scrambled to his feet. "How did your meeting go, sir?"

Valerius glared. "Report, soldier."

The coastal breeze shifted, carrying the enticing smell of grilled fish from the other side of the ramparts. Severus' stomach burned with hunger. "Report, sir? Uh, nothing to report."

Valerius paced a tight line before the conscript he had not asked for and did not want. He looked Severus up and down, trying to find merit, but was clearly displeased with what little he had to work with. It had been a long time since Valerius had seen a worse conscript. He swatted some brick dust off of Severus' tunic and took a close look at the bloodstain on his shoulder. "So, you've been here the whole time?"

"Yes, sir, I mean, no sir. That is, not exactly," Severus stammered. "To be perfectly honest, sir, I got hungry so I ventured into town to find something to—"

"Hungry for what?" Valerius stomped his foot, accidently sending a plume of muddy water up his own tunic. "Wine? Wenches?"

"Both, sir." Severus played along with the notion that he was nothing more than testicles on legs. Anything was better than admitting he was a fugitive with a price on his head. "But I had no money for either."

"Any street urchin could lie better than you." Valerius stepped back onto a dry patch and scraped the mud off his soles. "I told you to stay here."

"Was that an order or a guideline?"

"Why is the whole bloody empire talking gibberish?" Valerius' remaining composure disintegrated as if suddenly crushed by the weight of his long trip, the unfamiliar terrain, and the cloud of mendacious nonsense that seemed to hang over Tarraco. He jabbed his stubby index finger into Severus' chest. "Hear this, you shifty weasel: there are no 'guidelines.' Everything I say is an order, and now I'm ordering you to start running."

"Sir?" Severus regretted not having deserted. He should have known better than to listen to Marius' hare-brained schemes about overthrowing the empire from within. A fly could sooner hobble a horse. "Where are we running to?"

"Put this pack on your back and start running around the field," Valerius shouted. He had enough worries without having to suckle a piglet like Severus. If no soldiers remained in the barracks, then maybe Fidelis Magnus could use a nosy kid to guard potted palms in front of the Villa. "The empire will not crumble on my watch."

"Is this my reward for being honest, sir?"

"For being insolent, quarry boy, you can add one stone to your pack with every lap." Valerius stormed away to find someone in the garrison who could take charge of the insubordinate conscript.

Severus began jogging and looking for the smallest stones to fill his pack. He tried to convince himself that training had begun, that he was on the path to becoming a warrior and not a spiral to nowhere. He assured himself that the pointless exercise would build fortitude. He would need more than just strength to help his kin reclaim their ancestral land. It would take grit and cunning to raise a rebel army. He and Marius would storm across the empire, free the slaves, and liberate Judea.

Then they would teach goats to sing.

His sandals thickened with mud and his optimism faded with each passing lap. Even the late autumn sun seemed to mock him by spending the last moments of the day behind a dark cloud.

Valerius returned an hour later to find Gaius Severus stumbling, barely able to walk. He followed the slow-moving conscript, careful to maintain enough distance so that if the boy fell, he would hit the ground. "Remember when I asked you about aqueducts?" Valerius asked.

"No, sir," Severus said, panting and hoping not to revisit the subject. He felt hollow with hunger, his knees ready to buckle backwards like a bird's. "Can I stop running, sir?"

"You call that running?"

"Do we get dinner in the legion, sir? I might like to eat a bit before I collapse."

The two boys they had seen earlier in the day ran along the edge of the parade grounds again, trundling their hoop and laughing as they hit each other with their sticks. Seeing the centurion, the younger one stopped and saluted with a loud *"Ave"* before charging off to clobber his sibling.

Acknowledging the lads, Valerius smiled for the first time since entering Hispania.. Turning back to Severus, the smile went flat. "Yesterday you said something interesting about stonework," he said.

"About quicklime?" Severus' voice quivered. What else had his loose lips let slip yesterday? "Amazing stuff, quicklime. It's cement that hardens underwater."

"Not about cement. You said something about your grandfather."

"Maternal or paternal?" Severus strained to speed up. He tugged at the pack straps but was unable to relieve the crushing weight of the accumulated stones.

"You said that he helped build the coliseum at Rome."

"That would be my paternal grandfather." Severus struggled to keep moving and not reveal his worry. Why the questions about his grandfather? Why would a centurion from south of nowhere care about who built Rome's mighty coliseum? Valerius must have spoken with the security forces. More than likely, he knew all about the proscription, the raids, and the arrests.

Swallowing his pain, hunger and fear, Severus thought through his cover story. The slaves who built Rome's giant coliseum were Jews. One of them, Severus' grandfather had been taken as a prisoner of war after the bloody revolts in Judea finally turned in Rome's favor over fifty years ago. When the time had come for Roman vengeance against the Hebrews, there was only one fate worse than enslavement.

After sacking the holy city, General, later Emperor, Titus' troops crucified thousands of Jewish prisoners along the provincial roads as a grim reminder to the surviving women and children. Gaius Severus' grandfather, thirteen-years-old at the time, was spared the cross but not the lash. He was captured and taken to Rome to build monuments.

Ten thousand prisoners, among them many of the surviving slaves from Judea, died in the elaborate celebration to inaugurate Titus' coliseum. A hundred days of blood consecrated the arena that their years of sweat had baptized. Gaius Severus' grandfather was one of the rare survivors. After a lifetime of working to buy his own freedom, he changed his name and slipped away to Hispania, as far from Rome as he could afford to travel.

Valerius grabbed the pack from behind and jerked Severus to a halt. "Your grandfather: slave or citizen?"

"And your grandfather, sir, what about him?" Severus countered, stiffening his shaking knees to keep from slumping to the ground.

"Slave," Valerius said proudly, "a Lusitanian slave, from the far Southwest. He earned his freedom by saving his master's life. The defense of Rome is an honor reserved for citizens. The penalty for a slave joining the legion is death. Now answer my question."

Severus pictured his father languishing in the governor's prison awaiting a fate that had been gathering for two generations. "I'd rather not talk about my family," he said.

"But you talk about everything else, don't you? You're a bloody authority on everything else, aren't you?" Valerius released his hold on the pack and, scarred and exhausted, Severus slumped to his knees. The centurion leaned over until he was nose-to-nose with the dodgy conscript. "What you don't say speaks louder than words."

Thirteen
XIII

The first thing Vindex noticed was the smell of death.

He struggled to stand but his wrists were lashed behind his back, bound to his ankles by a thick rope. He tried to rock onto his feet, but a kick in the back sent his face digging into the floor of the arena.

"Mock me not! Let me die with dignity," he bellowed, loud enough for the merciless crowd could hear his last words. Vindex had lived and would now perish by the gladiator's vow to die by sword, beast, or the will of Caesar.

In the silent certainty of his impending death, Vindex heard soft footsteps. Attendants, no doubt readying the arena for the next event, would soon spread fresh sand into his spilt blood. Men dressed as Charon, the shrouded boatman of the River Styx, would drag his maimed, lifeless body across the killing floor and into a mass grave outside the arena.

Vindex struggled again to move and tried to open his sand-filled eyes. The grim smell of the arena floor flooded him with vivid memories from his days of deadly glory. He had delivered the fatal blow enough times to know that in a matter of seconds, if the mob willed it, the tip of a sword would pierce his throat; his life would spill into the sand. There was peace in knowing that he would return to the sacred groves of his ancestors where his spirit would guide a new generation of warriors to fight the cursed Romans.

"Behold, the mighty Vindex. You've fallen off your pedestal."

Vindex recognized the nasal voice, but in his misery could not place it. He knew this opponent; they had locked horns before. "Coward!" he shouted.

"The only slave who didn't escape. You're in a bit of a bind, Vindex."

Vindex twisted his neck and looked up at his tormentor. For Vindex the only shame worse than being bested, was living to see Winus Minem buzzing above him like a parched mosquito.

"Surprised?" Minem said. "Brains always triumph over brawn."

Vindex tried to piece the puzzle together but could not remember how he had been defeated. He recalled delivering the governor's slaves to the arena. He recalled a scuffle, and his throbbing head told the rest of the story. Judging from the pain, someone had hit him with an anvil.

"Knocked out cold," Minem said. "Face down on the floor. Just like the night you were supposed to be guarding the old governor. You need to be more strategic, Vindex. It's a mistake to use the same alibi twice."

"I'm no assassin." Vindex attempted to wriggle free, but it just sent the pain pulsing down the back of his neck. The rope binding his wrists was tight enough to cut into his flesh.

"A murderer—but not an assassin … how many of your victims can appreciate the difference?"

"I was a famous gladiator."

"No one remembers a defeated gladiator. Where's your fame now?" Minem paced a triumphant arc around Vindex's fallen frame and raised his tiny hands in triumph. "Can't you hear the crowd? Now they're cheering for me. Imagine the applause erupting for the small Macedonian that brought down a warrior twice his size. They're calling you a murderer. They want me to finish you off."

Vindex twisted his head to avoid having to look at Minem's smug face. "Go ahead and finish me. The gods know I'm innocent."

"Don't be stupid. Your gods can't help you here."

"I'm not making any deals with you." Vindex tried to relax his muscles and wriggle free of the knots, but his body was stiff and the rope held tight.

"You're hardly in a position to make deals, old crow." Minem leaned down and whispered in Vindex's ear. "I'd say you're barely in a position to beg."

Vindex whipped his head around and sent a plume of sand into Minem's face. He flipped onto his back, looked into the stands, and saw the rows of wooden benches reserved for the nobility. Squinting upwards, he imagined the remaining seats filled with bloodthirsty spectators quaffing watered down wine and tearing at loaves of bread as they watched the carousel of death unwind beneath them. Children would be running up and down the stairs, cheering for their favorite gladiators; women would be gawking at the lunchtime executions.

Vindex tried to wriggle free but only dug himself deeper into the moist sand. He wanted to escape the stench that hung so close to the ground. If only senators could smell this, he thought. If only.

Something moving in the stands caught Vindex's attention. From above the imperial box, Fidelis Magnus, the security chief, watched the proceedings and gestured for Vindex to keep quiet.

Vindex assessed his predicament. This was the second time in less than a week he had taken a fall. For whom? Vindex no longer understood the rules of the game he once dominated. He knew that Minem had always hated him, but what was Magnus doing there? Did he, too, suspect Vindex of having assassinated the ex-governor? Was Magnus in league with Minem? It would be no surprise to discover that the security chief and the top advisor had a stake in framing an innocent bodyguard. It added up quickly: He would be their scapegoat.

"You can't frame me."

"It's not hard to frame such a perfect picture," Minem said. "You're the biggest killer in the province. How many of your victims pissed themselves and begged for mercy before you—"

"You're the assassin!" Vindex starred straight into the gray sky and shouting for the gods to hear. "I saw you in the Villa the night the governor was murdered."

"Did you?" Minem came around and positioned himself over Vindex's face. "And who's going to believe anything that comes out of your mouth?"

Vindex spat a mouthful of wet sand into Minem's eyes.

"You fool." Minem wiped the sand and spittle from his face. "Learn to recognize your allies."

"You're no friend. Snakes like you are the real killers."

"Tell it to Charon, Vindex." Minem stood tall and scraped his sandy foot triumphantly across Vindex's face, taking time to grind his heel into the fallen man's forehead. He raised his arms in victory, calling out to an imaginary emperor, "*Avé, Imperator*! I offer you the life of this fallen gladiator."

Vindex tensed his thick neck, jerked his head, and launched Minem like a stone from a catapult. The advisor sailed backwards and landed flat on his back.

"Bravo!" Applause rang forth from the stands where Fidelis Magnus stood on a bench cheering. He scrambled over the stands and dropped down into the arena. Clapping his hands and laughing, he ran over to where the tiny advisor lay. "Quite a show, Minem. A big moment for such a little man."

Rising slowly, Minem caught his breath, dusted himself off, and tried to smile. "Just having a bit of fun, Magnus. You know how it goes."

"Indeed," Magnus said, his good eye bearing down on the advisor. "I see exactly how it goes."

"Then you can see that it goes badly for you." Minem eyed the security chief with sudden steel. "I'm sure the governor will be interested in how you let this fiasco happen."

"Here's my knife." Magnus pulled a tarnished blade from his sash and handed it to Minem. "If you believe Vindex is guilty, go and finish him off."

The angry advisor did not take the blade. "Don't tempt me, Magnus. The governor wants this one for the games. See that he's locked up tight."

Magnus looked down at the bound gladiator. "He's tight enough for the moment. Someone has seen to that. Before I put him away, take a little walk with me, Minem. Tell me what brings you here."

Magnus took Minem's arm and in spite of the smaller man's resistance, easily dragged him towards the imperial box. Vindex could see that there was no love lost between the two men. If they were in league together, it was a marriage of convenience and nothing more. By calming his breathing and turning his head, Vindex could overhear their tense conversation.

"The imperial box has been unoccupied since the days of Augustus." Magnus pointed up towards the stands. "In the front rows, the wives and mistresses of senators and magistrates would be watching the games. Inhale, can you smell it? Slaves would be spraying perfumed water over the crowd and fanning the stench away. On an important day, the Vestal Virgins would have graced the games, hovering like angels above the carnage. Ever sleep with a Vestal, Minem?"

"You find sacrilege funny?" Minem pulled free from Magnus' grip.

"Where were you the night Biberious was murdered?"

"Where were *you*, Magnus?" Minem said.

"I'm asking the questions here."

"Are you?"

Vindex heard the change in Magnus' tone. He had long suspected Minem of being complicit in the assassination and now Magnus seemed to share his hunch. The game of cat and mouse had shifted. The security chief was no longer sparing; verbal punches might soon lead to real blows.

Magnus picked a half-buried brick out of the sand. "A little David could use something like this to bring down a big Goliath." He tossed the brick to Minem who caught it with one hand and quickly let it fall.

"Do you really think I dropped Vindex with a brick?" Minem asked. "Do I have wings? He's twice my size."

Minem tried to leave, but Magnus followed. Vindex rolled to one side so he could hear them better. As he turned, he saw a small shadow drift across the sand before him.

"Tell me," Magnus continued, "when did you arrive in Hispania?"

"Don't interrogate me," Minem snorted.

"It's a simple question." Magnus reached forward and spun Minem around to make eye contact. "Give me a simple answer."

"I'm an advisor." Minem smiled. "I don't give simple answers."

Distracted by the passing shadow, Vindex looked up and saw a crow silhouetted against the gray sky. He watched the black bird circle and tried to fathom its arrival. In the east, the crow was considered a messenger, entrusted by the sun to demand sacrifice. In Hispania, the arrival of the black-eyed, carrion-eating bird portended only death. It occurred to Vindex that the two interpretations—death and sacrifice—were not too different. There was no doubt that crow signified a transition from this world to the next. The only question was for whom.

Magnus continued probing Minem's defenses. "Does Rufius know that your former client died while you were under contract?"

"People die all the time. This is all very intriguing, but I can't stay and chat. The new governor is expecting me."

"Expecting you to kill him?"

"Cute, Magnus. Cute as piglets."

The crow landed near Vindex's feet without disturbing so much as a grain of sand. The broad-chested bird strutted around the still gladiator, shifting its head from side-to-side, reviewing Vindex like a general looking over a battlefield. It cawed once before extending its wings and rising into the air.

Vindex looked up at the crow and felt an eerie peace. If this dark angel of the afterlife bore him any malice, its sharp beak would have made it clear. Instead, the bird's underbelly revealed iridescent hues of indigo and blue that radiated like midnight along its wings and tail feathers. When it drew close enough to obscure the sky, Vindex saw stars and constellations shimmering along its wingspan as if the bird's body were a deep black window into the night.

Vindex felt as though he were falling upwards into space until the sound of the two men arguing brought him crashing back to earth.

"I think that the same person that hit Vindex the night of the murder hit him again today." Magnus stopped, picked up the brick that Minem had tossed, and turned it in his hand. "So where were you the night of the murder, Minem?"

"What kind of security chief lets a murder suspect wander freely through a governor's mansion?"

"Whose side are you on, anyway?" Minem's voice cracked with frustration.

"The side that should arrest you right now."

"At your own peril, Magnus." Minem stomped away towards the exit, leaving a sparse cloud of sand in his wake. Once a comfortable distance away from Magnus, he turned and said, "Think, man. Use the half of your brain that hasn't been pickled. How would I profit from killing a governor? Do I look capable of flooring a monster like Vindex?"

"You've made a career out of overcoming your inadequacies."

"And you haven't."

After Minem left the arena by the Death's gate, Magnus was surprised to find Vindex in dark communion with a circling crow. Magnus laughed nervously, but it was hard to avoid the obvious: if the crow had no hunger for Vindex's flesh, it might still be thirsty for his spirit.

"Defeated by a crow?" Magnus waved his arms and the shimmering bird rose and sought refuge on the curved wall above the killing floor. "Or did a ragtag band of house slaves bring you down?"

"Ambushed." Vindex arched his neck to see where the crow had gone. "Hit in the back of the head with a brick."

"The great Vindex? The giant who fought before Emperor Trajan himself?"

"I should have killed him."

"Such empty blasphemy." Magnus inspected the area around the fallen gladiator, but aside from the crow's tracks found no footprints or evidence of a scuffle. Either the person who hit Vindex had brushed over his footprints, or Vindex had hit himself. "It's not smart to threaten an emperor," Magnus said, "even a dead one."

"I'm tired of this game. Just slit my throat and get out of here."

"I'm happy to do as you ask, but something doesn't quite add up." Magnus drew the sharp knife from his sash and held it so Vindex could see that the gray blade was the same color as the sky. He ran his thumb across the edge and looked away for a moment. "Guarding the old governor should have been easy. Delivering the slaves to the arena should have been easy. Why do you keep falling on your face? Have you lost your balance, Vindex?"

Vindex heard the bird caw from a distance. Now understanding why the crow had come, Vindex opened his eyes to look death in the face. Though bound and defeated, he would not flinch or beg.

"Go ahead and get it over with."

"And ruin the new governor's celebration? I might lose my job," Magnus said. "With any luck, you'll get to fight a lion for Rufius' inauguration. Ever fought a lion before, Vindex?"

"Lions are overrated."

"So is Rufius, but we need him alive." Magnus leaned over and cut the cords from Vindex's wrists. "We need Minem alive, as well. Politics isn't a gladiator's game. The stakes are higher and you're outmatched."

"The shadow of the crow passed overhead and Vindex stood up slowly, letting the blood flow back into his ankles. He looked up to see the crow rise above the top of the arena, tip its wings as if saluting, and fly away. "I didn't ask you to spare me," he said. "Don't do me any favors."

"I won't," Magnus said. "I promise."

"I'm in no one's debt," Vindex insisted.

"As long as you think like a slave, you're in everyone's debt."

Magnus turned away and walked towards the exit.

Fourteen
XIV

Imperial Associates, or "IA" as it was known, had become so influential in the colonnades of commerce and halls of government, that the organization was almost an empire unto itself. Its origins shrouded in myth, IA traced its beginnings back to the time of Alexander the Great. Careful and clever, they had remained wisely aloof from scandal and intrigue over the past few centuries, preferring to profit in the shadows of history rather than roast in its capricious flames.

To Winus Minem's dismay, the new Governor of Hispania was not impressed with IA. Senator Rufius, a longtime IA client, had paid for only one month's consulting services to get his underachieving son Festus' career unstuck. With Security Chief Magnus now on his tail, Minem knew he was racing against the water clock to bring the reluctant governor and his resource rich province into the IA fold.

Noting that Rufius' eyes had started rolling behind his heavy lids, Minem tried to liven up his presentation. After piquing his interest with an undiluted pitcher of imported wine, Minem kept Rufius awake with short hand claps as he stepped through a gauntlet of essential, though previously unheard of, IA concepts and services.

"You're talking pish-posh." Rufius was not paying attention. He shifted the cushions about on his cane chair and tried in vain to stop Minem's intricate presentation. "Two days on the job and I'm already bored to tears. I swear this tacky villa feels like a tomb."

"Let's go into town," Minem said, changing tactics. The sales pitch could wait. Rufius clearly needed some distraction and a bit of fresh air. "We'll wander the forum anonymously."

"Dressed as slaves, perhaps?" Whatever his father saw in the animated advisor was not obvious to Rufius. Minem had arrived as a gift, but he was the kind of gift that eats. "I'm a governor, not an actor."

"*Incognito ergo sum,*" Minem said, visibly taken with the revelation.

"Your Macedonian logic escapes me." Rufius stood up to leave the room. "I'm going to take a bath. See that no one disturbs me before my next promotion."

"Trust me on this sir." Minem jumped in front of Rufius, preventing him from leaving. "You'll never get the true picture stuck inside this villa. By wandering around, disguised as a normal citizen, you'll learn what the real people think."

"As long as they pay their taxes, I don't care what they think."

"But people aren't paying their taxes and your tribute targets have doubled. I dare say you're in a bit of a bind."

It took the promise of fine food and seeing dancing girls from Cadiz in an upscale tavern to loosen the governor from his lethargy. The two men donned bland cotton togas and slipped by Security Chief Magnus, who was snoozing in the guard station with his lazy eye half-open.

The men walked downhill along a worn cobblestone path toward the once-elegant administrative district of Tarraco. They passed under the arched entrance to the central plaza and saw the tail end of the funeral procession disappear down the *Via Augusta*.

An oversized statue of Augustus, the deified Father of the Empire, stood near the end of the elongated plaza. Offerings of flowers, fruits, and assorted entrails were scattered around the pedestal. Puddles on the pavement conjured the illusion that Augustus walked on water.

Rufius stopped and tried his best to draw inspiration, but Augustus was the man who had driven Cleopatra to clutch a deadly asp to her breast. Rufius found it impossible to admire the dictator who, when given a choice between bedding a sultry Egyptian queen and conquering the world, had not done both.

It struck Rufius that early November was traditionally a time for popular games and celebration. In Rome, the mood would have been festive, the circus overflowing with gaily dressed citizens. Unlike the dull, unfashionable people milling around Tarraco's drab forum, the stylish Romans would have been gleaming.

November. The ninth month should have been joyful, but Tarraco was dour. To take his mind off his exile, Rufius went over the months of the year in his head. July and August bore the name of the first two Caesars. March and June were named after the god of war and the wife of Zeus. This left eight months still available; surely, one could be named Rufius.

"The Divine Augustus passed two years in this very place," Minem said.

The sudden sound of a flat, jagged flagstone whistled over Rufius' head but he was too deep in thought to take notice. The spinning paver hit the ground and smashed into pieces that skidded and bounced towards the giant statue of Augustus.

Minem turned around to see who might have thrown the flagstone, but everyone on the plaza looked equally suspicious.

An old woman in an elegant *stola* was helping herself to salt from an unguarded spice cart. Nearby, two dockhands were roughing up a fruit vendor, demanding reimbursement for mealy oranges they claimed to have bought a week earlier. Hoping to see the argument turn violent, a small crowd had gathered to goad both sides.

Minem ushered Rufius away from the growing disturbance. "Lord Augustus lived in your villa. It augurs well that you walk in his footsteps."

"It augurs poorly that my feet hurt." Rufius kicked a fragment of the projectile that had landed seconds earlier. "Call in a maintenance crew. This plaza needs to be re-grouted."

It was mid-afternoon and the smell of sheep head pudding lingered in the air. Among the statues in front of the courthouse basilica, one in particular attracted Rufius' attention. The once painted figure had been left fade under a white patina of bird droppings.

"That's Vespasian," Minem said. "He restored the empire after Nero."

A passerby put an apple on Vespasian's pedestal and murmured what appeared to be a prayer. Noticing Rufius and Minem watching, he nodded. "Hispania needs someone like him now," he said, indicating upwards. "You won't be seeing any statues of old Biberious here."

"Not exactly loved, was he?" Minem asked. He glanced sideways, winking conspiratorially at Rufius.

The man's face turned cautious. Informers and secret police had prospered under Biberious and there was no telling what the new regime would bring. "Not from around here, are you?" he asked.

"Pilgrims," Minem answered.

The man nodded and backed away. "Watch out for thieves," he warned. "Lots in the plazas and more in the Villa."

As Rufius and Minem wandered through the crowded colonnades, they picked up falling snippets of conversations. Without exception, the former governor was universally despised. The poor hated him for cutting back on their entitlements, the rich for his merciless taxes.

Everyone in Tarraco seemed mad about something. Some bemoaned the lack of a funeral feast, others complained that the popular games of November—the *Ludi Plebei*—had been cancelled. The discontinued bread dole elicited steady murmurs of discontent as much from those who owned the ovens as from those who received the loaves.

"It's plain as cotton that Biberious fleeced the province," Rufius muttered. "Hispania has been looted." He noticed an outsized man in a tight-fitting toga entering the treasury, opening the only gilded door in the long row of administrative buildings with vaulted entryways. "That fellow looks healthy."

"That's Cassius Kleptus, the tax collector." Minem nodded sideways towards the thick man with the thinning hair. "Beware a fat taxman, I always say. His prosperity probably explains your deficit."

"*My* deficit? Does Rome expect *me* to fill the shortfall?" Rufius asked. "Being a governor's one thing; being a God quite another."

"You're close to having a God in the family, but if you don't fix Hispania, your brother will never become emperor."

As they wandered along the colonnade and peered into the upscale pharmacies, jewelry shops, and bodegas that were still open, Minem picked up where he had left off earlier. "So you see, Excellency, Hispania and, in fact, Rome herself are at a critical juncture. It's well known that—"

Rufius stopped and looked back at the statue of Vespasian. "If he's so important, how come there's no month named after Vespasian? Why do we have eight months with stupid names like 'October' when we've had so many powerful emperors since Augustus? October, November, December: eight, nine ten. Is that the best we can do?"

"Interesting question." Minem saw that his pitch would have to wait until later. "Vespasian surely deserves a month named after him. He restored tranquility after the disastrous year of the four forgettable emperors who floundered in Nero's bloody wake. We could call it 'Vesember.'"

"Shouldn't his son, Titus, have a month? Rufius asked. "Titember," perhaps?

"I think Trajan deserves a month, too."

"Trajanuary." Rufius stopped to watch a prostitute work her way across the plaza and then looked up to make eye contact with the Divine Augustus. Perhaps the real answer was that no emperor since Augustus had dared hang his name on a month for fear of overshadowing the great Father of the Empire. Though the paint had faded, the marble monarch still loomed larger than this life and the world beyond.

The thick, distracting smell of grilled onions made Rufius hungry. Why didn't the fare in the Villa smell this good? Something was definitely wrong in his kitchen. Perhaps in his passion for justice, Rufius had accidentally condemned the only competent cook. The Gods only knew what sorry hacks were now preparing his meals.

Rufius looked over the dowdy citizens and the drab architecture. "What a backwater. Provincial, provisional, predictable," he said. "Call this a capital? All I see is stone. Where's the marble? Why aren't the statues gilded?"

"Rome gets the gold."

"But I'm entitled to a percentage." The hunger gnawing at Rufius' sour stomach overwhelmed his outrage. "Do I smell mushroom stew? Let's get something to eat."

"I know just the place. Good food and a delightful floor show. It's just on the other side of the forum."

A blind and deep-wrinkled woman with an incense burner bumped into Rufius and reached into his toga folds. "Charms, fortunes, hexes?"

Rufius pushed her away and rubbed the smoke out of his eyes. Midway across the crowded plaza, he stopped to consider the silent, sacred temple of Jupiter. Its six uneven columns supported a skewed pediment that suggested a crooked priesthood.

"That's where my inaugural parade should start," Rufius said. "The priests will bless me at the top of the steps. Next, I'll ride through town on a gilded chariot, and then preside over the most elaborate games this dump has ever known."

"You should also consecrate a new temple, too," Minem said. "And when you do, think Saturn, God of the Harvest."

"I'm partial to Jupiter."

"Temples to Jupiter are everywhere—Jupiter's old toga," Minem said, glad for the toe hold. "The God of the Harvest can make money grow on trees."

Rufius nodded and did his best not to reveal that, in addition to starving, he was also baffled.

"We'll find some investors to run Saturn concessions all over the province. It's kind of like issuing contracts to tax farmers, except there's a catch."

Rufius had no idea what a Saturn concession might be worth, but he suspected that Minem and his IA demons would be among the first investors. Saturn had to be a potential gold mine or Minem would have never brought it up.

"Here's how it could work," Minem continued. "We sell Saturn like nobody's business. You know, pump up his powers— emphasize his benevolence, create excitement. People start bringing in goats, money, and whatnot. As Saturn's popularity rises—and don't underestimate the Augustus tie-in here—we raise prices. "

"Saturn and the Divine Augustus: That's a good angle," Rufius said, happy to demonstrate a bit of insight.

"Exactly. And with the piles of sacrificed animal corpses, we start a rib shack across the street. It's a virtuous circle. You charge people to offer sacrifices, and then you sell the grilled bits back to them on their way out the door."

Rufius was no longer paying attention. Attracted by the savory smell of grilled lamb, the governor had disappeared into the sea of moneylenders and fly-by-night astrologers clustered at the edge of the square. He emerged under the colonnade where a sullen pimp was loitering in front of a tavern.

Barring the door, the pimp grabbed Rufius by the sleeve, and prevented him from entering. "No tunics," he said.

"Let go of me, fish breath."

With no apparent strain, the smaller man lifted Rufius by the lapels and slammed him into the wall behind them. The two dockhands who had previously been arguing about oranges emerged from the passing crowd and flashed their knives close enough for Rufius to smell the rust.

"What did you call me, fatso?" the part-time pimp and full-time thug demanded.

"He's with me." Minem intervened by dropping some coins in the pimp's pocket before Rufius could get into more trouble. "No floor show today? What happened to the dancing girls of Cadiz?"

"They turned out to be boys." The man lowered Rufius to the ground and waved his unpleasant associates away.

"Don't blow our cover, sir." Minem dragged the angry governor inside before he drew more attention.

"Brilliant idea coming here dressed as commoners," Rufius muttered. He brushed the dust off his shoulders and inspected his elbows for abrasion. "Next time, let's dress as prisoners of war and visit the arena."

Minem took advantage of the confusion caused by a pregnant pickpocket to cut in front of the small crowd waiting for tables.

The two pushed their way into a dark corner and sat down at a musty table.

A slave with stained hands ran over with pitchers of wine and water. "Sorry," he said, mixing the contents back and forth. "There was a bit of a row last night and all the cups are broken." Before leaving, he reached into his pocket and sent some grilled almonds spinning across the table.

Minem returned to the pitch he had been trying to start since they had left the Villa. "An empire is like this table, sir. You can only pile it so high with food before the legs buckle and break."

Rufius sorted through the nuts and finally found one that met his rapidly falling standards. He tested it with a long fingernail, popped it in his mouth, and washed it down with a swig from the pitcher. "This wine is awful."

"The Greeks, the Sumerians, the Phoenicians," Minem continued, "it's the same story over and over again. They couldn't integrate fast enough. Expenses grow, revenues fall, challengers emerge and— boom!—down they went. Every past empire has collapsed like a skinny-legged fat man."

"So you're saying that the Greeks ate faster than they could digest, choked on their own lunch, so to speak?" Rufius studied a handful of nuts, but found none worth eating.

A kitchen slave slapped some charred brochettes on the table but, before Rufius could grab one, a nearby patron stole the entire platter. The man stuffed a chunk of meat and gristle into his mouth, swallowed it whole, and tucked greedily into the next. Barely a second later, he was writhing red-faced on the floor.

"I'm burning!" he shouted, clutching at his throat. "I'm dying!"

The two dockhands who had threatened Rufius at the front door ran over to investigate the noise. They let the man convulse at Rufius' feet for a moment longer, then dragged him out the back door.

"Make mine less spicy," Rufius told the waiter who had just arrived with a steaming platter of grilled pig's feet.

Minem reached for one of the fatty pork trotters and sniffed it carefully before sampling it. Satisfied that it was edible, he began to speak and chew excitedly. "Your work here is critical. This province has been a drag on the empire for years."

Rufius bit into a pork morsel and winced. The meat had been marinated in *garum*, probably the same rank sauce that had sickened him on his trip across the Mediterranean. He had no choice but to rinse his mouth with watered-down wine, and use a long fingernail to pick at the gristle now stuck between his two front teeth.

Minem appeared not to notice his patron's discomfort. "Augustus pacified Hispania over a century ago, yet it continues to underperform the more recently civilized provinces by a factor of ten. To be honest, you're not exactly exceeding the emperor's expectations out here. It's well known that Hadrian wants more tribute."

"That's unfair," Rufius objected. "I'm sure we're not the worst … I mean, Rome isn't exactly losing money in Hispania."

Minem wiped the grease off his bony chin and dropped his voice an octave. "Between us, Excellency, my analysis suggests that a fertile province of this size should be leading, not trailing the empire. You need to fix this place, or Rome might simply divest."

"Divest? What in Pompeii's ashes do you mean by that?" After half a pitcher of bad wine on a burning stomach, following Minem's logic was like chasing a squirrel through bramble.

"Sell it off." Minem bit into another grilled onion, this time chewing it before continuing. "Sell it off chunk by chunk to the highest bidders. Believe me, I've run the numbers: Hispania is worth more in pieces than it is as a whole. The olive-oil sector alone floats half the province. And my preliminary assessment is that your wine industry is bleeding."

"Spanish *vino* tastes like blood." Rufius clapped his hands to summon a waiter, but none came. "I don't know how these yokels can drink this stuff."

"Very perceptive," Minem said reverently. "Hold that thought, Excellency. Wine is the ultimate solution."

Fifteen
XV

Festus Rufius spent half the night steaming in the Villa's private *tepidarium* and rose at mid-day feeling like someone was drumming on his skull. His head throbbed so loud that he could not hear the cries of angry commoners gathered in protest outside the Villa.

"Bread!" People shouted and stomped their feet around the perimeter of the mansion. While others chanted to restore bread dole, at least one thin fellow was still frustrated that Biberious had been skewered without leaving a morsel behind. "Where's the funeral feast?" he demanded, "Bring back the bread!"

Cassius Kleptus, the portly taxman who had eaten well under the previous administration, pushed his way through the throng and arrived at the gates just as people recognized who he was. "Open the gates!" he shouted.

No longer able to ignore the noise, Fidelis Magnus stirred from his morning nap in the guard station. "Maybe I should leave you to the crowd," he said, one eye regarding the taxman while the other floated to the side. "After all, you're the one who turned off the bread dole."

"Open the gate!" Beads of nervous sweat wicked along the folds of the taxman's forehead, as the crowd pressed against his broad backside. "Feeding these freeloaders is a waste of money,"

"Render unto Caesar, after you've helped yourself. You're an inspiration to hungry citizens everywhere." Magnus unlocked the gate just enough for Kleptus to squeeze through sideways.

"If you want free bread, go to Rome," Kleptus muttered. He flattened his thin hair, cinched down his toga, and waddled away towards the Villa.

Emboldened now that the *vigile* raids had ended and no soldiers had been seen for a week, the hungry crowd congealed into an angry mob. The lawless wind that inspired the governor's slaves to escape from the arena now whispered to Tarraco's hungry citizens. All at once, the crowd fell silent and began tearing up the cobblestones.

Fearing a stampede, Kleptus locked the gate. "They're quiet. The rabble has stopped rousing."

"Calm before the storm." Magnus ran ahead and opened the front door to the Villa.

Kleptus looked forward to seeing the fine furnishings he had sold to Governor Biberious. His family ties to the former governor had been instrumental in winning the concession to farm taxes in the province. This lucrative contract gave him the right to keep any additional funds he could collect above the ever-rising quotas.

Instead of buying the franchise with a direct kickback to the former governor, Kleptus had promised his homely daughter, Egnatia, and a substantial payment to Biberious' buck-toothed son. Unfortunately, the bridegroom absconded with the dowry and Egnatia reverted to the taxman.

Kleptus knew Rufius was married and had a wealthy wife in Rome so pawning off Egnatia was not an option. From what Kleptus had heard of the ambitious Rufius clan, he reckoned that they were not overburdened with a sense of fiduciary responsibility to the empire. Hanging on to the tax concession would be a simple question of price.

Confused for a second by the empty atrium, Kleptus shifted his bulk towards the great hall where he found Rufius sitting on the edge of a daybed, cradling his head like a scorned child. Something smashed loudly onto the roof, but the governor did not acknowledge the clatter or the visitor.

"Excellency." Kleptus bowed as much as his distended gut permitted. Like the gold rings on his fingers, his bulk was one of many outward signs of success. He looked around the great room that had once housed his high priced goods, but most of Biberious' former finery was gone. Only a chipped marble bust of Augustus and two heavy candelabras remained where gilded statuary and solid lemonwood furniture had once graced the hall. A solitary table laden with untouched food stood in the center of the room. The once glorious hall now looked like a barracks.

"Where did everything go?" Kleptus gasped.

"My shipment sank in a storm," Rufius said, barely acknowledging Kleptus' substantial presence. "My most valuable possessions, and a handful of decent slaves, are at the bottom of the sea.'

"Insured, no doubt."

"Insured by weight, but most of my slaves were too skinny to break even." Rufius stared at the floor as if every grout line led farther away from Rome. "To make matters worse, no one in the whole Roman Empire responds to my queries."

Kleptus deposited his bulk into an armless chair. He was too large to stand on decorum or his own aching feet for very long.

"You came alone?" Rufius rose stiffly and squinted as if the man's outsized appearance might have been a trick of the shadows passing over the skylights. "Where are the others? You were supposed to bring my top taxpayers here for a little chat about the future."

This was news to Kleptus. The messenger from the Villa had not mentioned this, but the tax collector knew better than to contradict a hung-over governor. "Regretfully," he said, "no one could come."

"I see that you take up enough space for three." Rufius beckoned to Carbo and the kitchen slave filled a goblet with equal parts wine and water. Not offering drink to his guest, Rufius tossed back the libation and chased it with a wince. "What I don't see is how you're going to restore the treasury and double the emperor's tribute in this blighted province if you can't get a few landowners to show up for a little lunch."

"Lunch?" The tax collector shifted his bulk nervously and his chair groaned in protest. "The problem," he said, improvising, "is that distrust runs high in Hispania, memories run deep as a showgirl's…" Seeing the pacing governor look down in anger, Kleptus decided to tack in a different direction in case Rufius didn't fancy girls. "Put yourself in their sandals," he continued. "Why would the growers and vintners of Tarraco accept a mysterious invitation from a new and unknown governor whose primary role is to scrape tribute from their hides? Where's the incentive?"

"Keeping your job. That's *your* incentive." Rufius shuddered as another stone hit the roof. "As for those vexed landowners, if free lunch with the new governor doesn't bring them in, what would? Seeing you crucified?"

"Such dark humor." After a burst of feigned laughter, Kleptus inhaled deeply, loosened his sash, and ruffled his tight toga to draw some air in against his clammy skin.

"Why is the treasury empty? You and Biberious cleaned up and left me with a mess."

"Biberious tried but couldn't take it with him," Kleptus said. "Listen: I've worked this territory for years and the *Pax Romana* has been profitable for all concerned. There's no reason it should end now, Excellency. Remember: Rome wasn't built—"

"Neither was your villa and I hear it's nicer than mine."

Another roof tile shattered above and the impact echoed through the great room.

"Did you hear that?" Rufius asked. "Honestly, I'm not sure if those crashing sounds are coming from inside or outside my aching head."

In response, a cobblestone came smashing through an alabaster skylight like the head of a comet flung earthward by an angry god. Festus Rufius watched the stone bounce across the floor towards the taxman.

Before either man could react, Security Chief Magnus ran into the room. He seemed gleeful, as if every time things got worse, he got better. "I'm sorry to interrupt you gentlemen, but there's a riot going on."

The shouting outside grew so loud that it shook the air inside the Villa. Rufius clutched his head involuntarily and slammed his eyes shut. "Do they really need to yell so much? Can't those bastards riot quietly?"

"It's the bread dole, sir," Magnus said, glaring directly at the taxman.

Kleptus made the international sign for money with his thumb and pudgy forefinger, hinting with his every pound of body language that Magnus would be wise to forget recent history. While Rufius cradled his head, Magnus played coy, until Kleptus doubled the offer.

Once the bribe was established, Magnus gently shifted blame. "Your predecessor stopped doling out free bread to the masses," he said.

Rufius waved one hand and held his fleshy forehead with the other. "Send out a cohort, Magnus. Restore law, order, but most of all, restore quiet!"

"You don't have a cohort." Kleptus shifted in his chair until the legs splayed. "With all respect, Excellency, the bread dole mob is mad at a dead man. This is your chance to kill a big, hungry, pregnant rat."

Magnus' lone deputy, a former thief, ran in, whispered something, and disappeared down a corridor as a downpour of alabaster, stone, and plaster plummeted to the floor.

"It's spreading." Magnus stepped into the safety of a doorway. "If the mob moves into town, they'll burn it down."

"After Rome burned, Nero rebuilt it in marble." Rufius joined Magnus under the lintel.

Unable to climb out of the low chair, Kleptus rolled forward onto his knees and began crawling towards the doorway. "If they trash Tarraco, we'll be eligible restoration funds from Rome. Maybe tribute will be waived, too—a potential windfall."

"Rome will never spring for fancy stone in Tarraco," Magnus said. "Unless you want to preside over a modern ruin, you'll need to take action."

"They've got a lot of nerve attacking my mansion." Rufius watched another stone skid across the floor leaving shards of roof tiles dancing in its wake. "Why can't these beggars just trash their own neighborhoods?"

"Bread!" The mob's stones and shouting thundered through fresh holes in the roof. "Give us our daily bread!"

"Let's send all the freeloaders to Rome!" Kleptus yelled. A cobblestone bounced off his back, but he barely felt the blow. "Let them join the other thieves."

"Rome's part of the problem. We already send Rome half of our harvest for their dole," Magnus shouted to the governor above the clatter of raining projectiles. "Your last cohort is halfway to Gaul. The police have turned to piracy. Even your slaves have escaped."

"Escaped slaves? What are you talking about?" Rufius rubbed his temples, but there were already too many mysteries swimming around his head to worry about this new one. "Murders, riots, and the fattest taxman in the empire. The Gods must truly hate me."

Plaster drizzled down from the ceiling as Kleptus crawled forward. He inched across the remaining expanse of broken tile, and crossed the threshold just before a cobblestone crashed behind him and shattered into fragments.

"Enough!" Rufius stomach rumbled with such rage that the previous night's wine burned the backside of his tonsils. His head felt like an overripe melon. Hugging the walls to avoid falling debris, he stumbled away towards his bedchamber. "Is there no escape from this noise? For Jupiter's sake, what will it take to shut them up?"

"Bread, sir," Magnus answered.

"Then stuff it down their throats!"

Sixteen
XVI

Twenty years of service defending the southern edge of the empire had been rewarded with an unexpected detour. His pension denied and his loyalty questioned, Centurion Marcus Valerius found himself sodded off on a fool's mission accompanied by a scrawny informer who talked nonstop nonsense.

Severus could not keep quiet. Every time he stopped talking, the cold made his teeth chatter anyway, so he put more words in motion. After slogging through the rain for two days with the silent centurion, Severus was now repeating himself just to stay warm. "I've heard that collisions are a constant danger on these mountain roads. Most chariots and carts aren't up to official standards, and even if they were, people think nothing of speeding around sharp turns without regard for their own lives or anyone else's. For a province where time is so abundant, it's a mystery why people insist on driving so fast."

"Stop jabbering and keep that donkey cart on the right side of the road."

"Fortunately for human progress, the empire doesn't depend on the cooperation of donkeys." Gaius Severus did his best to follow the centurion's orders, but the donkey had no more grasp of military discipline than he did. He whacked it with a stiff switch which convinced the brooding beast to stop and drink from a rain-swollen pothole.

Seeing Severus struggle with the obstinate donkey was Valerius' only light moment on an otherwise dark day. He walked ahead, out of range of the boy's chatter. Finding Tarraco's garrison empty, he had tried to leave Severus with his old friend, Magnus, but the security chief had insisted that Valerius take the greenhorn. Valerius now wondered why Magnus had been so adamant. There was something shady about the boy, something unquestionably off kilter. Perhaps Severus had cut a deal with Magnus. Maybe they were both informers. Waiting for the other sandal to drop was eroding Valerius' patience.

"So, what do you think is really going on?" Severus asked. "What's this *imperial transformation* stuff really about?"

"Money." Valerius wondered if money was Severus' true motivation. The empire was infested with fast-talking parasites and profiteers specializing in trumped up charges of sedition. Severus' mindless chatter was probably intentional, designed to catch Valerius off guard and lead him into a trap. Like a shipwrecked astrologer, something about this conscript did not add up. "No more questions."

"There's no question we're heading north."

"No more chatter!" Valerius had heard stories about extracting confessions through steady, grinding interrogation, but he had never imagined it could be this severe. What man could endure such a slow drip of mindless drivel without cracking?

"Well it's not hard to figure out," Severus continued. "The sun rose on our right; that means we're headed north. Since we've been marching uphill for two days, I'd say we're headed towards the border with Gaul."

"If you're ever captured by the enemy," Valerius warned, "you must bite off your own tongue."

They continued onward, avoiding the mud and potholes, struggling to keep the donkey from feeding on every bramble that tore through the road.

Valerius said nothing. Instead of sailing back to the warm shores of North Africa, he was trudging through cold, unfamiliar terrain with a nattering kid who seemed bent on wearing down his mental resistance. Physical torture would have been preferable.

"Perhaps we should have taken the coastal route, sir." The eerie trek punctuated by footsteps, creaking branches, and the farting donkey had grown too quiet for Severus' comfort. "It's winter. These mountains get so cold that frozen water falls from the sky."

"Stop your superstitious chatter." Concerned about being followed, Valerius looked back but could see no farther than the last bend in the road. "Our orders are to take the mountain route while our cohort follows the coast. We'll meet them on the other side of the border."

They ascended the steep road through the bare forest, making their way through the thick carpet of fallen leaves that stuck to foot, hoof, and cartwheel. Valerius watched the sky for omens, but saw none that he recognized. The unfamiliar territory unleashed a fearful thought: what if he was surrounded by portents he could not interpret?

"Strange," he said. "The trees are all dead. I've never seen anything like this. Dead leaves, bare branches—it doesn't bode well."

Severus perked up. "The trees are alive, sir. These trees sleep in the wintertime."

"That's ridiculous! Trees don't sleep." Valerius stopped and pointed forward up a straight stretch of the ascending road. "Look up at the mountainside—the trees up there have leaves, no? Something's wrong in our part of the forest. I'm sure of it."

"It's November, sir," Severus said. "That's what happens in November."

November! Suddenly it all made sense. Of all the tainted days in the year, and there were many, November was host to the worst. "What's today's date?" Valerius asked.

"I don't really know, sir. One day seems like another, but I think you picked me up on the Kalends."

Valerius did a quick calculation. The Kalends, the first of the month was exactly a week behind him. The dreaded eighth of November, the day when the gates to the underworld opened had finally arrived. On this terrible day, spirits of the dead walked among the living, often dragging them under before nightfall. Of all the terrible, vexed days to be lost in a dark, unfamiliar forest, this was the worst.

A dense blanket of fog unfolded above the treetops. Within an hour, the soldiers could see no more than ten feet ahead. The misty silhouettes of trees reached over the path like the bony arms of death.

"Why is our cohort running ahead of us?" Severus asked. He peered into the gray forest as if expecting visitors. "Where do you think they are?"

"Stop asking questions!" Valerius shouted. His eyes darted in the direction of a cracking branch. "Your job is to clear the path and keep your eyes peeled for suspicious characters." An ambush was a possibility in the best of times. On such a cursed day, there was no knowing what form an assailant might take.

In confirmation that something was amiss, even the flatulent donkey grew silent.

The gray gloom infiltrated every wet breath that Valerius sucked through his teeth. The haunted woods reminded him of a recent nightmare. In the dream, he was leading a fierce desert battle. Stung, but not defeated, the enemy regrouped, blurred, and transformed into a blinding sandstorm. With the biting sand swirling around him, Valerius fought on, finally stopping when he could no longer see or hear anything. When the air cleared, his troops were petrified in their final positions. Some were contorted; others were cleaved in two, their bodies strewn about like discarded stumps. Smashed helmets, broken shields, and shredded armor lay scattered about like fallen leaves. Above the carnage floated a bearded demon with purple eyes. Valerius alone had survived.

"Speed up!" he ordered, trying not to reveal his discomfort. Had the dream been a premonition? Had Fortune, always a harsh Goddess, decided to let him die in these dreary woods, or was he dead already? In either case, this was clearly his final road. On the eighth day of November, no other interpretation held water.

"So you see, sir," Severus was saying, "I could contribute a lot more to our mission if I understood it better. Why are we looking for our cohort? Are they lost? And this cart, what exactly are we transporting?"

The older soldier forgot about the eerie vision and focused on the disturbing present. Whatever Severus was—a spy, an informant, or an assassin—he was first and foremost a ball-breaker. Valerius cursed his own misfortune and directed a few choice insults at Governor Festus Rufius, thanks to whom he was now walking a waking nightmare on the most dangerous day of the year behind a farting jackass and a chattering lunatic.

"This must be the highway to Hades," Valerius said, wondering why the sun had abandoned him. How had he ended up on a lost road to perdition? He had always obeyed orders, fought bravely, and honored Rome; eternal damnation did not logically follow from his twenty years of selfless sacrifice. He was due to retire in North Africa, raise olives and father children but something had gone terribly wrong. His exemplary life was not supposed to end like this.

A shrill scream ripped through the fog and filled the dead canyon. Valerius looked but could not find its source. Above him, bare branches creaked with arthritic malevolence. He drew his knife and steeled his nerves.

"Not to belabor the point, sir," Severus said, "but your friend Magnus back at the Villa told me that the more I understand our goals, the more I can contribute to our success."

"Contribute by getting us the hell out of this dead forest!" Valerius ordered. Magnus—that double-talker!—he had to be behind this mess. It stood to reason. Security guards were never far from conspiracies.

The hungry conscript continued to talk as he bent down to untangle weeds from the cart's axle. "Now that I know we need to rejoin our cohort, I can better perform my function as a team member."

"Good. Now get the donkey to perform his."

The donkey soon stopped to gnaw at a nettle bush obstructing the path. Before Valerius could reach for his *gladius*, Severus was already hacking the weed with a small knife.

"The better informed I am, the better I can do my duty, and the higher your expectations can be," Severus said. "It's what your friend Magnus called a virtuous circle."

Valerius pulled the donkey back so Severus could remove the bush. A crow, the only portent that had been missing from the dark mosaic of malice, laughed down at him from a low branch. He looked up uneasily and squeezed the hilt of his short sword.

"A soldier needs to make quick decisions on the battlefront, sir. When the fog of war descends, we'll surely be cut off from the command post. With a battle raging, we can't stop and wait for new orders, no sir! By knowing the goals, a soldier can make quick judgments. The alternative is an entire legion paralyzed with indecision. The fog—"

"Stop talking about the vexed fog!" Valerius shouted. He tried to suppress a shiver by telling himself it was only from the cold, but he could not suppress the feeling that he was adrift in a nightmare with a demon named Severus. Valerius stiffened at the thought that somehow they had crossed into the underworld together. Could there be any worse way to spend eternity?

The slope grew less forgiving. The soldiers spent a fearful hour climbing slowly through the gloom until they finally emerged into a deep, gray valley surrounded by snow-laden peaks.

Valerius stopped and stared. He had never witnessed anything like this. All his touchstones had turned to dust. Beyond the forest of petrified bodies, a world without color was exactly how his battle nightmare had ended. The terror that had awakened him in a cold sweat now lay frozen before him. Marcus Valerius wiped ice from his eyebrows and stared blankly at the lifeless world.

"It's beautiful in a strange way," Severus swept his walking stick like a paintbrush across the monochrome vista. Cold and impatient, he waved a hand in front of his commander's face and shook the veteran's hard shoulder. "Shouldn't we start marching, sir?"

Valerius did not respond. He had spoken little among living and there was no reason to start jabbering in hell. Instead, he devised a simple test to determine if he were dead or alive. Since a dead man cannot die twice, Valerius would kill himself once. The logic was flawless. His spirit thawed just enough to trudge along the ridge top and look for an opportunity to disprove his existence.

Severus followed, guiding the donkey cart along the icy path until a deep crevasse blocked their progress. Proceeding carefully to the edge, he looked down and probed it with his long stick.

"Centurion!" he shouted to be heard above the wind. "I'll bet this chasm drops straight down to the underworld! If you squint, you can just about see the River Styx."

"The underworld?"

Confirming all the omens so far, three screaming crows emerged from the fog and traced a slow arc back into obscurity. Needing no further signs, Valerius stepped to the edge of the abyss and jumped in.

Seventeen
XVII

After one week on the job, Festus Rufius was already sick of trying to drag Hispania into the future. The once bright promise of a sun-drenched sojourn had quickly clouded over. The trivial issues of a backwards province were enough to turn his hair gray at the roots. Being governor was all pits, no olives.

Hispania was mired in problems created and left to fester by the previous administration. The locals were restless, the grain stores depleted, and the treasury drained. Taxes were impossible to collect without soldiers and even mercenaries were nowhere to be found. Since the masons had marched north to build Hadrian's Wall, all construction projects had fallen permanently behind schedule. The simple act of restoring the bread dole, Rufius' only gesture of goodwill, had already cost a mint because Hispania had to import grain all the way from Sicily.

Fidelis Magnus was useless as a security chief, Vindex, the bodyguard, was a murder suspect. The meals were tasteless and the servants were shifty. Shards and rubble from the bread dole riot still littered the floors and water pooled under the holes where the skylights had shattered.

Rufius wanted to throw lavish parties, import a decent theater troupe, and host elaborate games in the arena. Instead, he was stuck with a thieving taxman, scheming servants, and self-serving advisors. His plans for an elaborate inaugural celebration had stalled like a mud-stuck chariot. The province was broke and he was expected to fix it so the rest of the empire could play while he languished.

Festus Rufius burned with resentment at his old friends, and Rome herself, for feeding at a trough that he was now expected to fill. He barely recognized his grim reflection in the bedroom mirror. "I work like a dog so Rome can eat like a hog. One night I'm the life of the party, the next I'm expected to pay for it."

If Rome was a capricious mistress, the emperor was even worse than Rufius' nagging wife. The two would make a perfect couple. She had hounded Rufius out of Rome and Hadrian was demanding that Hispania double its tribute.

"How does Hadrian expect the governors to cover his booty without putting any muscle behind it?" he muttered. "Rome wants money. My wife wants money. Hadrian wants money. I want money. Where's all this money supposed to come from?"

Rufius' anger at undeserved wealth eventually led his thoughts back to Cassius Kleptus, Hispania's corrupt, corpulent, and predictable tax collector. Rufius knew his kind only too well. Kleptus was the kind of self-serving functionary, who grew fat suckling the great, lactating breast of the empire. Increasing tribute to Rome could be as simple as reducing Kleptus' appetite for luxury and luncheon. Maybe it was time to pay him a personal visit, seize his assets, and throw his bovine backside in jail.

"I'm going to die here," Rufius moaned to the mirror. He tightened his jaw, but his once-cherubic face had begun to sag. He crawled back into bed and stared at the coved ceiling. "Goose shit yellow," he said, commenting on the color. "This place needs some fresh paint."

Early the next morning, Winus Minem woke the governor to present a detailed plan for revitalizing the province. For over an hour, the tiny advisor peppered Rufius with plans, catch phrases, and platitudes. He paced around the bed, waving his hands and wagging his finger while Rufius' sat trapped in a silver-spun web of incomprehensible proposals and catch phrases.

Rufius desperately wanted to escape from Minem's tyrannical facts, figures, and mind-boggling flights of fancy. Anything would be more enjoyable than listening to the tiny advisor rant about civic improvements that most Spaniards were too content to appreciate.

Rufius' stomach growled so loud that he stopped listening to the gesticulating advisor. Through the haze of hunger, he realized that Minem thrived on minutiae like a rodent on refuse; feeding on the day-to-day details that made Rufius gag. Rufius began to see that the mouse-faced huckster might actually prove useful. "There may be an ongoing role for you here, Minem, if you can ever get to the point."

"I'm honored by your directness," Minem answered. Closing time had come earlier than expected and Minem caught the cue. He pulled a scroll out of his tan-trimmed toga. "We have some breakthrough proposals here that you'll find quite intriguing."

Feeling hungry enough to place his official seal on anything, Rufius signed the document and watched in dismay as three slaves marched in with a half-dozen painted panels littered with vivid colors and primitive motifs. The brightly colored charts clashed with the earthy paintings of wood nymphs, girls, and goddesses that graced the yellow walls. Rufius cringed at yet another assault on his sensibilities. The bedchamber was the only place in the Villa that had a shred of style and Minem was ravaging it.

"I don't want another presentation."

"Trust me, sir, this is worth your while," Minem insisted. He licked his hand and drew it across an unruly lock of his scrub brush hair.

Before Minem could continue, a young bath attendant burst into the room.

"Begging forgiveness," he said, "but a merchant in the atrium is demanding payment for a dozen ostriches he sold the former governor. He says the money's overdue. Asking for interest as well."

"Send the bill to the afterlife." Rufius waved the servant away. "The former governor's debts are of no concern to the living and all this talk of ostriches only makes me hungry."

Lost in thought, Minem scratched a few more numerals into his wax tablet, pausing occasionally to pull at a tuft of ear lobe hair and reconsider his calculations. When satisfied with his sums and differences, he positioned himself in front of the first panel, looking it over as if it told a revealing story that he alone could unravel.

"Just tell me your conclusions, Minem."

"Of course, Excellency." Minem smiled from canine to molar. Eschewing the charts and figures, he stepped into the corridor and returned with a carafe of wine. He filled two thick glass goblets and passed one to Rufius. "I'd like you to try this."

Rufius held the goblet up to the garden window and swished it around. He watched the thick purple liquid recede along the glass and waited to imbibe until after Minem had taken the first sip. "Delicious." he said, and finished it in two greedy gulps. "Another glass, perhaps, or does listening to your proposals require temperance?"

Minem refilled the glass, barely able to hide his delight as Rufius quenched his early morning thirst and held out his goblet for more.

"Excellent wine. Much better than the swill they drink around here."

"It comes from Southern Gaul. Simply put, the Gauls make the best wine in the world."

Festus Rufius tipped back his goblet until the last drop found his tongue and nodded his agreement from the bottom of his glass. He sighed with contentment, but his serenity was shattered when a heavy hammer struck the outside wall.

The bedroom shook as if Zeus himself was smashing the wall between the bedchamber and the governor's private garden. Rufius peeked out the window and saw two burly workers swinging iron sledgehammers at the exterior stone. The crew had finally arrived to start work on the door that Rufius had requested days earlier.

"Let's go up to the roof," Minem said. "The sun is out, the view is incredible, and nobody will bother us up there."

"A bit of fresh air to clear away the cobwebs." Tipsy and agreeable, Rufius wobbled over to the window, opened it, and climbed out. He was careful to avoid the men with hammers as he stepped into his private garden. "Bring the jug," he said, returning to recover his glass from the windowsill.

Minem followed Rufius into the garden. "If wine is the lifeblood of civilization, what do you think of the local wine, the fruit of your own province?"

"The local stuff tastes like sewer water. I'd rather drink horse sweat." Rufius examined the ruby rim of his glass before handing it to Minem and climbing up a wisteria trellis leading to the roof.

"It's a shame," Minem said, calling up to Rufius. "This region grows and ferments more grape than the rest of the empire combined, but only the locals can stomach the results."

"That might explain their temperament." Rufius swung his leg over the top of the wall and fell with a thud onto the red-tiled roof. After a few seconds, he peered down at Minem whose toga had snagged in a twisted branch. Happy for a chatter-free moment, Rufius reached down to take the wine jug from Minem. He took a swig directly from the jug and watched Minem wrest his toga free. "With wine like this on the market, it's no wonder we can't sell the local swill."

Minem clambered climbing onto roof and sought a tenuous balance on the rounded tiles. "I must commend you, Excellency. You've actually identified the same opportunity as my team of IA experts."

"Imagine that." Rufius looked up at the sky and wished he could fly home like an eastbound bird.

"What would you pay for a decent amphora of Gaulish wine?" Minem asked. He extended a hand to help the governor stand up and take in the view.

The capital city shambled seaward from the forum, just below the governor's mansion, to the harbor at the southern edge of the slums. From his vantage point, Rufius saw the small, skewed Temple of Jupiter that he and Minem planned to convert into a tavern.

By Roman standards, the oval circus just beyond the forum did not seem large enough to run full-sized horses, but, then again, the provincial forum did not seem large enough for full-sized people either. Perhaps the tiny Iberians just raced rabbits. Perched on the western coastline beyond the city wall, the half-finished arena would have fit into Rome's great coliseum like a thimble in a bathtub.

"Practical." Rufius groped for something complimentary to say about the tiny, coastal stadium. "The blood drains right down to the sea."

Rufius' attention returned to earth when he saw that the gently sloped roof was littered with cobblestones and tile shards, jagged reminders of the bread riots two days earlier. In spite of repeated requests, none of the shattered alabaster skylights had been replaced. Work had barely started before it stopped for another holiday Rufius had never heard of.

Rufius cursed under his breath, while Minem launched into his pitch. "Normalized for import duties and transportation costs, the worst Gaulish wine, the dregs of Gaul, would easily cost double your best local drink."

"Double?"

"The worst of it is they could sell more if they wanted," Minem said. His voice crackled with disdain. "With that wine, the Gauls could rule the world."

Festus Rufius watched a trickle of spilt wine wick down a divot and drip through a broken skylight. He shifted from side-to-side, trying to maintain his balance as the red fog of fermentation settled over him. Looking across Tarraco's jumble of crooked streets and tenements, he shook his head in disbelief. "Hispania's a backwater if this is the best she has to offer."

The acrid odors of a less-than-noble luncheon wafted upward from the Villa's outdoor kitchen and the smell made Rufius dizzy. Unable to find his equilibrium on the concave roof tiles, he angled his backside into a terracotta trough and drank what was left of the wine. Squinting, he looked across the sea hoping to catch a glimpse of his beloved Italia.

"We can beat those arrogant Gauls!" Minem's upper lip trembled and his normally infectious smile curled under at the corners. "They didn't exactly welcome Julius Caesar or thank him for bringing the benefits of civilization."

Concerned that Minem might be an angry drunk, Rufius attempted to change the subject. "Are you getting hungry, Minem?"

"Hungry to whip the Gauls." Minem's tiny eyes glowed like a trapped ferret. "Hispania has fertile land, cheap labor, and easy access to the sea. You could out-produce and under price the Gauls without breaking a sweat. If we could just figure out why the local swill is so bad, we could dominate the table top."

Swollen with inebriate enthusiasm, Rufius he tried to stand up but Minem quickly pulled him back down to safety. "There's only one flaw in your logic: Our local wine isn't fit to piss in."

Rufius began crawling back towards the trellis, struggling against what now felt like the mountainous slope of the roof when a dark figure appeared at the top of the tiles.

"Hello, Governor," the cloaked man said in a cold, unforgiving voice. As he climbed onto the roof, he took care to kick the trellis away from the wall, destroying any possibility of retreat.

"Nice costume," Minem said, trying to suppress his panic. "Black tunic, red sash. Positively stunning."

Surprised by the mysterious visitor, Rufius remained supine and silent. He considered his escape options but found none to his liking. Jumping towards the garden would require a dangerous leap of faith. Fleeing towards town invoked a thirty-foot drop to the pavement.

"Hadrian hands you your head, Governor," the visitor said. He removed a terra cotta head from a satchel and held it aloft to reveal a perfect likeness of Festus Rufius.

Still sprawled across the tiles, Rufius looked up at the clay head and laughed at the novelty of seeing his own likeness. The intruder tossed the head towards him, but Rufius fumbled the catch. His terracotta countenance smashed onto the roof.

Rufius noticed a piece of papyrus among the clay fragments. He picked up the small note and read it aloud. "Don't lose your head over missing tribute. You've got one month to render unto Caesar."

"That's how Hadrian cures headaches." The trespasser laughed, jumped down into the garden, and left the two men stunned and stranded on the roof.

Eighteen
XVIII

The leap ended with a blast of sharp pain followed by calm darkness. Death answered the question of whether or not Marcus Valerius had in fact been alive. His confusion was over until a dim light leaked through the void.

Someone or something was prying at his eyelids. Perhaps it was Charon, the river guide, looking for payment. Valerius had forgotten this detail; he had no coins. Was passage across the River Styx negotiable? He opened one eye and saw Gaius Severus' pale forehead hovering above him. He slammed his eyes shut but could not shut out the terrible truth that the boney-nosed demon had accompanied him to the afterlife.

"No," he moaned, "it can't be." Valerius ground his chapped fists into his frozen eye sockets. He drew a cold, biting breath and looked up into the trees for an indication as to which side of existence he now haunted. The drooping branch above him strained under a giant white talon of accumulated snow. The forest canopy bore an army of sculpted white creatures and nightmarish forms twisting inward upon themselves. Each treetop was more gnarled and menacing than the next. Dead spirits would have no trouble hiding in such a nightmare.

"I'm sorry, sir," Severus said. "I didn't mean to hit you so hard. When you stumbled towards the chasm, I used my walking stick to stop you," Severus said. "I meant to catch you in the chest ... not in the forehead."

Valerius used Severus' walking stick for support and stood up slowly. His head was throbbing, his dead heart broken. As he began to walk, Severus positioned himself and the donkey between Valerius and the chasm's edge. They inched along the crevasse until they found a place to cross safely.

Severus broke the windswept gloom after another half hour of cold, silent trekking "Look, sir," he said. "There's a sign by the side of the road."

"What does it say? 'Welcome to the afterlife?'" Valerius chided himself for being caught in such an intolerable predicament. A centurion in the Roman Legion was expected to know at all times if he was alive or dead. He mulled over the two possibilities until an uplifting thought took hold: If Gaius Severus could hear his words, the two of them might actually be alive. The other possibility, that they were together in Hades, bothered Valerius more than if he alone had died. Perhaps they had both been killed or, more likely, they had finally killed each other. Either way, Severus was clearly some kind of hellhound whose teeth dripped with torment. Valerius was out of options. Only one way remained to resolve the mystery. Gaius Severus had to die.

Valerius reached for his *gladius* and Severus struggled to make out the faded letters on a broken plank nailed into a nearby tree.

"I don't understand it," Severus said, "but the sign says, 'HANNIBAL SLEPT AT THE PONUS INN.'"

"Elephants," Valerius muttered. He sheathed the *gladius* and reached for his throwing knife "That would explain this awful road."

As if spurred by the possibility of refuge, the donkey attempted an uncharacteristic trot, but the deep snow and the moribund cart checked his pace. Severus slogged alongside and Valerius, his head still pulsing from the blow, followed with murder on his mind.

Valerius maneuvered carefully to avoid skewering the donkey and compromising the overall mission, but Severus kept bending and twisting as he trudged through the knee-deep snow. Valerius was further jinxed when a stiff wind shot up the trail, kicking a cloud of snow into their faces and thwarting any chance at a clear shot. The trees groaned and unloaded the snow that had accumulated in their boughs.

For a few seconds, Valerius stood blinded, shivering, and more disoriented than ever. As he fought to maintain balance, frozen particles stung like a sandstorm against his exposed face. Teeth chattering, he drew his thin cloak over his chapped lips and nostrils to keep the biting snow from entering his lungs

If killing Severus were even possible, it would have to wait. For now, finding shelter was all that mattered.

"What is this cursed stuff?" he asked, once the wind abated. He brushed ice from his nose and eyelashes. It was now clear that hell was simply the opposite of everything Valerius had known in life. Having spent his existence battling the heat of the desert, he would now spend his afterlife freezing on a mountaintop. In spite of his closed-toed boots and woolen cloak, his stiff toes made it painfully clear that he was ill-equipped for eternal rebuke.

"It's snow, sir, the frozen water I mentioned, at least that's what I think it is. I've never actually seen it before," Severus said. Tiny icicles frosted his hair and eyebrows.

Valerius sucked the snow off his lips. Frozen water was consistent with his theory that hell would be the inverse of everything he had ever known. In life, his soldiers had obeyed him. In hell, he couldn't get Severus to stop talking. In life, water was liquid, in hell it rained down like frozen blades. In life, the sky was blue and the world had color, but here monotony reigned. It all added up to the same cold conclusion. Eternity was going to last a long time.

Gaius Severus tried to stay warm by walking close to the donkey, but the beast was more bothered by the conscript than the cold. Whenever Severus approached, the donkey brayed, kicked, and pushed him away.

"Look, sir, another sign," Severus said. He trudged over to read the letters carved into a ragged plank nailed to an ancient pine. "This one is easier to unravel," Severus said. "'PONUS INN: BEST PRICES BEFORE BORDER.'"

Even the donkey was now shivering. While Severus unhitched the beast and rubbed its flanks, the centurion crept towards them. Still determined to test his theory, Valerius drew his short sword just as Severus tried to climb on the donkey's back. The uncooperative beast bucked and kicked his rear hooves directly into Valerius' chest.

Hearing the dull thud of Valerius landing in a snow bank, Severus ran over and pulled him upright.

"Over there," Valerius whispered once he got to his feet. He pointed into a snow-bound thicket. "Something moved in the woods."

Valerius pulled his bow off the cart and knocked an arrow. He drew the bowstring taut and took careful aim in the direction where he had detected movement. At the instant Valerius released the arrow, Severus pushed the commander's arm aside. The stray shaft hissed away into the forest.

"Why did you do that?" Valerius growled.

"I don't think it's an animal, sir."

"It was covered with fur." Valerius drew another arrow. "If it isn't dinner, it's dangerous."

Knowing that baneful creatures populated the underworld, Valerius scanned the woods for signs of movement. The desert tribesmen spoke of sulfurous lions covered in serpent scales. He had also heard tell of two-headed dogs and dark-winged vultures with talons so strong they could tear a man in half.

The creature he had just seen was not like any of these, but the Eighth of November offered no reason to look on the bright side. Valerius' brief glimpse suggested an unlikely possibility: perhaps the small intruder—a pan, perhaps?—bore no malice. A pan, half boy, half goat, would augur well. Pans were harbingers of lust, debauchery, and the land of eternal reward. When something brushed against the small of his back, Valerius spun around and drew his *gladius*. Heart pounding, he waved his short sword at the small, child-faced creature who had snuck up behind him. "Are you a pan?"

"Yes." The rascal jumped back, laughing and hopping from side-to-side. He looked to be five years old and his playful smile revealed a missing front tooth. "Remo!" he said.

"Is that your name?" Seeing that the creature was neither meal nor menace, Valerius sheathed his blade.

Severus ran over to his commander's side. "Jove!" he said, "It's a child."

"Remo," Valerius said. "A freckle-faced monster wrapped in animal fur." Disappointed at not finding dinner, but relieved at not having skewered a child, Valerius wiped a bead of cold sweat off his forehead.

"Do you speak Latin?" Severus asked.

"Yes!" the boy said. He stuffed a shock of unruly red hair back under his cap.

"Is there a town nearby?" Valerius asked.

"Yes."

"Somewhere we can find a good meal and a warm fire?" Valerius insisted.

"Yes."

Severus intervened. "Is your father a she-goat?" he asked.

"Yes." Remo bobbed gleefully for a second before spinning about and skipping away down the frozen road.

The soldiers followed Remo into the Ponus Valley, a border enclave largely uncorrupted by the benefits of the Roman Empire. He escorted the exhausted, half-frozen men all the way to the weathered front door of the Ponus Inn and then dashed away.

They hitched the donkey and brought the strongbox safely inside the dark establishment. The room was big enough to house a score of men with no expectations of comfort from the dirt floor and drafty stone walls. The low, sloped ceiling's rough-hewn beams showed no strain under the weight of the snow that had piled above. The hearth was full of recently turned coals.

"Hannibal." Severus said, pointing at a dusty elephant tusk hanging above the mantle. "He slept here?"

"Don't be so gullible." Valerius stirred the embers and warmed his hands.

Relieved to be sensing his toes again, Severus thawed in silence, exhausted from the day's trek. A pile of bearskins attracted his attention. If they were to survive another day in the mountains, they would need to exchange their cotton tunics and thin cloaks for more suitable apparel. He looked around the room, inspecting the sparse furnishings and squinting into the dark corners. The gaps between the wall stones were stuffed with mud and straw in an ongoing battle against the wind.

"Why would anyone want to live in a place like this?" Valerius asked.

"Snow must serve some purpose," Severus answered without conviction

Remo burst back in the room followed by an intrepid looking old man wearing rough woolen trousers and a bearskin cloak. He gave Remo a pat on the head and sent him skipping back into the blizzard.

"Ponus," the man said in a thick mountain accent. He looked the two travelers up and down with naked disbelief. Everything in his manner suggested that he had seen worse looking voyagers, but not recently. "You are having reservations?"

"Sorry," Severus began, "we weren't aware—"

Valerius shifted his foot and let the entire weight of eternity pass through the conscript's big toe. Severus winced and the doubting veteran felt momentarily alive again.

A tawny-haired girl, roughly the same age as Gaius Severus, poked her head out from behind the central hearth. She wore a tight fitting tunic made from the hide of a mountain cat and had a sprig of pennyroyal behind her ear. She smiled at Severus, and, noticing her father scowling, disappeared.

"Let's stay here tonight," Severus said. The cold day melted away as if boiled by lightning. The girl's pearly skin made the finest alabaster look like discarded quarry stone. His heart flopped like a fish out of water, twisting and breaching to keep from drowning in a sudden sea of love.

"Sorry. All full up," said the old proprietor. His tone was as sharp as the end of his nose. Beckoning the men to follow, he walked quickly towards the oak door.

"We are Roman soldiers and we'll be staying here tonight," Valerius stated with martial authority.

"Closed for season," Ponus insisted. His fur-lined cap hunched over his forehead to the point where the bushy tufts of his eyebrows emerged like untrimmed hedges. His dark, deep-set eyes gleamed with the anticipation of a hearty profit.

Valerius forgot about crushing Severus' toe and stomped over to confront the innkeeper. "We are Roman soldiers on Roman soil," he said. "You are obliged to house and feed us."

"And tend to our donkey." Severus added, visibly pleased to be exercising military authority for the first time in his career. He edged towards the hearth trying to see where the girl—a vision, perhaps?—had gone. She was like no girl he had ever seen which suggested the possibility that, in fact, he had not really seen her. After such a cold and exhausting day, it was entirely normal to imagine seeing a goddess.

"You are in Roman territory. You enjoy the protection of the Emperor, may he never hear of your impudence," Valerius said. "You have no choice but to offer hospitality."

"No is Rome here." The old mountain man stomped his foot and stood his ground.

"Please don't beat the little villain, sir," Severus whispered, after catching another glimpse of the girl. She was lithe as a lynx and twice as silent. He hoped she was not the old man's wife, but who ever knew with these mountain people? Severus had heard about one such village where brothers married their sisters, children had two left hands, and wolves walked on their hind legs. Given how backwards things could be in remote villages, he reasoned that the young girl might even be the old man's mother.

The girl emerged again to turn the embers. She shot Severus a quick glance and flicked her long braid like a whip. The herb sprig she kept behind her ear fell to the floor. Severus darted over to pick it up and hand it back to her.

"My name is Gaius," he said, blushing like a summer sunset.

"Go away, Lena!" the old man shouted. He shooed her away, muttered something sounding equal parts curse and incantation, and then spat into the fireplace. "Soldiers bad for business. All trouble, no money."

"We have money," Severus said.

At this, Ponus broke into a broad, mostly toothless smile. "Why you no saying before?" He removed his cap to reveal a shock of thick, uneven gray hair and then slapped it back on his head. "Waiting here only one minute. I am finding my son to help."

He ran out into the cold leaving the door open just enough for a blast of icy wind to swirl into the room. The inrush of cold air offered the soldiers a graceless reminder that life or death depended on nothing more than the whims of winter and the crotchety old innkeeper.

The fire shuddered and then sparked to life as a log crackled and took flame.

Severus looked behind the hearth for the intriguing girl with the long braid, but could not find her. Where had she gone? How had such perfection sprouted on a frozen and forgotten mountain? What tethered this goddess to such a conniving old man?

"Learn to keep quiet, won't you?" Valerius grumbled when Severus returned after rounding the fireplace. "We don't pay for lodging. Soldiers travel free."

"Well, it's not really fair, is it?" Severus said. "I mean the poor old codger has to earn his keep, doesn't he? What if an entire cohort passes the night here? Would he have to feed and shelter eighty men for free? No wonder Rome has to fight so hard to expand the empire. What's in it for the little guy?"

"This 'little guy' gets reimbursed by the local garrison," Valerius explained. "He's trying to tickle some tax-free cash by bamboozling us. If we can't stay for free, I'll negotiate a good price and we'll eat our weight in porridge to even things out."

The heavy door creaked open and the largest man that either soldier had ever seen entered the inn. He was so big that he had to turn sideways to squeeze through the doorway. More than entering the room, he filled it like smoke. He had tiny black eyes and wiry black hair that shot out in all directions. His thick beard left only a small gap for his nose—a keel-sized copy of his father's. He was covered in animal furs, and like all northern barbarians, wore rough woolen trousers. He ambled over to the hearth, threw a large chunk of dry wood on the coals, and shook his head so violently that ice crystals flew out of his beard and hissed onto the steaming fire.

"Excuse me," Severus said. He approached the big fellow who looked like the spawn of man and she-bear. Perhaps a forest creature had left him by the tavern's doorstep as a cub. "I saw the sign on the road. Is this the Ponus Inn?"

"Ponus not in."

Worried that the outsized fellow might be turn out to be Lena's beastly husband, Severus fought to maintain his composure. Upon closer examination, he could find no family resemblance between the goddess-like girl and the god-awful young man. Severus hoped that they were nothing more than brother and sister.

To his delight, Lena returned to hang a pot of water over the fire. She gave the big man a hefty shove but could not move him out of the way.

Seeing Ponus the Younger as a possible path to Lena, Severus tried to make conversation. By reaching out and befriending Lena's grizzly brother, she might in turn be swept away by the wiles and wisdom of such a worldly young soldier.

"The Ponus Inn?" Severus asked again.

"Is not Ponus in," the big man grunted. When Lena jabbed him in the fleshy neck with an extended finger, he rose reluctantly, towering over the soldiers like an ancient oak.

"We are in the Ponus Valley, aren't we?" Severus asked. He smiled and tried to locate Lena beyond the big man's shoulder.

"Ponus out," the giant said. His tone made it clear that he did not want to discuss the matter any further, especially after Lena gave him some sharp-tongued instructions in their harsh local dialect before disappearing again.

"I don't think this big hedgehog understands you," Valerius whispered.

The furry colossus stomped across the floor, picked up a heavy section of a tree stump from the corner, and moved it effortlessly to the center of the room. He dropped it in place with a loud thud, dusted off the surface with his forearm, and fetched two smaller stumps for the soldiers to sit on.

"Sit!" he growled in the local tongue, stretching the word into three equally threatening syllables. He then took an earthenware jug from the mantle and threw back a swig of something that caused one of his eyes to bulge. He slammed the container down and a dollop of clear liquor sloshed over onto the table, filling the room with an odor that evoked equal parts piss and pine resin.

"I wish I could speak a few words of his language, sir. There's so much he could tell us." Gaius Severus watched the small puddle wander along into the wood grain. At young Ponus' insistence, he sniffed at the jug and pretended to take a swig while keeping his lips closed tight against his host's preferred poison. Feigning enjoyment, he passed the jug to Valerius. "The empire is so vast … so many peoples, languages, and cultures. We need to reach out to them, bring them into the fold. How can we help these people become good citizens if we don't understand each other?"

"The sword is understood everywhere," Valerius sniffed at the jug, took one sip and then another. He held the jug at arm's length, considering whether to drink a third shot when the donkey's snow-covered snout pushed open the door.

Within a second, the beast was in the room, shaking off the snow and nibbling at a handful of thatch stuffed in the wall. Ponus the Younger washed another mouthful of liquor down his throat and gargled with laughter as it burned past his windpipe.

"See to it that your animal doesn't freeze tonight." Valerius shoved the jug back to Severus and put his head down on the table. It had been a long day and the liquor was strong. Within seconds, he was snoring.

Leaving the sleeping centurion, Ponus the Younger shuffled over to where Severus was struggling to push the donkey out of the warm room. The bulging barbarian took a swig from his jug, wiped a drop of the resinous liquid from his beard, and stroked the donkey's head. "Donkey eats?"

"Yes." Severus said. Eyeing the strongbox and the sleeping centurion, he declined the jug. "Donkey. Hungry."

"Donkey. Eat." The bushy-faced behemoth tucked the donkey under his arm and lugged it towards the door.

"Feed him some grain," Severus said with tired satisfaction in his voice. Things were going well. Already dreaming of Lena, he arranged a pile of bear skins near the strongbox, lay down, and drifted off to sleep.

Severus woke an hour later to the sound of a crackling fire and a snoring centurion. His hunger was stoked by the smell of smoke and stew meat. Seeing Valerius head down on the table, he shuffled over and shook his commander's shoulder. "Wake up, sir."

"Dinner cooking, nice stew." Ponus the Elder said. The old proprietor sat by the hearth, content to stir a large iron pot that bubbled over the fire. "You stay with us here few days?"

"No," Valerius said. He stood up and shook off the thick afterglow of whatever had been in the jug. Still stiff after the cold day's trek, his knees cracked like the burning logs. "We leave tomorrow."

"Good deal on weekly rates," Ponus said, dredging up something from the bottom of the charred pot. He looked at it, threw it back in to simmer, and banged the ladle against the iron pot. "Best deal on mountain. Third night free."

"No." Valerius stepped on Severus' foot to keep him quiet. "One night only."

Lena reappeared and threw some chopped roots into the stew pot. Severus watched in fascination as she pulled a few stray hairs back across a translucent ear and crumbled a handful of dried herbs into the pot. The stew pot bubbled over and filled the room with savory steam. Circling closely, Lena brushed against Severus' shoulder as she left.

"We did offer to pay," Severus said. He smiled at Lena and ignored his commander's sharp elbow. "I've heard that prices nearly double as you go north."

Valerius grunted in exasperation. The promise of a warm bed, the glow of the wood fire, and the fact that he had no tenable fallback position, all conspired against his ability to negotiate. His stomach growled in anticipation of a hot meal. Tomorrow, they would need to get out of these mountains, but tonight there was no alternative to the Ponus Inn. Throwing caution to the howling wind, he continued the negotiation. "How much for one night?"

"One silver Caesar." Ponus answered. "Each."

Valerius pounded the table and stood up. "That's robbery."

"Robber?" Ponus swelled with the confidence of a seasoned haggler. "You are robber!"

The two men faced off just as Ponus the Younger squeezed back through the door, shifting his bulk into the room one leg at a time. The veins on his snow-covered nose glowed like a coal in ash.

"Five silver ... best offer," the mountain patriarch insisted. He opened his hands to reveal his weathered palms were empty of deceit.

"Five? But you just said 'one.'" Valerius sat down and whispered to Severus, "It's like haggling with Hades himself."

Severus stayed quiet. Not only was this an opportunity to watch and learn from his mentor, but Lena had just returned and her conspiratorial smile set his heart pounding so loud he no longer heard the two men arguing. She was everything his father had warned against, and more.

"Three silver is best price," the innkeeper insisted. "More good than after before."

"Two." Valerius said. He glared at Severus to keep still.

"Two? Is joke, no? You make joke?" Old Ponus laughed.

"Joke!" Young Ponus joined his father in laughter.

Lena giggled loudly, causing Severus to start in as well. Within a second, everyone but Valerius was smiling.

"No joke." Valerius slammed his coins on the table. "Two and that's my best offer." Valerius stared at his adversary with a look that could have skinned a live hyena.

The old man slapped his hands against his thighs in a gesture that signified agreement and exasperation. "Two is special rate for Roman soldier. We have deal."

Ponus the Younger jumped up from the corner, raised his stocky arms in the air, and rumbled like a dislodged boulder. "Deal!" he shouted, waddling towards the fire like an erect elephant.

Content that the negotiations had ended, Ponus the Elder yelled for his daughter to serve dinner. Lena emerged from behind the central hearth with a large spoon and a lilt in her step. She ladled the scalding stew into large earthenware bowls, and waited by the fire as the four men tucked into their meal. Before anyone could finish, Lena replenished their bowls with boiled meat, steaming broth, and fibrous roots.

"I'd really like to come back here someday," Severus said after tipping his bowl into his mouth to drain the last few drops of much-needed sustenance into his hollow torso. He wiped his lips and tried to engage the mountain dwellers in conversation. Trying to determine the distance from the Ponus Valley to the coast, he was obliged to describe what a coast was. This led to a vivid description of what a sea was, which, in turn, led to thunderous laughter from their hosts who enjoyed the description of an unbelievably large body of water full of strange creatures.

"Biggest water," repeated the elder for his son's benefit. "Big like sky!"

Severus heard the girl's intoxicating giggle from behind the hearth. Her mirth transported him on downy wings until her brother's volcanic coughing brought him crashing back to earth. Ponus the Younger's loud convulsions reverberated off the walls of the room with avalanche-loosing power. After his snorts subsided, he stuffed more meat into his mouth and vibrated contentedly.

"It's pointless," Valerius muttered after supping on his fourth bowl of stew. "These people don't even know what's in the next valley let alone what a coastline is." He pushed aside his bowl and took to gnawing on one of the hefty bones left on the table. His full stomach left no doubt that he was, in fact, quite alive. The cursed eighth day of November had ended. The gates to hell had closed without taking him under, though hearing the winter storm raging across the Ponus Valley, Valerius was unsure if remaining among the living offered much of an advantage.

Gaius Severus watched with fascination as Lena cleared the table. His stomach ached from the hearty meal and his heart strained against his rib cage like a prisoner doomed to die alone in a tiny cell. He wanted to follow her behind the hearth, take her in his arms and tell her that she was perfect as a summer moon. Instead, he sat paralyzed and dizzy as facts crowded out fantasy. He was an accidental conscript, a Jewish refugee bound for Londinium. She was an illiterate mountain girl, a virtual slave of her crooked father and mongrel brother.

It was a match made in heaven.

Lena covered the coals with ashes to keep them hot until the morning. As much as Severus tried to catch her eye, she did not return his glances. When she left without so much as a flick of her braided hair, Severus bid her a silent farewell. In spite of her brother's large presence, the room now felt empty.

The big brother threw a few bearskins on the ground near the hearth. "Sleep," he ordered, apparently willing to back up the command with a smack on the skull of anyone not dozing off immediately. His inebriation had passed the giddy summit of rosy joy to a darker state of drunkenness. The clouds forming in his dark eyes suggested he would be easy to anger.

Satisfied that Lena was safely away, the large man lumbered over to the front door, fiddled with the handle, and exited the room one hemisphere at a time. The inn fell silent except for the occasional burst of wind howling outside the thick walls. A last smoldering coal in the fireplace crackled in the darkness as the soldiers settled in for the night.

Though exhausted, Severus could not sleep. Sleep would bring the morning, and the morning meant leaving behind a mystery named Lena that he longed to unravel. "Centurion," he said in the darkness, "are you awake?"

"No."

"Maybe we should stay here until the weather clears."

"For Saturn's sake ...." Valerius shifted his position and began snoring.

A burst of cold air whistled through a crack in the wall. The storm outside masked the sound of the innkeeper's fetching daughter sneaking back into the room to stir the embers.

Nineteen
XIX

Vindex had met the black-clad messenger before. Prowling the perimeter on the last night of the governor's weeklong inauguration party, he was surprised to find the former arena executioner sneaking into the Villa.

"I got here first." Vindex stood his ground and barred the executioner turned messenger from scaling the Villa's garden wall. "Besides, you owe me a favor."

"You were stupid to spare my life," the messenger said, imitating Vindex's mossy accent. "Lucky for Hades, I'm not here for you." The man twisted his red sash to reveal an embroidered patch bearing an eagle. "Imperial courier."

"I'll go with you. I've got a message to deliver."

"Sorry, old vole. I work alone."

Quick as a cobra, the man grabbed Vindex by the wrist, jammed a stiff thumb into his pulse, and brought him to his knees. Before Vindex could rise, the cloaked menace had disappeared over the high wall.

Once inside the Villa, the intruder found Festus Rufius pacing and yelling at the taxman. Immune to the governor's tirade, Cassius Kleptus barely looked up from a tray of twice-poached lampreys.

"You again?" When Rufius saw the dark messenger looming before him, his heart dropped into his empty stomach. "Stranding me on the roof with Minem was a dirty trick."

Rufius tried to leave, but the messenger blocked the exit and tossed a tightly wound scroll to the governor. From the dull thump and the way the package skidded across the tiled floor, Rufius surmised that the document contained more than just words. Shaken but defiant, he kicked the scroll back towards the messenger and a tarnished blade clattered onto the floor.

The messenger left quietly as Rufius scanned the papyrus, blanched, and handed it to Kleptus.

"There are only two ways out of debt," Kleptus read. "Alive or dead."

"Sage advice for a wealthy taxman." Rufius peeked around the doorway to see if the messenger was still lurking, but the corridor was empty. "Paying off the deficit is your problem."

Kleptus burped quietly and kneaded the folds of his forehead. "Bring back the legion, so I can collect taxes," he said carefully. "Without soldiers, I'm toothless. I need—"

"You need a big bathtub where you can slit your wrists with that rusty knife," Rufius said. He scowled at the well-fed bureaucrat who had woven his toga by robbing the treasury. "If you can't collect taxes, I'll—"

Before Kleptus could respond, Winus Minem burst into the room, breathless as if he had been chased by an enormous, hungry opportunity.

"Our distinguished advisors are here!" Minem smiled at the perspiring, red-faced taxman. Caught up in his own excitement, Minem whisked Rufius away through the Villa's confusing corridors. Gasping for breath, he explained that two highly paid experts in the art of winemaking were waiting in a small vestibule off the atrium.

Minem pushed Rufius into the waiting room and two pale women stood up to great him. Both nursed overbites and one was nervously curling a lock of frizzy hair around her finger.

"Sorry." Rufius turned to leave so fast he nearly flattened Minem. "Must be the wrong room."

Insisting that Rufius was in the right place, Minem tried to pull the governor back into the vestibule by the tail of his toga, but Rufius kicked the door shut and refused to budge.

"Those are your experts?" Rufius folded his soft face into hardened disbelief. "Those two can't be experts ... they're women!"

"I'm not sure I see your point, Excellency," Minem said. He put a hushing finger to his lips lest the dark-haired sisters overhear and take offense. "Tabia and Lavinea were the only two souls in Gaul willing to share the secrets of winemaking."

"Women don't even have souls." Enunciating slowly and speaking loud enough for his voice to echo down one corridor and return from another, Rufius held firm. "They can't be experts. They're women."

Minem stiffened like a full sail. "Do you think the Gauls were eager to help us? I was lucky to make it back here alive." He waited a second to regain his composure and then offered a comforting fact that, while untrue, would be impossible to verify. "Besides, in the Winemaking industry most of the great noses are women."

"Great noses?" Rufius hunched his shoulders and clasped his arms across his chest. "All I see are big noses, pasty-faces, and stringy hair. They're ugly as hyenas."

"They're the best I could do." Minem was no longer straining to keep his voice down. "Short of torture, there was no other way to get help from the Gauls."

Rufius considered his options for the better half of a second and then stomped away. "It will only work if they disguise themselves as men," he said, before turning down a dark hallway.

After a few moments lost in the Villa's winding corridors, Rufius arrived at the entrance to the gaily-decorated dining room. Slaves dressed as Persian eunuchs pushed past him, ferrying ornate pitchers, silver plates, and glass goblets. Halfway across the threshold, he stopped and stared bug-eyed at the lavish spread overflowing the many platters and tables. Stuffed dormice—Rufius' favorite—peeked out of poached goose eggs. Mouthwatering pastries floated like pleasure craft on a soft rolling sea of imported cherries, apricots, and peaches. Chickpeas and lupines, lamb nuts and kidneys, sow vulvas and peacock tongues spilled over onto the sofas where richly dressed men and their barely dressed consorts supped like camels at an oasis. Bacchus himself could never have imagined or paid for such a party.

Rufius lost his appetite to see the freeloading gentry perspiring like old cheese as they groped his food and their mistresses. After a week of festivities, none of the guests remembered or cared why they had been invited to the Villa. Two fat plantation owners tossed pearl onions into each others' mouths. Like a plague of rats, the ungrateful guests ravaged a large platter of green and black olives that had been arranged in mosaic fashion to resemble the pointed boot of Italia, the very boot that threatened to grind Rufius into powder.

Rufius took a deep breath and steeled himself for the task of rallying the local gentry to his vision of a greater, less insolvent Hispania. Captivating their spirits was the first step towards capturing their cash and, given their gluttony, both would be a challenge

As Rufius proceeded towards the rostrum, Vindex cut across his path carrying a steaming platter and a disgruntled demeanor. He was dressed as a harem girl and wore enough clattering jewelry to wake a dead banker.

"Sausages," he said to Rufius, "made from arena predators like you."

Vindex shoved the platter at Rufius but a gluttonous reveler jumped between them. Others followed to grope and gobble sausages made of bear meat, hyena, and Nile crocodile. Vindex was quickly surrounded and Rufius took advantage of the excitement to scurry out of the room only to crash into Winus Minem.

"Vindex is back," Rufius whispered, extracting himself from Minem's toga folds. "He's come to kill me."

Both men turned to escape down the corridor, but Vindex, his usual menace tempered by garish mascara, a silk sash, and false, lopsided breasts grabbed them by the scruff of their togas. He dragged them back into the banquet hall and, much to the crowd's delight, lifted them into the air.

"Put us down, you murderer!" Minem squirmed and twisted until he was cheek-to-jowl with Vindex.

"I've killed no one," Vindex growled, his accent thick and truculent. "Not yet."

"Why not start now?" Rufius said. "You'd be doing me a favor. Being murdered on the spot would solve most of my problems."

"You planned on letting me rot in jail and killing me in your inaugural games."

"Not at all, my dear Vindex," Rufius insisted. "How you misunderstand me!"

"Then give me my old job back." Vindex's false breasts sagged like bean sacks as he raised the men higher and smiled at the cheering crowd. To further titillate the guests, he shook his hips and shifted his lumpy corset from side-to-side. While they laughed, he continued to work his advantage over the two dangling captives. "I want to be paid so I can buy my freedom. And no more costume parties."

"Of course," Rufius said. "If I make you a security guard and pay you a stipend, will you put me down and promise not to kill me?"

Vindex lowered Rufius to the floor.

"What about me?" Minem asked.

"You? I'll twist your neck like a chicken." Vindex held Minem a moment longer and shook his tiny sandals loose with a spine-wrenching shake.

"Unlike you, I'm not an assassin," Vindex said to the terrified advisor before dropping him. Satisfied at seeing Minem scurry away like a drenched mouse, Vindex ripped off his harem girl costume and made great show of tossing all but the most valuable accessories to the mistresses and trophy wives swooning nearby.

Rufius took refuge at the rostrum and tried to get the crowd's attention, but they were slow to settle down. The women were distracted by the sweaty sheen of Vindex's marble torso, and the men were lost in wine and jealousy.

"Enough!" Rufius shouted. He pounded the rostrum, rubbed his dry elbows, and glared at the guests. In spite of Minem's assurances, the august gathering had not served to propel Hispania, or its newest governor forward. The only consensus the tax-avoiding freeloaders had reached was on how best to gorge themselves on delicacies never before seen in their dead-end province. If his lavish party had borne any fruit, the guests would have devoured it and washed it down with free drink.

Rufius noticed Vindex propped against a column, flexing for the attentive ladies. Restored to his skintight tunic and reveling in his status as a paid bodyguard, he no longer represented a threat.

Slaves with veiled faces delivered plates of steamed eels and grilled cod livers.

"Friends, Citizens, Winemakers," Rufius shouted. "After a week of fine fare and gay festivities, it's now time for the last event. You've probably been wondering why I asked you to bring samples of your best wines to this noble gathering."

"So we can booze it up," Cassius Kleptus, the taxman, said in between handfuls of cumin scented quail eggs.

"Our goal must be nothing less than seeing our radiant emperor drink from Hispania's next crush!" Rufius announced to the disbelievers.

Cassius Kleptus, whose mouth was never less than half-full, nearly choked on the notion. "Hadrian can afford anything he wants. Why would he drink our stuff?"

"Simple!" Minem reappeared and, to avoid Vindex, jumped up to the rostrum. "Indeed, citizens, in a year or so, your wine will grace the table of the emperor himself, long may he imbibe."

"To the emperor!" Rufius raised his glass and sloshed a few wayward drops onto Minem's light brown toga. "May his nose ever shine with the fruit of our vines!" He drank deeply and, for a second, imagined returning to Rome triumphant before reality drained his glass.

"To the emperor!" Winus Minem raised his glass and drank in approval. He had rehearsed this speech a number of times and the crowd seemed to be lapping it up.

"Fellow citizens," Rufius said, launching a solemn crescendo, "for over two hundred years the empire has expanded in constant triumph. Our ancestors brought new territories and subjects into the vivid fabric of modern civilization. The Roman formula has been consistent: reward collaborators and grind enemies to sausage! If a man doesn't grasp the olive branch, we nail him to it."

The thundering call to arms woke those who had been sleeping and Minem nudged Rufius frantically. "Wrong speech," he whispered.

Guests shifted nervously on their sofas. Some men left their perches and wandered over to the wine-laden tables that the noisy servants had arranged along the walls.

"If I might have your attention for just one more moment," Rufius continued. "For the next hour, I ask you to keep your minds open. Trust the refined tastes of our esteemed experts. There is much to learn even if at first you don't like the message. Remember: We are in pursuit of truth, and truth will lead us to greatness!"

"And the truth," Minem whispered, "is that Hispania's best wine could kill a mother cobra."

Rufius elbowed Minem and stepped off the rostrum. "Citizen Minem will now explain the rules of the game," he said. "May the best wine win!"

"This is my kind of game." Kleptus stood up and rocked his volcanic hips. "What's the prize?"

Minem ignored the interruption and explained the basic procedure to the few puzzled participants who were still listening. "All of the containers are numbered but otherwise unmarked. Your job is to sample and rank the various wines. The goal is to select the best wine from among the dozen samples."

"What if I already know the answer?" Kleptus asked.

"When the tasting is complete and our votes have been tallied," Minem continued, "I'm going to bring in two connoisseurs from outside the province and compare our results with theirs."

Knocking Carbo and the kitchen slaves aside, the men threw themselves into the exercise with newfound enthusiasm. They rushed from table to table, pushing and shoving, slamming goblets of the various wines down their fleshy gullets and never bothering to rinse. When the first empty pitcher crashed to the floor, Carbo crawled out of the scrum and went to fetch another.

"This one has no taste," Kleptus complained after sampling something unfamiliar. "Are you sure it's wine?" Disappointed, he moved on to the next sample and, after a tentative sip, arched his thick neck to let the pungent crush coat the full length of his throat. "Now this," he shouted, "this booze has balls! Come on over, boys, and have a snort of Hispania's hardiest hooch!"

Men gathered around the taxman and drained the pitcher. The pattern continued until all the wines had been ranked, and the men were thoroughly intoxicated for the third time that day.

While the guests sucked down wine and gobbled a fresh platter of fruits, Minem and Rufius reviewed the rankings. Neither was surprised to see that the fine Gaulish fare had finished dead last in preferences. Hispania's foul wine emerged as the undisputed winner.

"I'm not surprised," Minem said. Seeing Vindex fast approaching, he looked for something with which to defend himself but all he found was a long wooden spoon dropped by an overburdened slave. He picked up the implement and gazed up into the sober, pale eyes of the ex-gladiator now looming above him like a thundercloud.

"You tried to lock me away." Vindex yanked Minem upright. He pulled a knife from his sash and twirled it in free hand. "I should skewer you like a rabbit."

"Good idea if your goal is to die poor," Minem said. "But here's a better idea: Spare me, and you'll die with enough gold to buy your freedom twice over."

"Why should I trust you?" After considering the proposition and the room full of potential witnesses, Vindex put the knife away and smiled. "Let's see a down payment."

"Good boy," Minem said. "Now you're thinking." Minem dropped a few *sesterces* into Vindex's giant hand. "Now scram or we'll both be broke."

"This buys you half an hour, mousey man." Vindex palmed the coins and returned to the kitchen.

Still shaking from his introduction to the gladiator's dagger, Minem pushed through the crowd and jumped up to the rostrum. He waved his hands and tried to organize the drunks for the next round in what they thought was just a fraternal drinking game. "In just one minute we'll bring out our special guests to evaluate these very same wines."

"Bring out your so-called experts!" Kleptus was less lucid than he had been all week. His wineglass could barely navigate home to his sagging lips. "If these geniuses know wine, they'll love ours."

The Gaulish sisters wore loose fitting, floor-length brown tunics, men's sandals, and white sashes. Long, bent and nearly identical noses protruded from underneath tightly wound turbans parked on their tiny heads. Stiff and far from home, they made eye contact with no one as they shuffled into position.

The crowd hushed as the two experts began the wine tasting ritual with an air of religious devotion. After cleansing their palates with water, they slowly swirled and sipped the first sample. First Tabia, then Lavinea sucked air through pursed lips, sloshed the wine around in her mouth, and spat into an empty pitcher. This final step surprised the men who, moments earlier, had been keen to swallow as much plonk as possible.

"Wine number one," Tabia said to the stunned room. She spat again, rinsed her mouth and lowered her eyes as the crowd leaned forward to hear her quiet judgment. "Wine number one is full-bodied to the point of obesity."

The men cheered. Wine number one had been one of their favorites. Some reacted to the expert's verdict by pushing closer to the table. Knocked off balance, Cassius Kleptus fell forward onto his fleshy knees.

After repeating the ritual with the next sample, Lavinea paused and did her best to speak with a throaty, gruff rasp. "The pleasure … the nuance … the nose ... this is the true fruit of Gaul!"

"Stuff Gaul!" Cassius Kleptus shouted. Three nearby drunks helped Kleptus back to his feet while he wobbled and yelled. "Gaulish wine is for girls!"

Lavinea glared at him. "Half the world is female, you oaf!"

Tabia nudged her and whispered, "Double fees, sister. Don't let these vinegar drinkers get under your skin."

Tabia moved on to the third sample, took a sip, and spat it out immediately. "Disgusting! This tastes of pitch." She rinsed her mouth out twice. "What was it fermented in, terra cotta? Don't you cads know that wine should be aged in oak barrels?"

"That's my wine!" Cassius Kleptus nudged the man next to him. "Who are these village idiots?"

Minem edged closer to his patron. "Did you catch that, Excellency?" he asked. "Your wine shouldn't be aged in terra cotta. The pitch that seals the amphorae may be our problem. We need to find some oak barrels."

"I need to find a better advisor." Rufius beckoned to Carbo who had been cleaning up another spill. "Find Security Chief Magnus," he whispered. "Tell him to get his bovine backside over here immediately."

Carbo bowed and shuffled away with a half-full pitcher of the finer wine.

"Once Magnus disposes of Vindex," Minem whispered to Rufius, "Have him ride north, catch up with the Scipio cohort, and bring back a few oak barrels from Southern Gaul."

"Hadrian's Wall can wait another week." Rufius agreed. He watched the two women spit and condemn another local wine. "Did you pay these so-called experts in advance?"

"Only half."

"So far, that's twice what they're worth. They really put the con in connoisseur."

"Wine number seven." Lavinea's voice cracked as she strained to be heard. "Delightful. Herbaceous. An initial hint of oak finished with a burnt cherry nose. It's a shame to spit this one out."

"So swallow, damn it!" Kleptus shouted. Prodded by the crowd, he waddled over to the table and guzzled the wine left in the container. "Lovely!" he said in a snide falsetto. "It's simple, yet complex; old, yet young. It could strip paint off of a statue, yet it's gentle enough to wash a hooker's hiney!"

Kleptus took another swig and spat a mouthful at Lavinea. Fed up with his ignorance and swagger, she emptied a pitcher over his head, sending wine spraying in all directions. The crowd cheered and laughed as, drenched with wine, Kleptus raised his arms in triumph.

Unwilling to endure another ill-mannered minute, Tabia grabbed Lavinea by the arm and pulled her away. "Let's go," She said. "There's no price high enough to justify being abused by mud-mouthed southerners."

"Hey! I'm a wine expert too!" Kleptus threw his glass at Lavinea and the projectile knocked the turban off her head.

The room went silent as her black, stringy hair unraveled like seaweed around her shoulders and her face ran pale with panic.

"Women!" Kleptus shouted. "They're female!"

A few men cheered and rushed forward to get a better look at the defrocked experts. Others attacked the remaining wine. One confused guest grabbed the spittoon and drank it down.

"Barbarians!" Tabia backed towards the exit as the men drew near. "Curse your mother's milk!"

The drunks cursed and shoved forward, sloshing their pitchers and glasses as they reached for the women. Drink splashed high into the air, staining togas and spotting the walls. Within seconds, the floor was redder than the blade of Brutus.

"Rufius, you old trickster," Kleptus shouted. He crawled over a fallen colleague in pursuit of the last full pitcher. "This is the best party ever!"

Rufius wrestled Tabia free from the clutches of an ill-intentioned guest and tried to drag her out of the room. "Good job, girls," he said. "You really know how to work a crowd."

"Get your sleazy southern hands off me!" Tabia yelled. Mistaking Rufius for one of the aggressors, she slapped his face. "Is this how you treat your betters? Why not just throw us to the lions and make the day complete?"

"You're finally making sense." Rufius wrestled her towards the corridor and slammed the door before her sister or the crazed crowd could follow. "But you can't imagine how hard it is to find lions on such short notice."

Twenty
XX

In spite of the falling snow, Marcus Valerius and Gaius Severus were dripping with sweat as they wrestled their cart towards the border between Hispania and Gaul. Remo the mountain boy trotted alongside them, happy to have company.

"Vex you," Valerius said to Severus.

"Vex you!" Remo repeated. He gathered snow into a ball and threw it at Gaius Severus.

"I can't believe you let that hairy ogre cook our donkey."

"I don't understand it. We seemed to be communicating so well."

The cart slid sideways across an ice patch. Severus struggled to pull it forward, but only managed to get it stuck. Valerius put his shoulder to the cartwheel and the two tried to dislodge it from a snow-filled rut.

"'Donkey? Hungry? Eat? That was quite a conversation." Valerius threw his angry weight against the cart and it finally lurched forward.

"My father used to say that we learn more from our mistakes than from our successes." Severus paused to consider if this were actually true and quickly decided he would prefer to learn less from an occasional success than volumes from his frequent failures.

"At least you knew your father."

"Father," Remo repeated, and threw another snowball at Severus.

"To be honest, sir, donkey meat didn't taste so bad, did it? Surprisingly tender, no?" Severus wiped the snow from his shoulder and groped for a handful of hope in what was clearly a terrible setback for the mission, "At least the innkeeper was good enough to sell us these bear furs at a discount. They might save our lives."

"Or attract a love-starved she-bear," Valerius mumbled.

"The weather's getting worse," Severus said. Even the warm memories of Lena, the innkeeper's delightful daughter, could not calm his shivering.

"No surprise. Everything gets worse as you head north." Twenty years of desert nights—bone chilling as they could be—had not prepared him to maneuver in such bleak misery.

"I feel like I've compromised our mission, sir." Severus reached in his pocket for a leftover chunk of donkey meat, and continued speaking as he gnawed on it. "On the other hand, how can I compromise the mission when I don't know what it is?"

"Your mission is to shut up and pull this vexed cart!" Valerius kicked a mound of snow, sending crystalline spray into the air. "Our mission is to get this cart to our cohort. Is that clear?"

"Clear? Just out of curiosity, sir, what's in the box we've been transporting?"

"Classified information. If you're captured and tortured, just die quietly."

Valerius rubbed his half-frozen eyes and tried to imagine a sunny day free from Severus jabbering. Something about the boy still refused to ring true. His endless chatter was enough to drive a man to suicide. He was too incautious to be political, too loud to be a spy, and too misinformed to be an informer.

Remo ran ahead, leaving the men to muddle onward. After navigating a frozen bend in the miserable road, Severus noticed a sign nailed to a nearby tree.

"'LADY RIVUS BIG BORDER CART MART,'" Severus read.

Valerius muttered a southern curse in anticipation of more northern nonsense.

The soldiers approached the border station where Remo and a prim, well-fed woman waited. A quick look at her bushy eyebrows suggested that she was a relative of Ponus the Innkeeper, perhaps his younger sister.

"You'll surely want to exchange your cart at the border," she said with a thick mountain accent. Her broken Latin was clear enough for commerce. She passed an experienced eye over the two soldiers and the cart they had dragged into her orbit. "Lady Rivus, that's me, has what you need."

"No, thank you." Valerius wiped the sweat off his face and motioned for Severus to stay quiet and mind his manners in the woman's presence. "We've no need of a new cart, though an able donkey would be of interest," he added.

"You need both," she said. "The road changes width on the north side of the border. Your southern cart is too wide."

Remo prepared a snowball, but Lady Rivus smacked the back of his head before he could throw it at anyone. The boy scurried off to play among the carts, spare wheels, and broken axles while the two cold soldiers walked off to verify that the road narrowed abruptly and inexplicably, exactly as she had said.

"What do we do now?" Severus whispered to his commander. "I don't see any donkeys."

"She probably ate them. Now stay quiet. That's an order."

Lady Rivus was smiling when the soldiers returned. She had looked over their rig to assess its value and uncover its contents. "Pity your rims are wood. Lucky for you I have hob-nailed wheels to get your cart down the mountain."

"All we need is a cheap cart and donkey." Valerius was quickly losing hope of getting off the mountain with his dwindling sanity and few remaining coins before the falling snow forced them back to the Ponus Inn for another miserable night.

"Short on cash, are we?" Lady Rivus smiled. "Perhaps you can trade some of your cargo."

"Cargo," Remo echoed. Freshly fallen snow bounced off his fur cap and onto his nose.

"Our cargo isn't for sale," Severus said. The centurion had insisted that spies and rebels could come in all shapes so he was careful not to reveal an important, though still mysterious, military secret.

The clouds parted momentarily and Severus caught a glimpse of the icy road ahead. How would they ever descend such a steep path without studded wheels and a sure-footed beast of burden? The true cost of the donkey dinner churned in his gut.

"Cargo not for sale, eh?" Lady looked the fur-clad men over again, up and down, side to side, taking special interest in Valerius. "You'll have to show your goods to my husband at the checkpoint so there's no need for secrecy."

"We are imperial soldiers traveling on official military business," Valerius said.

"Soldiers? I've never seen soldiers wearing bear skins. Who's the enemy, a rabbit?"

Valerius was colder than he had ever been in his life and had no patience for games with coy civilians. "We are legionaries. You are obliged to help us."

"In a hurry to join the fighting?" Lady Rivus' dark eyes seemed to light up with intrigue.

"Fighting," Remo repeated, dancing in place. He twisted his face into a scowl and punched Severus in the leg to show that he knew exactly what the word meant.

"Fighting?" Valerius considered her face carefully. Because she looked like Ponus, he suspected trickery.

"What fighting?" Severus asked.

"Down in the valley," Lady Rivus said when it was clear that there was no profit in holding back the rumor or the soldiers any longer. "I heard that soldiers are attacking a small town."

Twenty-one
XXI

Festus Rufius was angry that his lavish inaugural feast had produced no results beyond putting him deeper in debt. Days after the last guest left, the Villa still stunk of fraud and fermentation and Rufius longed to breathe air that did not reek of bad memories. The lethargic servants had barely started scrubbing away the stains of overindulgence when another local holiday stopped their progress.

He blamed the entire debacle on Winus Minem, the Macedonian millstone whose free advice was less that worthless. Rufius had a growing desire to toss Minem into a tub full of starving lampreys. The tiny advisor was inept in every sense but his uncanny timing.

"A gift, Excellency!" Minem banged on the bedroom door and, when it did not open, began to shout. "Open up! I've got the perfect diversion for you."

"Suicide?" Rufius buried his head under a pillow. "I've already got a rusty knife."

"Bulbul."

"The Imperial Falcon Master?" Rufius jumped out of bed, unlocked the door, and almost jerked his shoulder loose prying it open. "This better not be a joke."

"Fortune favors the fortunate and Fate favors Fortune's favorites!" Minem said. He pushed past the doorway, and handed Rufius a scroll whose imperial seal had already been broken. "Once-in-a-lifetime opportunities don't come often. How quickly can you get ready?"

Bulbul, the emperor's falcon master, was a small, sinuous Nubian with eyes like new moons. He was silent as sunset and agile as a fox. After two hours of trekking through the coastal foothills with Rufius, he had not spoken a word or cracked a twig underfoot. The two hooded falcons perched on each of his leather shoulder pads rode along without agitation. Though his stride was short, Bulbul maintained a rapid pace that soon had Rufius in a sweat.

The air was fresh, the sky was clear, and the recently harvested fields of winter wheat meant that hare and other small creatures would be easy prey for a novice. Rufius took heart to see a gull, a good omen, tracing wide, rising circles overhead. It was his happiest moment in Hispania.

Without looking up, Bulbul unleashed the larger falcon and tossed it into the air. The bird of prey shot into the sky and brought back the broken gull before it had had time to squawk. Bulbul tucked the carcass into his sack for later use.

"Perhaps gulls aren't such good omens, after all," Rufius said. The brisk pace through the brown hills suited him well. Far from the dull chatter and intrigue of the capital, the sweat and silence restored his soul. All that mattered now was learning to hunt with the emperor's enigmatic falcon master.

The emperor! Rufius tried not to think about provincial affairs, but Minem had shared a rumor that bore promise. Hadrian, it seemed, was travelling through Gaul on one of his grand, sweeping tours of the realm. There was even talk of him coming south to see his homeland. Could it be true? On any given day, the emperor was generally believed to be in three places at once, but if one of them was Hispania, it would be a thick stroke of fortune

"Tell me about Hadrian," Rufius said.

Bulbul cleaned his teeth with a small stick and padded along without acknowledging the governor's presence. The hooded falcons on his shoulders were silent as sculptures.

"What luck to learn falconry!" Rufius sucked fresh air into his lungs and exhaled with explosive vigor. "I hope you know enough Latin to teach me the essential vocabulary, Master Bulbul. Can you picture me talking falcons with Hadrian, bonding like birds of a feather?"

The more Rufius reflected upon it, the more excited he became. "What if it's true that the emperor is coming to my humble province? Jove! What a lucky draw it was to get this assignment. Thank the Gods I wasn't dumped in one of those soggy northern provinces where I'd have been stuck indoors, bored to death by dull architects droning on about roads arches and sewers. Instead, I've got an easy post, a mansion by the sea, and a golden chance to impress Hadrian, may he remember me favorably."

Bulbul led Rufius through the forest until he found an ideal spot for a first lesson. He proceeded to the center of a small meadow, held his creased palm open and upright, and spoke for the first time. His Latin was sparse and heavily accented with the deep, muddy drawl of the upper Nile. "Here stopping," he said.

Bulbul borrowed Rufius' knife, cut two bent saplings, and drove them into the ground. He slipped the knife in his sash, lashed each bird to a perch, and removed two long goatskin gloves from his sack. The hunter put one of the gloves on his right hand and indicated for the governor to do the same.

Rufius looked at the birds, the gloves, and Bulbul's small leather sack. It dawned on him that there were no porters, no cooks, and no entourage. In his excitement to depart, he had overlooked his own comfort. "Vexation," he muttered. "Someone's paid a fortune for this hunting trip and it isn't even catered?"

"Before hunt you must master bird." Bulbul took the smaller bird from its perch, threaded a length of leather cord around her ankle, and tied the other end around the governor's gloved wrist. As soon as Bulbul released her, the hooded falcon let out a shrill cry, flapped her wings madly, and tried to fly in a tight circle.

Bulbul caught the nervous bird and produced a soft, scratching sound from the back of his throat. "Schhhrrrr, schhhrrrr," he whispered. He positioned the bird onto the governor's forearm and held her until calm. "She senses your fear," he said.

"I'm not afraid," Rufius protested, holding the small falcon at arm's length. "A bit concerned, perhaps."

151

Bulbul raised his weathered hand to silence Rufius. He pressed the falcon's hooded face into the governor's glove until the scent of the familiar kid leather reassured her. The reluctant bird rocked cautiously on Rufius' trembling forearm.

"Schhhrrrr, schhhrrrr," Bulbul said. "Be still with falcon."

"But how do I—?"

"You must first learn her name." Bulbul walked away, taking the larger bird with him. Before disappearing into the woods Bulbul looked back over his shoulder and smiled for the first time. "Remember: you are her master."

The minute Bulbul vanished into the woods, the young bird dug her talons into Rufius' forearm. Attempting to take flight, she beat her wings and traced a crazed radius before the cord snapped her back. She strained against the lash and clawed at the glove.

Rufius panicked. Unable to prevent the attacks, he flailed both arms widely to avoid the bird's sharp talons. "Carbo!" he shouted, hoping against reason that his recently promoted valet, might be nearby. "If only I hadn't yelled at him yesterday," he cried, keeping the bird at a distance. "When I said I wanted some time alone, I didn't mean *this* alone."

Eventually, the young falcon tired of beating her wings. She came to rest on Rufius' forearm, dug her talons into the goatskin glove, and pinched to the point of pain. Rufius winced and reached for his knife, but Bulbul had taken it. There was no way to cut her loose. He inched his free hand towards the bird, but when his fingers reached the knot, the winged demon grabbed hold.

"Mother of Jove!" Rufius screamed, trying to wrest his fingers from her grip. A fine plume of blood shot out of his forefinger as he ripped it free. "Carbo!" he shouted. "Carbo if you're out there, help me! Help me and your grandchildren will be free men."

The bird took wing again. She circled and menaced Rufius from every angle. Each dive brought her sharp talons stabbing down into the glove and Rufius waved his arms like Icarus falling, flapping in counterpoint to avoid her strafing. After a dozen dives, she tired and came to rest again on his gloved hand, twitching as the tantrum subsided.

The lull gave Rufius a moment to examine her closely.

"You little monster," he said, softly.

The hooded bird reared and clawed at his face, but he yanked her back before she could seize his lip.

"Carbo!" Rufius yelled. "Help me and I'll wed you to a free woman!"

The small falcon wrapped her talons around his ulna, squeezing his forearm and loosing another shrill cry.

"Calm down my little princess of pestilence." Rufius tried to sooth the falcon. He felt sorry for the hooded bird in spite of her belligerence, "Scared of the dark, are you? Stay still and I'll untie your hood. You'll feel better when you can see, won't you?"

During an instant while the bird was calm, Rufius managed to snag the hood and yank it off her head. Delighted to be out of the dark, the falcon chick drove her beak into his free hand. She tore at the tender skin between his thumb and forefinger and beat her wings, twisting as if trying to gut a mouse in flight.

"Carbo!" Rufius shouted, trying to shake her loose. "Save me and you're free!"

The falcon screamed with hatred and stabbed at Rufius' exposed wrist. He pulled his flesh away and the leather cord went taut. Cackling with rage, she circled and attacked again.

"Stop, damn you! You want me to bleed to death?" Rufius remembered the calming sound that Bulbul had made. "Schhhrrrr, schhhrrrr," he gurgled, half-choking on the consonants.

To Rufius' surprise, the falcon calmed down as if struck by magic. She returned to Rufius' forearm and cocked her head to one side, a bit of his flesh still hanging from her beak.

"Schhhrrrr, schhhrrrr," he whispered again.

Seeing that the sound soothed her, Rufius repeated the calming noise and took a closer look at her. "Schhhrrrr, schhhrrrr, calm down little one, that's better."

The falcon eyed him cautiously and then struck his cheek like winged lightning.

"You shitty bird!" he shouted. Blood dripped down his cheek. "I'll kill you!"

The falcon shrieked and turned her attention to the glove. She bit, clawed, and tore feverishly at the thin layer of protection.

"Schhhrrrr, schhhrrrr," Rufius whispered frantically, but the incantation had lost its power. "Vesuvius!" he cursed, waving his arm to avoid her fury. "This is the worst vacation I've ever had!"

There was no longer any question in the governor's mind that the tiny bird was his mortal enemy. Roman tradition offered many noble ways to die, but being pecked to death was not one of them. Hadrian's rusty knife would have been preferable.

"Bulbul! Help!" Rufius cried. "Bulbul!"

The bird continued to attack with increased verve and violence.

"Schhhrrrr. Schhhrrrr." Rufius growled, but the falcon grew more excited by the minute. "Bulbul," he cried, and then it occurred to him: Bulbul would never return. It suddenly added up. Bulbul had trained the deadly bird. He had vanished after taking Rufius' knife. Bulbul knew this would happen—he wanted it to happen. Bulbul was more than just Hadrian's falcon master, he was an assassin. Rufius' panic rose as the sting of betrayal set in.

"Bulbul! Whatever they're paying, I'll double it!" Rufius struggled to keep the bird at arm's length. If the falcon failed to finish him, her master would. Rufius looked around, frantic to find a hard surface against which he could pummel the winged savage. "I'll triple it your blood money," he shouted. "Name your price, you feather mongering bastard!"

Movement among the trees distracted him long enough for the bird to strike and bite into his free hand, nearly taking one of his fingers as a prize. Before Rufius could react, she ripped into his gloved wrist and blood wicked along its length. Keeping the falcon arm extended, he wrapped his lips around his finger to quell the bleeding. For the first time in his charmed life, Festus Rufius looked into the face of death.

And death looked like Vindex.

"Help me," Rufius whimpered. Bleeding and afraid, he dropped to his knees.

"I'm not a killer." Vindex stepped from the forest into the light and walked across the meadow.

Blood gushed from Rufius' wrist and the bird flailed wildly, tracing a blinding path around his outstretched arm. "Save me," he said, faintly. "I'll give you anything you want."

"I want freedom." Vindex pulled out a long knife.

After Rufius nodded his meek agreement, the Danubian distracted the falcon and deftly slashed the leather cord. Rufius fell backwards and the bird shot into the sky like a fan-tailed arrow.

Vindex tore off a swatch of his tunic and wrapped a tourniquet around Rufius' bleeding wrist. Offering no comfort, he picked up the trembling governor and stomped away towards the woods.

Drops of blood marked their retreat.

"We need to move fast," Vindex said. "If Bulbul feels like hunting, he'll have no problem tracking us."

Twenty-two
XXII

The soldiers descended a winding canyon that scarred the underbelly of Southern Gaul. The high peaks above traced the jagged border between ancient tribes and rival provinces. The trickle of river below would soon divert the snowmelt and spring rains, bestowing fertility unto Gaul that Hispania could only envy.

Valerius was in a hurry to investigate Lady Rivus' rumor of a skirmish below. Unable to procure a narrow cart and donkey, he had had no choice but to suspend the mission and hide Rufius' wide cart and precious cargo under a tarp in her parking lot. He intended to return within a day, retrieve the cart, and fulfill his last mission.

Emerging from the canyon just after nightfall, they saw flames rising from a small town tucked against the foothills. The stone perimeter wall suggested that the enclave housed something worth coveting. It may have escaped notice from Roman tax collectors, but not the small-time brigands that roamed the hinterlands.

The light rain returned skyward as steam rising from burning dwellings. A lone flame shot skyward, illuminated the rooftops. A projectile rumbled like thunder smashing through terra cotta and timber. The town was under siege.

A legion standard, visible in the flames, confirmed Valerius' worst fear: his new cohort, *Scipio IV Hispania*, was orchestrating the assault. "When we get to the ramparts, we'll separate. Try to find out what's happening and who's in command," he ordered. "Understood?"

Severus nodded. His face was flush with fear and excitement.

They ran downhill and were stopped by a rotund man in a mud-splattered tunic who appeared to be guarding the gates to town. In addition to his width, a cart loaded with furniture and amphorae blocked the entrance.

"Ten percent on booty, twenty percent on prisoners." His fleshy smile was sparse and wide, his girth suggested someone who could conjure coins from crevasses. "Twenty percent is my best offer,"

"Move aside," Valerius ordered. "You're interfering with military business."

"Military business is my business!" The man's gap-toothed smile consumed the lower half of his face. "I can see you're a tough customer. Fifteen percent, that's the best I can do without slitting my own wrists."

"Slit them and stand aside!" Valerius shouted. He tried to shove the cart out of the way but it was too heavy.

Severus threw his insubstantial weight against the obstacle. "He seems willing to negotiate, sir," he whispered. "It might be faster to settle."

The large middleman planted his porcine face between the struggling soldiers and extended his wide smile beyond the bounds of credulity. "Since you good fellows are in a hurry, I'll give you twenty percent of face value on any loot or prisoners you bring out."

Valerius straightened and glared. The man's chubby face was unfamiliar, but he knew the type well. Every battle scene had a profiteer who waited at a safe distance, ready to convert the spoils of war into a handful of coins. These despicable characters often turned around and sold looted goods back to their original owners. Profiteers claimed that they provided a useful service as no soldier could be expected to pack his own plunder, but to Valerius, men such as these were no better than dung beetles.

Unable to move the cart or its owner, Valerius was obliged to play along until he could find a different angle. "Fine then, twenty percent," he said. "Now move this cursed cart or there won't be anything left by the time we get in!"

"Twenty percent, two X's!" the man agreed. He extended a flabby hand and relaxed his fleshy smile. "The cart is stuck. You'll have to enter the town from the other side."

Valerius considered twisting the man's arm off, but there was no time to throttle the trickster. A town was burning and cries were rising from inside the wall. After agreeing to meet on the far side of the town, the soldiers ran off in opposite directions.

Severus pushed forward through the stream of terrified villagers escaping through gaps in the crumbling wall. The night pulsed with the sounds of large stones smashing through roofs. An occasional flaming arrow streaked across the smoke-filled sky. As he rounded the far side of the perimeter, Severus found a soldier struggling to lift a large river rock into the sling pocket of a catapult.

"What are you doing?" Severus asked.

"Lugging stones." The soldier nodded towards a pile of rocks. "And I'm loading them onto the catapult. Lugging, loading, and launching."

"I can see that." Severus had never witnessed a Roman catapult in action. There was something elegant about its simple design, something intoxicating about its ferocity. He thought it sad that the Romans had invested more ingenuity into destroying homes than building them.

"Make yourself useful." The soldier strained to load another large projectile. "Help me with this rock."

Severus offered no assistance. "Why are you attacking the village?" he asked.

The soldier managed to lift the stone onto the business end of the siege engine and ignored the question. "Fire!" he shouted.

The ratchet released, the winch spun, and the small boulder traced a fatal arc through the sky. It smashed explosively into the wall.

"Direct hit!" The soldier clapped his hands with satisfaction.

Severus felt his stomach tighten as a piece of the stone wall crumbled. He had no idea why Spanish soldiers were attacking a Gaulish town, and neither, it seemed, did anyone else.

"Stop!" Severus shouted. "This makes no sense."

But the soldiers seemed deaf to reason and drunk on destruction. They fired stones, shot arrows, and celebrated each impact with war whoops and raised fists. Men who might have never harmed a rabbit grew more bold and sadistic with each hit.

On the other side of the wall, timbers groaned, smoke spread, and flames scratched the dark, murderous night.

"Stop!" Severus could barely hear the sound of his own shouts as he tried to silence the battle and assuage his conscience. He was caught in a nightmare where the dark, violent urges that most men learn to ignore had taken command of their souls. Where one man might resist blind impulse, eighty men could not escape its contagious power. Severus watched the men goad each other into madness and fought the urge to run away.

A woman waving her infant child like a white flag ran towards the blood-crazed soldiers.

They cut her down like a weed.

"This isn't Jericho!" Severus shouted, but the ground seemed to part beneath him. His knees buckled and he dropped to the dirt. He tried to pray instead but found no faith. Any God who had created such fools as men was not worth worshiping. He could not get the taste of war out of his mouth. Though his eyes were flushed with tears, he saw a man take an arrow and fall from the ramparts. The dead would soon outnumber the living and Severus no longer cared which group he was in.

Severus lay down, planted his face in his hands, and sobbed.

"This is no place to sleep!" A soldier kicked Severus in the side, and rolled him over to see if he was dead and worth looting.

"Why are you attacking an innocent town?" Severus wiped his eyes and sat up slowly. His mouth tasted of smoke and bile. "What's the mission?"

The soldier looked at Severus suspiciously. "Load the catapult. Fire the catapult. That's my mission."

Another projectile crashed behind the broken wall. The roof of a dwelling where a family had once scratched out their lives crumbled like an anthill under a Roman boot.

"This makes no sense," Severus insisted.

"Doesn't have to," the soldier answered.

Feeling feverish and queasy, Severus stumbled from post to post, counting corpses and accumulating contradictions. By the time he found Marcus Valerius on the opposite side of the town, the fragmented story he had assembled made less sense than a nightmare.

"What in Mars' name is going on here?" Valerius asked. He was out of breath and very angry.

Severus' stomach rolled like a pig in mud. The smoke phantoms rising above the town mocked him for having ever imagined himself a soldier.

"Report!"

Valerius' shouting brought Severus back to the present.

"Hundreds dead." Severus said. He tried to stop his eyes from tearing, his lips from trembling. "A massacre."

"Sometimes the fog of war turns to fever," Valerius said. He gripped Severus by the shoulders and shook him sternly. The veteran had seen it before: A boy on the threshold of manhood could lose his footing. A greenhorn soldier crushed by the weight of war could be defeated by delusion. "Most of the villagers escaped. The survivors outnumber the fallen. Now straighten your spine and tell me what you learned."

The certainty of Valerius' grip helped quell the acid panic pulsing through Severus' veins. One-by-one, the smoke phantoms dissipated, leaving him confused, exhausted, and ashamed.

"Report!" Valerius ordered.

"*Scipio* soldiers are laying siege to the village."

"I can see that." Valerius shook Severus' shoulders as if trying to wake him from whatever demons still danced inside his eyelids. "Why are they laying siege?"

"Mistreated," Severus mumbled. He wiped his eyes on his sleeve and tried to make sense of what he had witnessed. "The soldiers needed food and shelter, but the townspeople treated them with disrespect. They—"

"Disrespect?" Valerius interrupted. "What kind of disrespect could justify laying waste to an innocent village?" Valerius tried to recall the rules of engagement for attacking civilians, but there were none. "Did you find out who is in command?"

"You won't like the answer." Severus pointed to a small roadside enclave beyond the edge of town. "The command post is in that tavern."

The voyager's tavern at the edge of town had been doing a brisk business selling drinks to the soldiers. Valerius pushed through the disorderly soldiers exchanging pitchers of wine and braggadocio outside the tavern. He ordered Severus to stand guard by the door and entered with caution. Once his eyes adjusted to the darkness, Valerius was stunned to find Fidelis Magnus slumped in a dark corner of the mud-floored room. Was Magnus, the soldier turned security guard, in command of this mess? Valerius' old friend looked oblivious to the one-sided battle raging outside.

"Magnus?" Valerius said. "What are you doing in this dump?"

"Drinking!" Magnus' speech was slurred and his good eye slow to focus. He raised his cup victoriously and sloshed drink in all directions. "You should try this stuff, Marcus. It has the most amazing little bubbles! It looks like piss, but tastes like wine."

"Your troops are attacking the village."

"And pigs are walking around ready-roasted." Magnus laughed and shoved a plate across the table. "Care for a snail?"

"A snail?" Valerius looked on in disgust as his erstwhile friend picked up a wet shell, sucked out the dripping insides, and smiled contentedly. Valerius shoved the plate away. "That's revolting."

"That was exactly my reaction at first. Turns out snails are just an excuse to eat salt with lard and garlic." Magnus washed down another slug, tossed the shell onto the floor, and stomped on it. He nudged the plate back across the table and encouraged Valerius to sample a slug. "A man could really grow to like this place. They live well here. When you retire, you should settle down in a town like this."

Valerius leaned across the table and shook Magnus by the shoulder. "Why are we attacking the village?"

"What are you raving about, you old piss pot?" Magnus squinted with his good eye and let the other wander.

"Innocent people are dying out there."

"Don't take it personally." Magnus drained his goblet. "People die every day."

Gone local, Valerius had seen it before. Far from civilization, uncertain about what the next minute would bring—when the world inverted, a soldier might lose his bearing, but a commander could not.

"I've seen drunk and I've seen disorderly, but I've never seen such disgrace." It was the lowest moment of Valerius' long career. "I have to relieve you of your responsibilities,"

"Huh?" Magnus sputtered. "What are you on about now? Loosen your leather, old chum."

"Listen carefully." Valerius leaned into his old friend's face until the two were nose to nose. "You've started a war between sister provinces."

Magnus pushed Valerius away and slurped another snail from its shell.

Seeing that the gravity of the situation was lost on his former friend, Valerius knocked the plate from the table. "You are unfit to lead. Fidelis Magnus, I hereby relieve you of your command."

Looking happier than Bacchus, Magnus smiled and pointed at his old comrade's untouched cup. "If you're not going to drink that …"

Disgusted, Marcus Valerius stormed out into the smoke-filled night where the wall was crumbling and the siege still raged. The thick air shook with the impact of each new projectile. Flames took purchase and extended their rampage to the few remaining structures. Somewhere in the maelstrom, a child howled for her mother.

Severus was waiting, balancing on unsteady legs.

"I found Habeas Novus, the second-in-command." Severus swallowed hard and spat out his report. "Novus won't reveal the mission to me. In fact, he doesn't even believe I'm a legionary."

Severus led Valerius through the archers and catapults to the location where Novus was proudly supervising the progress of the attack. The stiff young officer cut a dashing figure against the backdrop of destruction. Fire shone in his eyes as if this was exactly where the gods intended for him to be.

Novus saluted sharply. "Centurion," he said, "you are just in time to witness the culmination of our mission. Your elite troops are about to return from behind enemy lines with our prize in hand."

"What *is* the mission, soldier?" Valerius asked.

Novus whispered something in the commander's ear. He pointed into the village to where a small squadron maneuvered deep behind the broken walls. They were extracting something large and awkward from the burning remnants of a workshop.

As the squadron and standard bearer returned back towards the command post, Severus saw that they were wrestling with two burdensome wooden barrels. He ran to help the soldiers lift the casks and strap them down on the cart parked behind Novus' command post.

"Mission accomplished, sir!" the squad leader said crisply. The surrounding soldiers cheered and *Scipio IV Hispania's* standard, bearing the insignia of a scorpion, was raised high overhead. The proud young legionary saluted the old centurion. "Request permission to take prisoners, sir. Our men's heroism is worthy of at least one slave per person."

Valerius stared at the wooden barrels. "This is the prize? A town destroyed for a couple of wooden barrels. Are they filled with gold?"

"Wine," Novus said. "Governor's orders,"

Valerius brushed ash out of his eyes. "Order the troops to stand down," he said. "We march for the border immediately."

Novus saluted, and sped off to organize the retreat.

Twenty-three
XXIII

Ashamed to have been beaten by a bird, Rufius returned from falconing to find his mansion had been ravaged by a tide of unwanted renovation during his three-day absence. He tried not to reveal the extent of his open sores and frayed nerves as he wandered through the gutted villa, but everywhere he turned, local hacks were making a mess of the tile work, furniture, and frescoes he had commissioned. In the atrium, a marble stag had replaced a buxom nude. In the banquet hall, two self-proclaimed artisans armed with bits of charcoal and buckets of bad taste were roughing in a coarse scene of Mount Olympus over Rufius' favorite mural. His dancing virgins and lascivious wood nymphs now languished under two coats of whitewash from which they would never escape.

In spite of his best efforts to reverse the slide, the slippery slope towards mediocrity was now nearly vertical. During his short absence, the décor and ambience had gone Greek. Without a drastic infusion of cash and energy—both of which were in short supply—Rufius' home away from Rome would soon look like a historian's nightmare.

When Minem learned that the governor had returned in a sorry state, he raced through the corridors and found him shuffling, despondent and round-shouldered in the banquet hall.

"I'm so glad to see you, Excellency. I can't begin to apologize for the mix-up."

"Then don't, unless you're disappointed I survived."

Rufius kicked a loose tile across the floor and walked over to inspect the tasteless painting of Romulus, Remus, and the she-wolf. The founders of Rome looked rigid and heartless as if posing for an overpriced family portrait.

"Did Bulbul kill Biberious, or did you smother him with Macedonian mendacity?"

"Such dark humor. Who do you think sent Vindex to check up on you?" The tiny advisor's eyebrows crawled like black caterpillars across his forehead. Minem smiled and thin wrinkles appeared like hairline cracks across his normally unflappable optimism. "Unfortunately, I've got some awful news."

"What could be more awful than this?" Rufius pointed at the dull landscape underway on the far wall. "It's bad enough your friend Bulbul tried to kill me, but shouldn't you have waited for me to die before remodeling my villa? Who's paying for all this?"

Minem bowed his head, revealing a bald spot Rufius had never noticed. The tiny island of pink flesh would be the perfect place to plant a hammer. Unfortunately, none of the artisans had left one within reach.

"Your beloved brother, Consul Rufius—"

"My brother is second in line to the throne," Rufius interrupted. "He's got better things to waste money on than—"

"He was assassinated in Londinium while you were away," Minem's face was now gray and solemn as a rain cloud. "Murdered just like Governor Biberious. The Praetorian Guard thinks you're—"

Rufius blanched with panic and ran into the corridor.

"Wait!" Minem kicked a stray chisel across the dusty floor and scrambled after the governor. "Try to look on the bright side."

Minem caught up just as Rufius stumbled into the kitchen where servants were honing a pile of knives and meat cleavers. Fearing for his life, Rufius whipped around and sent Minem sprawling backwards.

"Disarm them!" Rufius shouted and sprinted back into the labyrinth. After a moment's confusion, he turned down a familiar corridor, darted into his bedchamber, and refused to come out.

Minem's staccato stride was too short to reach the room before the door slammed shut. "Let me in, Governor," he begged, knocking on a thick oak panel. "There's something else I need to tell you."

"Go away!" Rufius shouted. He blocked the door with a heavy chair and slumped down upon it. "It's so unfair," he muttered. "If anyone was going to kill my brother, it should have been me."

His head pounded with pain and self pity. "What have I done to deserve so much grief?" he asked. "It's as if the walls are closing in just as the rug's been pulled out from underneath me." He tried to wipe the tears and dust from his eyes, but his vision was clouded to the point where the yellow walls of his room looked blue. He experienced a sudden feeling of being underwater, falling like a stone in the sea. He gasped for breath and wiped a sleeve across his nose. Clearing his eyes, he confirmed that his room had indeed changed color. In his absence, a legion of idiots had transformed his sunny refuge into a drowning man's nightmare. "Who painted my walls?" he shouted.

"Blue is Hadrian's favorite color." Minem whispered from the other side of the door.

Rufius stood up and ran his hand along the ugly wall until he arrived at the broken plaster and exposed brick where the garden door was supposed to have been built. Moving over to the window, he saw that the latches had been removed and the casing nailed shut. Instead of a simple exterior door to bypass the Villa's tedious corridors, some ham-fisted carpenter had sealed off Rufius' only escape route.

"Listen carefully. I'm going to tell you a secret." Minem's normally shrill voice leaked through a crack in the door. "Jove be praised, the Emperor is coming."

The twitch taking root above Rufius' right eyebrow did not prevent him from seeing the pattern: Biberious, Bulbul, his brother. Two leaders were dead and Rufius was next in line, trapped in a blue crypt with a Macedonian assassin drumming on his door.

"You need to take action," Minem insisted. "Hadrian's entourage is running ahead of schedule, and Vindex wants to kill me."

"Tell Vindex to hurry."

"There's no time for joking," Minem said. He jiggled the door handle, but it held fast. "Hadrian, may his face outshine the sun, is coming to Hispania, returning home in triumph to the land of his forefathers."

Rufius sat down on the edge of his bed. He grabbed a blanket and brought it to his face, but found no comfort in the folds. On the other side of the door, the muffled sound of bare feet padding down the corridor approached like a slow death.

The door handle creaked and twisted. Someone had a key.

Rufius was trapped. The Fates had locked him in a forgotten room at the end of a dark labyrinth atop an insignificant capital at the edge of an indifferent empire. A Roman prison would have been preferable. His life had run its course and it would now end in obscurity.

"Enter, assassin," he muttered. "Make it quick."

The door creaked open and Carbo, the recently appointed valet, slipped into the bedchamber.

"So it's you," Rufius mumbled. "I should have known."

From the way the slave bowed stiffly, it was clear he regretted having ever left the kitchen where food was plentiful and abuse was scarce. The kitchen had always provided easy access to leftovers that he could sell for a small profit. The so-called "promotion" to valet should have given him access to more profitable goods, but the governor's personal shipment was at the bottom of the sea, and the cleaning crew had already sold off the Villa's remaining few trinkets. This promotion had put Carbo years away from raising enough money to buy his freedom and he could barely hide his resentment.

Carbo tried not to look at the scabs forming on Rufius' face. "Your bath is ready, my Lord."

"When I need my butt wiped, I'll send for your mother!" Rufius' resignation turned to rage at the Fates and everyone within shouting distance. "Now leave me in peace."

Minem ran in as Carbo ran out.

"Enter the true assassin." Rufius threw an angry look that the tiny advisor easily sidestepped.

"Time is short, Governor. Decisions need to be made, and if you don't pull ahead of history, you'll be lost it its fog."

"You're history!" Rufius lunged at Minem's throat, but the advisor easily sidestepped the attack. Furious, Rufius looked around the room for a vase to break over Minem's head but the chamber had been ransacked of anything useful. "Why did you keep Hadrian's visit a secret from me? Do you plan on murdering him, too?"

"Hadrian's activities are highly confidential," Minem backed away from the governor and spoke fast. "The imperial itinerary is not the sort of thing one talks about with killers like Vindex lurking about. Besides, haven't you noticed that the only way to get something done around here is to impose an impossible deadline and whip people into a state of panic?"

"Maybe you're right," Rufius sighed in agreement. He dropped onto the edge of the bed and dug his fingernails into his thighs. "Even the crops don't grow until a day before harvest."

"The harvest has arrived, Governor. It's time to stop moping and start coping." Minem picked the blanket off the floor and tossed it back onto the bed. "That's why I started the remodel and a few other projects while you were away hunting."

"The treasury has run dry." Rufius ground his teeth. Every coin filched for public works was another coin out of reach.

"You'll have to borrow, but consider it an investment. Hadrian's mother came from Hispania; his father still has extensive holdings near Cadiz. Our emperor came of age in your province. He still has a place in his heart for Hispania. Praise the Gods, Excellency! Our prince is coming home."

"Home. I may never go home." Rufius moaned. "We'll be ground to sausage if you don't turn this situation around."

"I've already started." Minem walked over to the door and signaled for Carbo to bring in a few tiny structures.

"Toys? You're going to save me with toys?" Rufius rose to investigate an elaborate scale model of a Greek theatre. He lifted the mock-up to eye level and looked inside the minute marvel. "What a wonderful little building," he said, distracted. "I've never seen anything like this. How did they manage to make it look so realistic?"

"We've got no time to lose." Minem tried to pry the model from Rufius' hands, but the governor was transfixed. "The emperor is running even more ahead of schedule than I'd previously—"

Rufius held the miniature theatre up to the light and turned it slowly. There were even tiny people milling around inside. "What did you just say?"

"Hadrian elected to take the river route. He's already in Southern Gaul, inspecting the remnants of a recently ransacked village."

"Vesuvius!" Rufius' face went white as a wedding lily.

"Exactly."

"How much time do we have left before you-know-who shows up to break our you-know-whats?"

"My sources are telling me he'll cross into your province in less than a week."

"One week?" Rufius handed Minem the model theater and took advantage of his proximity to grab the tiny advisor by the toga. He pulled Minem close enough to bite his head off, breaking the miniature building between them. "If your head wasn't flat, I'd make it roll."

Minem twisted free and brushed the debris off his chest. "Hadrian's keen to reach his father's birthplace," he said, moving towards the door. "He may only stay in Tarraco long enough to collect what you owe him or throw you in jail."

Rufius grabbed another architectural model. "What a lovely arch. Such artistry, such proportion, but it's time to face the truth: These will never be finished on time. Project cancelled!" He threw the scale model at Minem.

Minem ducked and the delicate arch smashed against the door.

Rufius watched the pieces scatter and, with them, all prospects of gaining the emperor's favor. The imperial visit could have been his big opportunity to ascend into the upper echelons of the Roman ruling class, his golden chance to penetrate Hadrian's inner circle without competition from his once-superior sibling. After losing himself in a momentary daydream about how he and the emperor might have become fast friends, Rufius returned to the cold, terrible truth: Hadrian would show no mercy.

"We'll need an emergency levy to raise enough funds in time," Minem said. "The cost of an imperial visit can be quite a strain."

"In other words, we're broke and sinking lower."

"The winds of change buffeting the empire had somehow missed Hispania." Minem tried to hold back the floodwater of failures welling behind his clenched teeth. Speaking without pause or punctuation, he recounted the list of false starts and setbacks that had blocked all forward progress in Hispania. The wine makers refused to age their crush in oak barrels. Slaves insisted on taking holidays. Taxes were later than ever and none of Hispania's citizens felt the need to change anything except governors.

The precarious state of provincial affairs had reached a dangerous point for Festus Rufius, but it still presented opportunities for Imperial Associates. Through Minem's clever clauses, IA now controlled the booming Temple of Saturn and adjacent snack shop. Rufius' missed payments gave IA a controlling share in the state-run olive groves. Hispania's next wave of defaults would give IA the majority share of customs duties flowing through the busy Port of Tarraco.

In spite of Minem's somber pronouncements, things were going quite well for his organization. But with Hadrian breathing down their necks and a possible war brewing along the northern border, Rufius' demise could drag IA down as well.

"Times are so tight that even the taxman's losing weight," Minem concluded. "But there's still hope: the imperial visit is your chance to rise like the sun or wane like the moon."

"Save it, Minem," Rufius said. "None of your poppycock pep talks please."

"Then if I may be so bold, Governor, your Spanish holiday is over." Minem paused to verify that Rufius was listening, and then continued with more direct talk. "Take charge. Learn from Hadrian. He would never hole up in his bedroom and wait for his subordinates and subjects to obey his decrees. Hadrian patrols his territory and imposes his will like a hammer. He makes it painfully clear what he wants, rewards those who deliver, and deals out swift consequences to those who don't."

Rufius cracked his fat knuckles loudly.

"We can turn this around, Excellency," Minem said. "But we have to act fast. I hope you won't mind, but in your absence, I've had to make a lot of fast decisions and judgment calls."

Carbo entered with a bathrobe and Rufius shooed him away again.

"How will you ever get the roads ready in time?" Rufius dropped his toga and slipped into the bathrobe. "The coastal route is a complete mess. If Hadrian sees the state of our roads, my enemies won't need to hire assassins."

"Workers are borrowing stones from the secondary roads and rushing them to the main vias. This will save you a privy-load in quarry expenses."

"What about the Villa?" Rufius said. His bathrobe hung loose and open. "It looks like the Fall of Troy in here. Where will you ever get enough talent to fix this place in time?"

Minem reached inside his toga for a new contract, and presented it to the distraught governor.

"Why do you keep shoving forms at me?" Rufius swatted the scroll to the floor. "If I wasted the hours required to read your stupid documents, I wouldn't have any time left for leadership."

Rufius' head ached too much to continue. If he could not escape from Hispania, he would do the next best thing: escape from Minem. He opened the door to his private bath and steam rushed into the room. "This mess is entirely your fault. Do what's needed to fix it. Sweep this province clean and let's hope Hadrian doesn't look under the doormat."

Twenty-four
XXIV

After a tense night of rapid retreat and two hours of dull sentry duty, Gaius Severus could barely maintain his balance. His feet were blistered from the forced march and his ears still rang with the boasting of soldiers who had just destroyed an innocent town and drank down the spoils. As he paced back and forth along the perimeter of the military encampment, only exhaustion kept him from abandoning the legion.

Severus peered into the night and tried to stay vigilant, but all he could think about was the fact that he was just an expendable soldier in a lawless regiment on the outskirts of an empire whose glory had faded. Being a conscript was like being a slave without the table scraps.

He stopped pacing. The thought of marching another minute behind swaggering soldiers and their incompetent commanders was too much to bear. The Roman Empire was an anthill on a dung heap; barely fit to live in, not worth dying for. How many soldiers before him had laid down their lives, duped or coerced into serving the false promise of Rome? It was one thing to play a role in a noble endeavor, another to be a pawn in a meaningless farce. At least his brother's foolhardy dreams of rebellion served some greater purpose.

All roads led to oblivion and no one's God—not Jupiter, not Jehovah, not Jesus—offered solace or explanation. All that any God seemed to offer humanity was to the chance to extend this world's pointlessness into the next.

The sound of voices in the nearby forest attracted his attention. He debated for an instant whether to leave his post to investigate. So far, his sentry shift had been so uneventful that he risked falling asleep in his boots. A temporary absence would present minimal danger to the snoring troops; besides, the sounds he heard might signify danger. He unsheathed his *gladius* and crept quietly between the trees. He drew near the source of the disturbance and concealed himself behind a bush.

A small, ragtag group of people had assembled in a clearing. Under cover of night, they listened to an old man wearing a skullcap and holding a lit candle. A dozen pairs of tired eyes peered through the darkness and followed the arc of the old Jew's illuminated gestures.

Severus knew his duty. It would be a simple matter to gather a few soldiers and arrest the docile looking mob but, instead of breaking up the secret gathering, he crouched and listened to the forbidden words.

"And the Lord presented himself in a fiery bush on Mount Sinai," said a familiar voice from the clearing. "The Almighty spoke and said, 'MOSES: I GIVE TO YOU THE LAW. THIS YOU MUST FOLLOW AND PASS ON TO GENERATIONS TO COME.'"

The Rabbi in the center of the small congregation looked over his flock. Upon seeing the old man's profile, Severus' heart thawed. He had been too tired and traumatized to recognize his father's voice.

Rather than feeling relief at seeing the old man alive, Severus flushed with anger. The fool! Hadn't his vocation for rabble rousing caused enough trouble already? If not for his father's obsession with the ancient God of Abraham, the family might still be together. Instead, his father was on the lam, talking treason less than a hundred paces from a camp full of legionaries who would happily tear him limb-from-limb.

Gaius Severus cursed the old man's audacity as much as he admired it. Against the tide of history and the weight of empire, his father still risked everything to pass the tribe's lore from one generation to the next. Unaware of the nearby danger, the old teacher blew out the candle and continued speaking in the pre-dawn shadows, altering his voice as he acted out the roles of God and Moses.

"'Excuse me, Mighty One,' Moses said, his knees banging together. 'The bush was crackling and I couldn't quite hear you. Would you mind repeating yourself?'"

"God's voice thundered, 'MOSES! I GIVE YOU FIFTEEN COMMANDMENTS.'"

Severus swallowed his frustration and sought refuge in the warm, familiar voice. He was happy to see his father standing straight and unbroken in spite of so much adversity. Forgetting his duties, Severus shifted into a more comfortable position.

"'FIFTEEN COMMANDMENTS THAT YOU MUST FOLLOW TO THE LETTER!' God said, His voice echoed off the very sky itself.

"'Are they complicated?' Moses asked, respectfully, 'Personally, I can only remember about three or four things at once.'

"'Write them down,' the Holy One answered. 'FIRST COMMANDMENT: THOU SHALL NOT KILL!'

"Moses' chest reverberated with God's eternal voice. 'That's very good, Lord. Clear, concise, logical, memorable ... are they all about this size?'

"'More or less.' God let the flames in the bush die down.

The old sage looked directly at the shrub behind which his son, the soldier was hiding. Gaius Severus held his breath. Had his father seen him? He longed to call out, to run into the clearing and embrace the old man, but he feared attracting the other sentries. His father smiled and continued embellishing the story.

"'Will you be carving the letters, or am I supposed to do it?' Moses asked. His back was already aching in anticipation of the trip back down the mountain with three heavy stone tablets. 'I should have brought a donkey,' he muttered."

Severus smiled and reflected on how naïve it was to have only one God. How could one lonely deity ever attend to such a crazy world?

"God bellowed out commandments and Moses chiseled as fast as he could," his father continued.

"'HONOR THY MOTHER!'

"'She will really appreciate this one,' Moses said, recalling the floating cradle and his long-suffering mother. 'Not that I would try to put words in your almighty mouth, but can we add something about fathers too, Lord?'"

"'Good point! Make it so.'"

The old man paused to draw on a goatskin full of sweet wine. He looked at his son and winked. Severus knew that the old man and his followers were in danger. God's promise didn't offer immunity from the wrath of the Roman Legion; Jehovah's justice was nothing compared to Caesar's. Overcome with concern, Gaius Severus tried to stand up, but a powerful hand slipped over his mouth. Two strong men grabbed his arms, and dragged him from his hiding place.

Severus looked up expecting to see the shimmer of a Roman *gladius* but instead the hand of his older brother motioned for him to keep silent. Only when Gaius acknowledged that he understood, was he released. Gasping for breath, he jumped up and embraced Marius.

"What are you doing here?" Gaius whispered. "Don't you know there's a legion camp through those trees?"

"What better place to hide than right under the empire's nose?"

Torn between the joy of reunion and fear for their safety, tears welled in Gaius Severus' eyes. "How did you get here?"

"An angry gladiator emptied the prison." Marius said, gesturing towards the former slaves enraptured by the story of Moses. "We left town, traveling by twos and threes, reuniting along the way like we're doing tonight."

"You're crazy! You may have escaped, buy you'll never blend in."

"Exactly. We're heading into Gaul to meet up with other Jews. We'll hug the coast until we can commandeer a boat and sail to Judea. We're returning home, brother."

"Home is Tarraco."

"Home is Jerusalem."

Gaius Severus shook his head. He had heard these dreams his entire life. Somehow, a poor and broken diaspora would squeeze out from under Rome's boot and restore an ancient prophecy. It was difficult enough to forge a path through the real world. Why did Marius cling to the impossible?

"If you want your life to mean something, I've got an important mission for you," Marius said. "But before I reveal it, you must swear in God's name that you're committed to the cause, willing to die if need be."

Gaius did not respond. Instead of arguing as they had done so many times before, the brothers fell silent and listened to their father's story.

"And so the negotiations continued," the old man continued. "Somewhere around the seventh commandment Moses asked, 'Is this an all or nothing deal, Lord, or can people fulfill, say, most of these rules and have a little wiggle room on the others?'

"'DID YOU LIKE LIVING IN EGYPT, MOSES?'

"'Understood.' Moses was smart enough not to haggle with the God of Justice."

The old man held his hands up and feigned fatigue. "By the time Moses chiseled Commandment Ten he was exhausted. 'I need to take a break,' he said. 'My elbows are aching and I'm thirsty as a fish.'

"'Squeeze any stone,' said the Lord.

"Moses picked up a stone and did as he was told. It was, after all, an age of miracles. Sweet water flowed from the rock. After quenching his thirst, Moses took in the view from high atop Mount Sinai: nothing but desert for as far as the eye could see. 'How long will we be wandering the sand dunes?' he asked.

"'ONE HUNDRED YEARS!'

"'A hundred years?' Moses dropped the wet stone. 'Sixty years would be more reasonable.'

"'No, Moses. ONE HUNDRED YEARS! It will take that long to purge the slave blood from your people.'

"'Let me get this straight: We have to subsist on brackish water and manna from heaven for a hundred years? What about you give us Five Commandments and twenty years, Holiness?' Moses bowed deeply. 'One generation is a long time to drag stone tablets around the desert.'

"'I'll meet you halfway,' answered the Lord after a moment's reflection. The burning bush roared and sent flames into the sky 'Forty years and Ten Commandments.'

Gaius Severus wondered what mission his brother had in mind. If he remained with the legion, he would die for nothing. If he followed Marius, he would die for a dream. All roads lead to death, he concluded. Some are just more direct than others.

"I'm willing to help, but I want to say good-bye to Father."

Gaius had barely finished his sentence when a skirmish broke out in the clearing. A *Scipio* sentry brandishing a short sword had stomped into the middle of the gathering. The legionary had barely a second to sneer before three slaves knocked him to the ground, bound and gagged him, and left him face down in the mud. Within seconds, the refugees were poised to flee.

"Go back to the legion," Marius whispered. "Learn to fight. Learn to kill. When you see the emperor, assassinate him. This is God's will, Gaius. I'm sure of it."

"Kill the emperor?" Gaius swallowed a burst of laughter. Marius continued to astound. "I'll have to think about that," he said after what seemed like a brief eternity.

"What's to think about?" Marius shook his brother by the shoulders. "You're such an onion-head."

"And you're a fool." Gaius Severus broke free. "You could have been a butcher or a carpenter's apprentice if you hadn't insisted on becoming a moron."

Marius spat on the ground. "A week in the legion and you've forgotten who you are. Let me remind you: You're a Jew. An outsider, No matter how hard you try, you'll always be a foreigner."

"And if you hadn't been born a Jew," Gaius said, straining to keep his voice down, "you'd be throwing rocks at me just like everyone else."

"Fighting Rome makes more sense than serving her." Marius turned to leave. "Are you a complete sell out?"

"Are you completely crazy?" Gaius stepped in front of his brother, clinging to a fading hope of talking sense into him. Why couldn't Marius see the folly of waging a shadow war against the strongest empire ever? The notion of killing Hadrian was almost as preposterous as the possessed look in Marius' eyes. Gaius took a step away from his brother, away from his kin, back towards the enemy into whose bosom Marius had pushed him. "When will *I* see the emperor?"

"He'll be in Tarraco within a month's time. Get yourself attached to the security detail. When his procession passes, be in position to knock him off his chariot."

"Tarraco?" Gaius was incredulous. "He's coming to Tarraco? Even if it were true, how would you know?"

"The movement is better connected than you realize."

"Movement? Now you're a *movement?*"

"Once you cut the head off the snake, come to Judea and help us slice its belly."

"Snake's heads? I don't know, Marius, this is all so ..."

Restless to catch up with the others, Marius sprinted away.

"Tell father I ..." Gaius Severus held back a tear. "I may never see him again. Take care of him, Marius, and you, too."

Marius turned for an instant longer. "Our people are counting on you, Gaius."

Gaius watched his brother follow the improbable band of refugees out of the clearing. The Jews were bound for Judea, the slaves for any port in a storm. Gaius wondered which of the two hapless groups had the more unlikely destination. The Jews might learn to fight, the slaves might stand up straight, and fish might start to dance.

Feeling no sympathy for the gagged soldier and not wanting to explain why he had abandoned his post, Severus left the unlucky sentry bound and squirming in the clearing. Saddened to have been close enough to touch his father yet unable to reach him, he crept back to the sleeping camp where the shadow of death rose with the dawn.

Twenty-five
XXV

Emerging from the haze of a midday nap, Festus Rufius felt back in form and ready to rule. He threw the linen bed sheets to the floor, rolled off the overstuffed mattress, and admired his expanding stomach in the mirror. Since moving Carbo out of the kitchen, the Villa's food had improved dramatically and now that the cuisine was in order, the rest of the province would surely follow.

Rufius' optimism had returned, sprouting like the sparse patches of whiskers that masked the scabs on his cheeks. In retrospect, the falcon attack seemed like a minor setback on the road to glory. The insults, assaults, and affronts he had endured since arriving in Hispania had tested him, made him stronger, and prepared him for assuming a greater role in the mightiest empire ever.

The emperor's impending visit offered a superb opportunity to scramble up the ladder of success, two rungs at a time. Now that Rufius' older brother, one of Hadrian's favorites, was gone, the emperor would surely see fit to bestow blessings and favor upon the family's sole surviving son.

By playing his knucklebones right, Festus Rufius would soon break bread with earthbound divinity. Having unlimited access to Hadrian would enable him to bypass all of the traditional, messy avenues for advancement. In a clean break with tradition, Festus Rufius might become emperor without having to murder anyone.

Rufius stood naked at the window, stretched his arms towards the sun, and accepted Apollo's tribute. *A leader needs to be like the sun*, he thought, *filling the world with blinding light from above.* With Winus Minem managing the drudgery, Festus Rufius, like Apollo, was free to rise above the humdrum.

He slipped into a day tunic and put his ear to the bedroom door where Vindex stood guard against assassins and other irritants. Hearing only Vindex's heavy breathing, Rufius cracked the door open.

"Come in quickly," he said, shooting a quick look past Vindex's bulk and down the dimly lit corridor. "Where's Minem?"

"Under a rock somewhere," Vindex answered, "visiting his mother."

"Really, Vindex, he half-believes you want to kill him." Rufius said.

"He's half-right."

Vindex stepped back into the corridor and produced a large sledgehammer, the sight of which made Rufius jump backwards. "That worm could sell water to a fish."

"You two feud like brothers," Rufius laughed. "But when I'm emperor, I'll need you both."

"Rufius Caesar ... exactly what the empire deserves." Vindex raised the hammer and let it rest on his shoulder. "Now, where do you want the damage done?"

Rufius pointed to the chipped plaster where an undependable mason had twice abandoned work on a new doorway.

Vindex swung the long hammer and sent a comet's tail of brick and plaster fragments flying backwards into the bedroom. Offended by the noise and debris, Rufius waved away the dust and covered his mouth with a sleeve. Sparks flew when the hammerhead hit granite.

"Can't you work faster?" Rufius said.

"Think you can swing this?" Vindex shoved the hammer towards the governor.

Rufius declined the offer and turned toward the mirror. "After my coronation in Rome I might return here just to savor the surprise on your tax collector's face."

Vindex resumed his pounding until a solid hammer blow broke through the outer rock and opened a jagged hole to the exterior. He paused with satisfaction as sunlight streamed like water through the opening.

"As emperor, I don't think I'll travel much," Rufius said. "I didn't enjoy my sea voyage to Hispania, and I can't stand horses. No, unlike our beloved, restless Hadrian, Emperor Divus Augustus Festus Rufius Caesar will stay put."

"The empire will thank you." Vindex used a chisel to expand the hole, but quickly determined that the granite needed attacking from the outside. He leaned the sledgehammer against the bedroom wall and raised another small cloud by slapping his dusty hands together. "By the way, how much do I get paid?"

"Why do you think Hadrian travels so much?" Rufius flicked tenacious plaster chips out of his thin beard. "Why does a man who has everything bother to visit every black spot on the map? I'll bet he never sleeps in the same bed twice. Why would a living god spend so much time away from Rome?"

"Two reasons," Vindex said, ducking under the lintel. "Moving targets are harder to hit and Rome is the world's biggest sewer."

"That may be the view from the bottom, but seen from the top, Rome is the greatest, richest, most magnificent place on earth. Parties, orgies, blood sports—every other day is a holiday. Why leave paradise?"

"May I leave?" Vindex asked. "The cooks need me to unlock their knives, and that stone can only be broken from the outside."

"Rome," Rufius sighed. "The center of the world from which all distance is measured. She's the daughter of Athens, the sister of Alexandria, the mother of mankind! I miss the gardens, the girls, and the crush of chariots streaking like lashed lightning around the Circus. How I long for the exotic smells of the marketplace, the warm marble of Trajan's baths, the silence of the monuments ..."

"The death-stench of the coliseum on a hot day."

"Surely, the emperor's visit will be my ticket home."

"Ever wonder who pays for the ticket?" Vindex stopped halfway across the threshold and turned back towards the bedroom. "And how do I get paid if you owe him money, too?"

"You don't understand anything." Rufius laughed and shuffled over to inspect the serrated hole in the bedroom wall. "In Rome a man can have a million in assets, a million in debts, and still call himself a millionaire. Once Hadrian sees what I'm facing here, I'm sure my sacrifice will be rewarded."

"Maybe you are the sacrifice." Vindex left without closing the door.

"Me? The sacrifice?" In a dark flash of clarity, Festus Rufius grasped the full sweep of Hadrian's game. His neck muscles tightened and dropped backwards onto the unmade bed and looked up at the coved blue ceiling as if it were the very dome of the sky.

It all made sense.

"Of course the Emperor travels!" Rufius said to no one. "He travels like a plague of locusts. Hadrian and his Praetorian horde ravage their way across the empire while I pay for the party."

Rufius sat bolt upright. The blood drained from his face and his right eye began to twitch. His upper lip trembled so much he could barely blurt out the obvious.

"From the first senator across my border to the last tail-dragging slave, I pay for the entire carnival. The minute those freeloaders enter my province I spring for their every bite, bonk, and bottle."

Carbo peeked through the open door but, seeing Rufius' foul mood, placed a steaming plate of grilled rooster combs by the threshold and disappeared. Within a minute, the oily smell added to Rufius' sense that the blue bedroom would be his tomb. Sickened by the odor, he pressed his face to the uneven hole in the bedroom wall and sucked fresh air into his lungs.

"It's all so clear," he moaned. "One year Hadrian has us building roads; the next year we're building temples. This year, we're building a stupid wall across Britannia. He stays on top by keeping us down and just as soon as a province digs out from his last visit, he comes back to empty the treasury again."

Still oppressed by the greasy smell, Rufius twisted his neck and stuffed his head through the jagged hole. He gulped another lung full of air and found, to his immediate distress, that he was stuck.

"Help!" he shouted, but no one heard him. His veins surged with panic, causing his neck to swell which rendered it impossible to retract his head from the serrated opening.

"Help me, I'm stuck!" Rufius shouted. He tried to extract himself only to realize that, in addition to being trapped in the wall, he was trapped in an imperial maze, caught in a contest more deadly than any gladiator had ever encountered. "How can I win a game where the rules keep changing?"

"Cheat," said a familiar, high-pitched voice before kicking Rufius in the behind.

Before Rufius could cry out in protest, another swift kick jarred his shoulders into the wall.

"It's my turn," someone else said, and hit Rufius with what felt like a broom handle. Within seconds, a seemingly endless supply of fresh blows rained down on Rufius' backside as a handful of house slaves queued up to deliver their anonymous punishment. Rufius cursed his own benevolence for not having condemned the lot of them back when he'd had the chance. He twisted and scraped against the sharp rock until his ears were bleeding. The beatings continued as Rufius shouted into the empty garden, panicking at the possibility that he might die a fool.

Twenty-six
XXVI

Though distraught over his brother's harebrained scheme to liberate Judea, Gaius Severus was nevertheless relieved to know that his kin were still alive. As night wrestled with dawn, he snuck back to his abandoned sentry post, expecting to find nothing but eighty exhausted soldiers sleeping in the afterglow of the wine barrels they had captured and quaffed.

Instead, he emerged through the trees, tripped over a dead man, and landed face down in the blood-soaked dirt.

"What was that?" whispered someone.

Severus held his breath.

"Come on," hissed a raspy voice. "Don't lose time."

A squat figure passed nearby. When no deathblow followed, Severus took a slow, shallow breath and, once the footsteps had faded, raised his eyes above ground level. The threat had passed, but from the edge of the darkness, a contorted legionary was crawling towards him.

"What's happening?" Severus whispered, barely able to force the words through his trembling lips.

"Surprise attack." The young warrior gasped and collapsed into the mud with a bent spear sprouting from his back.

Severus gagged on his own pounding heart. Beyond the fallen soldier, he saw four dark figures creeping from tent to tent, working in pairs to kill the sleeping legionaries. The camp he was supposed to have been guarding was now host to a quiet massacre.

Severus clenched his teeth and sought comfort in an old verse—a psalm of David, about fearing no evil—but it offered no solace. The angel of death was on a rampage and no prayer could save a soldier who had abandoned his post. Even if the one God of the Hebrews found cause to forgive him, the many Gods of the Romans would see him crucified.

Tears wicked down his mud-caked face. He heaved in revulsion and fought the urge to cry out loud when another man's life passed from this world to the next, his throat slit as if it were nothing more than a slab of meat on a butcher's block

As a shield against the stench and savagery, Severus tried to picture Lena, the innkeeper's heavenly daughter, waiting for him with a warm hearth and open arms. If only he could slip away unscathed, she would never have to know what a coward he had been.

Severus stole another look at the assassins prowling like jackals in the rising steam. Even from the depth of his inexperience, he could tell that these killers were no ragtag gang of bandits. Wherever they came from, they were well coordinated, disciplined, and deadly.

Severus clenched his fists and fought back the fear shrouding over him as cold does a cadaver. Through shear will, he forced his terror to stand down. Death might have scratched his shoulder, but it had yet to draw his blood. If he could not beat the assassins, he might still outwit them.

"This way," an attacker whispered. His boot—that of a Roman soldier—kicked mud across Severus' back. "Let's snuff the commander and get out of here!"

The standard and the centurion. Capturing the symbol of the legion would plunge the name of the *Scipio IV Hispania* into deeper disgrace. Killing its commander would decapitate the cohort. Revenge and Roman justice would be served.

Severus' fear turned to anger. By any measure of justice, the centurion did not deserve to die. He heard the sound of his father's voice saying, *"Justice, Justice shall thou pursue."* Justice, his father had said, is what set the Jews apart from all other nations. And justice was something worth fighting for.

Severus snaked through the red mud towards the command post, slithering between the empty tents and lifeless bodies. He stopped twenty feet away from the cohort's raised insignia, a poised scorpion about which the four enemy fighters hovered like hounds of Hades.

"Charge!" Severus shouted.

He jumped up, grabbed the center pole of a tent, and swung it like a flag over his head. With steel in his voice and short sword in hand, Severus ran roaring towards the attackers. "Follow me, men!" he called to the imaginary legion behind him. "I want them taken alive."

The sudden commotion startled the assassins. Severus' war cries and the sun rising behind him blinded them to the false onslaught.

"Attack!" Severus bellowed, running towards his commander's tent.

The four intruders escaped over the log they had put in place to bridge the spike-filled perimeter trench. They ran into the woods toward the clearing where, ten minutes prior, Severus had taken leave of his kin.

Before Severus could shout another battle cry, Marcus Valerius sprang from his tent, *gladius* drawn ready for action. Squinting into the breaking dawn, Valerius seemed unsurprised to see the thin silhouette of Gaius Severus running towards him, brandishing a tent pole.

For Valerius, the moment of truth had come. Severus had finally revealed his true colors. Until this moment, the young spy had played his hand perfectly, feigning innocence and building trust until Valerius' guard had finally dropped. Valerius ran forward and yanked the pole from Severus' hand. "You never had me fooled," he grunted. "Not for a Roman minute."

"Assassins," Severus said, voice quivering. "Soldiers, I think."

Valerius saw the tears streaking the boy's mud-caked face. A quick glance around the camp confirmed that death had paid a nocturnal visit. Valerius sheathed his blade. The moist morning air bore the terrible smell of defeat.

"They entered over there." Severus pointed to the makeshift bridge over the perimeter trench.

"Those vexed wine barrels worked better than a Trojan horse," Valerius said. The weak sunrise cast the massacre in eerie light. The devastation told a story that the veteran had no trouble reading. After assessing the extent of the disaster, Valerius clapped the trembling conscript on the shoulder. "Good work, soldier," he said before hurrying off to the worst looking corner of the camp.

Severus followed. Consumed with fear, he dared not speak lest he betray his own complicity. From the corner of his eye, Severus could see the second in command, Habeas Novus, approaching rapidly.

"A small band of highly trained killers," Valerius said. "If I didn't know better, I'd say they were Praetorian Guardsmen. Did you get a look at them, Severus?"

Severus was about to answer when Sub-centurion Novus interrupted, "I chased away a dozen of them, sir!"

Valerius looked up with evident sadness from where he had been examining one of the dead men.

"The attack was silent," Novus said, "but the smell of blood woke me. Good thing I'm a light sleeper, sir. I came out of my tent and saw cloaked assassins prowling the camp. I threw a few javelins in their direction to scare them off. I was heading for your tent when this half-wit started shouting."

"Anything to add, soldier?" Valerius asked, looking directly into the stunned conscript's eyes.

Severus stuttered, too overwhelmed to admit that men had died for his lack of vigilance. He tried to speak, but the thorny confession lodged in his dry throat.

"There's no time to send off our dead correctly. If the Praetorian Guard are behind this, they'll be back to finish the job." Valerius' attention returned to his second in command. "Wake the surviving men." he ordered. "We march for Tarraco immediately."

Twenty-seven
XXVII

Carbo chased the slaves out of Rufius' bedroom and gave his master one harsh and easily deniable kick after no witnesses remained. Once the beating's subsided, Rufius simmered in misery until Vindex arrived outside with a small hammer and chisel.

"They could have killed me." Rufius was nearly sobbing.

"I might kill you if you don't stop moving your head," Vindex said. He made his point by chiseling along a mortar line just above Rufius' left ear.

"I'm stuck," Rufius whimpered. He tried again to pull back, but the rough bevel of broken brick restrained him. "Stuck in this losing game."

"Without losers, there are no winners." Vindex planted his hammer directly above Rufius' head, sending dust and stone into his hair.

"Be careful, you oaf!" Rufius was hemmed in by hammer blows and rising mutiny. His remaining slaves had needed little provocation to wax violent. Minem could not be trusted and Carbo was probably a spy. Worst of all, the precious strongbox was on the road to nowhere. A terrible thought occurred to him: *What if that dull centurion was working for Hadrian?* The joyless old soldier might have already delivered the incriminating documents to the emperor.

The document proved that Hadrian had stolen the throne. Rufius' plan had been to transfer the authentic copy of Trajan's will, purchased from a reputable informer, to his now-defunct brother in Londinium. But his brother had been murdered, stabbed on the very same day Bulbul brought the birds to Tarraco.

"Stop hammering!" Rufius shouted.

"You prefer to leave your head in the hole?"

"Unless I get my strongbox back from that tight-lipped centurion, you might as well cut off my head right now."

"Just say the word." Vindex shrugged his shoulders and returned to chipping at the stone and mortar.

"It's so stinking obvious, how did I miss it?" Rufius was too agitated to stay still. He squeezed his eyes shut while more dust rained down on his head.

"Stop talking," Vindex said. "You're almost free."

Vindex pushed on Rufius' head as Carbo pulled at his hips. After a moment's effort, Rufius popped backwards into the bedroom and landed on the tiny slave.

After extracting himself from underneath his master, Carbo scrambled to his feet and poured a goblet of mulled wine. He tasted it first as Rufius had recently started to insist.

Rufius rubbed his kinked neck and brushed the debris out of his hair. He brought the warm wine to his lips and drew the comforting vapors into his nose. "I want the name of every slave who kicked me," he ordered.

"I'm the only one who didn't," Carbo said. He refilled his master's goblet and avoided his gaze. After gathering the soiled linens and food scraps from around the bedroom, Carbo shuffled off to fill Rufius' private bath with hot water. "You'll feel better after a bath."

Rufius turned his back to the mirror. He wanted to inspect his face for damage, but fearing derision from his own reflection, he paced the room instead. He hated the blue paint. He hated the Villa. He hated Tarraco and he hated Hispania. After his bath, he would return to Rome where at least the things he hated would be familiar.

The vapor rising from the adjoining *caldarium* offered no solace. Dizzy and disgusted, Rufius dropped onto his bed feeling like Icarus falling, feathers aflame. Staring at the blue ceiling, he realized that the game was rigged. If he played by Hadrian's rules, no road would ever lead to Rome.

"Vindex is right. Hadrian's a ball breaker."

Rufius lost himself in a treasonous train of thought. Hadrian had to be stopped. But how? Lacking soldiers, Rufius might enlist the help of his fellow governors. Hadrian had bled their provinces and drained their fortunes. Would their hatred for the emperor be stronger than their mutual distrust? No, they would sooner kill each other. If his father was any example, clearly no senators could be trusted. Every pretender to the throne was in the same sorry stew. Until Hadrian was ready for a successor, he would have no challengers.

Before Rufius could hatch a plot, Carbo emerged from the steam. "Your bath is ready," he said.

Rufius tore off his dusty tunic and kicked it across the room. A warm bath would calm his nerves and give him a chance to think. He stepped down into the bathroom and lowered himself into the sunken tub. "Lock the doors. No one is to disturb me."

Carbo placed a pile of fresh towels on a small bench, and adjusted the hot water faucet to assure that a steady trickle would keep the bath warm. Satisfied that all was to his master's liking, he exited the bath chamber and secured the door as instructed.

Rufius snuffed the lamp, closed his eyes, let the quiet comfort of the hot water relieve his aching backside. Finding no calm in the warmth and darkness, he submerged his head and remembered how, as a child, his brother would hold him underwater while their father laughed.

The memory brought him up for air, gasping. "Doesn't my father see what's happening?" he said. "It costs a fortune to climb Hadrian's flaming ladder. If Father has to bail me out of this province the way he's had to cover my previous losses, we'll both be ruined."

Rufius twisted the faucet handle and listened to the hot water flow into the tub. He recalled a time when he was just a boy and his father had lost him in Trajan's great bathhouse at Rome.

"Nero's nuts!" Rufius snapped back into the present and slapped the surface of the water with both palms. "Father is traveling with Hadrian. If I don't put on a good show, he'll be shamed and ruined, nailed to the same cross twice."

Finding no silver lining in the steam-filled room, he took a deep breath and slumped backwards, sending water splashing onto the heated floor. How hard would it be to skip town before

Hadrian's torrent washed him aside? He traced his toes along the tiles ringing the tub and wondered if it hurt to drown oneself. A warm death would be preferable to Hadrian's cold shoulder.

Rufius' backbone stiffened with a terrifying revelation: Death was a game that two could play.

"Brutus stabbed Julius Caesar in the broad daylight of the Senate," he whispered. "Praetorian Guardsmen murdered Caligula in a corridor. The empress poisoned Claudius ..."

Rufius ran a long fingernail along his neck and picked at a scab left by the falcon's talons. He listened to the tub fill with hot water, inhaled the healing vapors, and tried not to follow the risky stream of conscience to its homicidal conclusion.

"Hadrian's got me by the tail," he said. "And what if his Praetorian thugs decide that they actually like this blighted province? They'll swill my wine and shake down the locals ... it's no wonder that half the kids in the empire don't know who their fathers are."

Rufius reached over to turn off the faucet, but the handle spun loose and fell into the tub. Water overflowed onto the heated floor of the *caldarium* and the room went solid with steam.

"Vexed plumbing." Rufius climbed out of the tub but the hot floor scalded his feet. He tried to find the door but the thick steam made it impossible. Shouting in pain, he hopped around in the darkness until he bumped into the bench and took refuge upon it.

"Mother of Romulus!" He stood on the bench and shouted for someone to open the door before the rising flood engulfed him. The wet air was hard to breathe. Sweat dripped from the folds of his flesh. With any luck, the boiler attendant on the other side of the thick wall might come to his rescue.

But luck was in short supply, and Rufius knew it. Overheating and disoriented, he knotted his towel and threw it towards the door. He shouted again, but the steam and agitation soon rendered him unable to fight the fever. Trapped in the sunken bathroom, his death, like his life would look like an accident. He sat down on the bench, closed his eyes, and waited to be boiled alive like a lamprey.

After what seemed like an hour, a sharp pounding woke him from his stupor.

Vindex's sledgehammer broke through the door. He smashed a large hole in the door and stepped down into the flooded chamber. With two more hammer blows, only the doorframe remained. Vindex tossed the tool aside, picked up the trembling governor, and carried him to safety.

Rufius' poached face was redder than Vindex's hair. After catching his breath and realizing that he was naked, he wrapped himself in a bed sheet, lay down, and stared at the ceiling. Rufius' voice was barely audible over his wheezing. "What scoundrels designed this sadistic labyrinth?"

"How does this my salary work? When do I collect?"

"Not now, Vindex." Rufius turned onto his side to avoid the gladiator's gaze. When Vindex circled around to the other side of the bed, Rufius retreated into a fetal clutch. He wanted to sleep, but a new question gnawed at him. "Did Minem send you to rescue me from Bulbul?"

"That worm says you'll never pay me. Isn't my job protecting you more important than his job robbing you?"

"That scroll-toting snake robs me until I'm worth more dead than alive, then he kills me. Where did you say he was?"

"The taxman's villa. He's plotting with Kleptus."

Rufius sat up, cast the wet sheet aside, and stepped into the corridor.

"Put some clothes on." Vindex grabbed the wet sheet and followed Rufius into the long hallway.

"Find Minem … get me Minem!" Rufius ordered. He turned and ran towards the kitchen. "I want that rat-faced swindler right now!"

Twenty-eight
XXVIII

Gaius Severus marched in formation with the surviving soldiers, willing his shaky legs forward. His memories of the massacre refused to fade and his guilt grew deeper with each step towards Tarraco. He alone was to blame for the disaster; the inquest would find him negligent for letting assassins infiltrate the camp. He wondered if a full confession might not buy a quicker, cleaner death.

When Sub-centurion Novus grabbed his arm and yanked him out of formation, Severus knew his time had come.

"I accept my fate," he whispered. "I—"

"That was a tremendously successful defense I orchestrated back there, wasn't it?" Novus' black eyes bore down with soulless amusement. "If I hadn't acted decisively, more men would be dead, perhaps even our noble centurion."

Severus looked straight ahead. He willed his lips to stop trembling and vowed to die with dignity, if only as an example to the others. In a few moments, crows would pick at his worthless flesh and his short life would have been for naught.

"Those assassins were either fanatics, rebels, or both. Jews, Christians—zealots, enemies of Rome!" Novus tightened his grip, gave Severus a shake, and then released his arm.

The mention of Jews sent a shiver down Severus' spine. Had Novus discovered his whereabouts during the early stage of the attack? Did he know of his brother's ties to the rebels? Perhaps Novus had captured Marius. Was their father also in custody? Gulping back his fear, Severus stood ready to take responsibility for the whole tragic fiasco. The truth, his father once said, will set you free.

Free from the burden of living.

"... because after all," Novus was saying, "we saved their lives, didn't we? A few casualties are a small price to pay. We liberated a village held hostage by fanatics who placed no value on human life." Novus glared at the frightened conscript. "Is this understood?"

Severus strained against every frozen muscle in his neck and nodded in agreement. With a few artful words and veiled threats, his superior officer had transformed disaster into a triumph. Novus had rewritten history and conveniently left Severus out of it. If truth can set one free, it was clear that a lie might save one's life.

"Fall back in line, soldier." Novus shoved Severus aside. "I don't want to hear another word out of you for the rest of your short life."

Once Severus fell back into the jagged column of exhausted men, the trickle of joy he felt at having survived quickly dissolved into a river of shame. How long would he be able to hide in Novus' self-serving shadow? Could he live with himself knowing that truth and justice had not been served?

Of course, he could.

After all, he had not led the troops into reckless battle. Severus had not been drunk and snoring during the counter-attack. Had he remained at his post, he might have been the first to fall. If Novus saw fit to honey-glaze the debacle, why should Severus wallow in blame?

Novus had transformed the bungling cowardice of a lawless cohort into a tale of bravery. Attacking a defenseless village was not brutality; it was a justified security measure, the triumph of law and reason. The four assassins weren't seeking justice; they were crazed zealots who hated Rome. The wine-besotted soldiers, their throats slit while snoring, were valiant heroes who fell defending the Roman way of life. And Habeas Novus, the ambitious commander who had overseen the sadistic destruction of an innocent village, would be handed a promotion.

Severus marched in silence, wondering how long he would need to repeat Novus' lies before believing them. Was embracing falsehood the first step towards becoming a Roman? Once free of moral bearing, would all roads lead to Rome?

He marched with renewed vigor and tried not to imagine what could be less civilized than the defense of civilization. If he had blurted out a confession, his punishment would have been extended to others. After all, there had been four guards on duty when the attack hit. While Severus was listening to folk tales, he witnessed another sentry bound and gagged by a few escaped slaves. The other two sentries, smart or dead, had wisely remained silent. Gaius Severus resolved that for the good of all concerned, he would keep his mouth shut lest he wedge his muddy foot in it.

Severus reconsidered how quickly the slaves had subdued the sentry. They had struck with speed and determination uncharacteristic of the downtrodden. Could it be true that the slaves who worked in the Villa weren't slaves at all? Perhaps they were rebels, part of the loose fabric of fanatics that included his brother Marius. A fraught question knocked Severus' feet out of cadence, eliciting a shove from the soldier behind him. Was his father traveling with the men who killed Biberious?

Had his father been leading the dual life of a mild-mannered teacher by day and a rebel by night? If those slaves had killed Biberious then the allegations against his father might be true. Why else would the old man be running off to the Holy Land? Severus reflected on his father's possible involvement, until Valerius pulled him out of the formation.

"Looks like you've saved my life again. I owe you a favor, kid."

Severus shrugged, looked forward, and kept walking.

Valerius looked at the dazed kid in the soiled tunic and, for an instant, saw what no governor would ever understand: the true price of war. To the old veteran, Gaius Severus looked like every terrified conscript who had ever wet himself during battle. "I'll make you a deal."

"Do centurions make deals with conscripts?"

"I need to get that strongbox back, and you want to see that girl again."

His heart jumped, but Severus avoided the centurion's gaze.

"Just tell me the truth." Valerius reached over and squeezed Severus' shoulder. "Come clean and tell me who you are, and what you're up to."

"I'm just a—"

"Just a quarry boy, a stonemason's apprentice? If I were stupid enough to believe a story like that, I wouldn't have survived my first day in the legion."

"Really, sir, I'm just—"

"A poor village kid?" Valerius tightened his grip on Severus' shoulder enough to stop him and swing him around face-to-face. "What do you take me for? You know too much. You can read and write and your words are so big that your lips can barely wrap around them."

"I can't manage a donkey, either." Severus looked away. He liked the centurion, but could not risk revealing his secret. He was a Jew, the son of an outlaw Rabbi, the brother of a revolutionary, and he had just sworn an oath to kill the emperor. No Roman officer, no matter how Republican, could overlook the half of it. "I'm nothing but bad luck. Send me back to Tarraco."

"We need to continue the mission."

Marcus Valerius marched ahead to the front of the column where he transferred command of the cohort to Sub-centurion Novus. "Make haste," he ordered. "Forced march to the garrison."

Novus stiffened and saluted and before any of the dazed survivors could grumble about their empty stomachs, sore feet, or aching head, he led them away, southbound.

Severus and Valerius watched the jagged line of hung-over soldiers disappear across a field of dun colored boulders. The men were lucky to have survived, though the punishment awaiting them at Tarraco might prove to be worse than what they had just escaped.

Twenty-nine
XXIX

Vindex arrived at Cassius Kleptus' estate after a daylong hike across terraced hills of dormant vines and olive trees. Rather than tearing the gates off their hinges and barging in to snag his prey, he waited for a servant to fetch Winus Minem who had been sampling the taxman's wine, hoping to find a suitable vintage for the emperor's impending visit.

"Are you in some kind of trouble, Minem?" Kleptus asked when informed that the ex-gladiator was hulking by the front gate. Not fond of walking, Kleptus escorted Minem past the herb and vegetable gardens and then pointed towards the oleander-hedged entrance where Vindex was waiting. "I don't think Vindex likes you, but I'm sure it's just a question of price."

Once the taxman had waddled out of sight, Vindex seized Minem and dragged him away from the gate so fast that his toga clasp broke, leaving Vindex holding nothing but pleated yellow linen.

"You're under arrest." Vindex threw Minem's toga into the bushes.

Unfettered by the folds, Minem sidestepped the gladiator's lunge, but could not avoid capture for long. Vindex slapped loose-fitting manacles on Minem's thin wrists, and dragged him down the recently paved road to the Kleptus estate.

"What is the meaning of this?" Minem tried to free his wrists as he bounced along behind the gladiator. "I work for the governor, I'll have you know."

"So do I." Vindex jerked Minem's manacles. "You're just lucky he wants you alive."

Vindex swatted at Minem's head, but the quick little advisor sidestepped the blow and slipped out of the loose manacles.

Frustrated by Minem's thin wrists and thick skull, Vindex tied a length of frayed rope around his neck. Vindex tugged the leash, but Minem resisted like a goat going to market. "Faster!" Vindex ordered, but Minem sat down on the new paving stones and refused to budge.

"We'll go much faster if you untie me."

"Save it, rat face."

"It's not like I can escape from you." Minem jingled the coin purse hidden inside his tunic. "But if you're in no hurry …"

After a quick negotiation, Vindex agreed to untie Minem's wrists in exchange for a handful of *sesterces* and a sworn oath not to escape. "Not that your promise is worth anything."

"A complement, coming from a criminal."

Vindex laughed. "Just give me a reason, and I'll pound you into polenta."

"Have you murdered the new governor yet?"

"You better hope I'm not a killer." Vindex picked Minem up and shook him until his undergarments nearly blew away in the breeze.

"*Civis Rumanus sum!*" Minem whined. "I'm a Roman citizen!"

Vindex ignored his pleading and tightened the rope around his neck. At the junction with the *Via Augusta*, the coastal route, Vindex picked up a loose paving stone and tugged on Minem's leash. "I thought you were paving the main vias. How come the little road to Kleptus' plantation is the best in the province?"

"He obviously managed to siphon off materials and labor designated for the primary road to Tarraco."

"I wonder who let that happen."

After another hour of slogging southward, the pair came upon a large work party standing around in a torn-up section of the *Via Augusta*. Needing to confer with a construction supervisor, Minem bribed Vindex to wait in a ramshackle tavern that looked as if it had been thrown together just moments earlier.

"Take some refreshment." Minem offered his captor a few coins to spend on food and cheap wine.

"Refreshment costs more." Vindex removed the coin purse from Minem's tunic and tied him to a stone-filled cart.

SlavePower, a shadow branch of Imperial Associates, had won the concession to refurbish the *Via August*. IA got paid to administer the contract and received a commission for the inflated cost of the job. By hiring their own subsidiary, IA kept all funds in the family.

Minem smiled at the SlavePower supervisor who had been watching him negotiate with Vindex. "Release me and I'll make it worth your while."

The pale foreman wore SlavePower's distinctive orange and blue uniform. His name, "Palo," was embroidered on his right sleeve He bore the look of distrust common among low-level supervisors who compensated for paltry wages with the arbitrary exercise of authority. He ambled over to watch Minem struggle, but was in no hurry to assist.

Eventually, with the promise of a favorable commission for his troubles, and assurances that Minem's capture would bring no bounty, Palo cut the cord.

"You need to move faster." Minem peeled the rope off his chafed neck, and threw it to the ground. For all the apparent activity—neat piles of broken stones, strewn about picks and hammers, and the uninspired shuffle of a few German slaves—not one inch of new road was in place. Furious with the dismal prospects stretching out in all directions, Minem found himself at a temporary loss for harsh words. "Tell your crews to slap those new stones down fast as lightening."

"Where's the glory in that?" Palo's voice dripped with the accent, overbite, and smooth irony of a northern Gaul. "I want to do more than just pave a road; I want to make a lasting impact."

"Lasting impact?" Minem slammed his fists into his thighs and almost spat on the ground. "What the parade doesn't pulverize, souvenir hunters will steal. Don't worry about lasting impact. Worry about hurry."

Concerned about Vindex, Minem glanced towards the tavern where a gaggle of prostitutes and freshly paid laborers were milling around the entrance to the makeshift roadhouse. Depending on local prices and Vindex's appetites, the money Minem had given him might not last long.

"Palo," Minem said, softening his tone. "Why are workers getting laid when the road stones aren't?"

"We're investing a little extra time up-front to understand the true cause of road degradation," Palo explained. "Otherwise, our efforts might be wasted in solving the wrong problem."

"Your workers are overpaid, that's your problem. How on earth are you going to have a road in place before the stars go dim?"

"If there's time to do it wrong, then there's time to do it right." The bookish supervisor shoved his large, crooked nose into Minem's face. "Do it right the first time, that's what I always say."

"Slogans don't lay stone." Minem raised his eyes towards the clouds as if looking to conjure a bolt of lightening with Palo's name on it. "Just tell me how you're going to get the job done."

"Here's the trick." Palo crouched to trace a few intersecting lines in the moist dirt where the *Via Augusta* used to lie. "Everyone everywhere works on everything at once. We run all our crews in parallel."

"Parallel? The only people working in parallel are the prostitutes!" Minem pulled Palo upright by the scruff of his tunic. He began to shout but, remembering Vindex, dropped his voice into an angry murmur. "I need this road built and I need it now."

Palo wriggled free and stooped to draw a few intersecting circles in the dirt. "Given the short notice, it wasn't practical to quarry, cut, and transport new stone for the entire project. I sent raiding parties out to gather whatever decent stones they could find on the secondary roads."

"And somehow, all the good stones went to the taxman's villa." Minem trained his eye on the comings and goings at the tavern, wondering if he had given Vindex enough money for a second round. Vindex's mood may have improved, but it was best not to wait and find out. The time to flee had already come and gone.

"There's just one problem with our strategy," Palo continued. "The secondary roads—"

"Are worse than the primary roads?"

"Um, sort of … rather … the advance crews have already torn up the main roads in anticipation of a fresh supply of good materials. We may be lagging a bit, but we've learned a lot in the process."

"IA's not paying you to learn. We're paying you to work!"

Minem ground fist into palm and looked up into the darkening sky. He was distracted from bringing his fists down on Palo's head when the makeshift tavern began to shake so fervently that it seemed on the verge of collapse. From inside, the cacophony of drunks singing a popular tune about a pig and a magistrate reminded Minem that his freedom was more tenuous than Palo's plan to pave the province.

"Find me a cart and horse," Minem demanded. "I need to get back to Tarraco."

Palo pulled at a tuft of earlobe hair and gave an indifferent shrug, "All available carts are full. Stones have top priority."

Minem straightened his ruffled tunic, harrumphed, and stormed away.

"Funny you should mention carts." Palo said, following Minem after a moment's reflection. "Because of the spike in demand for stone, we were obliged to import cut rock from the neighboring provinces. Demand was high, supply was low, and prices … well, I'm sure you'll understand that we're running a bit—"

"Over budget?"

A loud crash inside the tavern convinced Minem to start running. To his dismay, Palo kept pace with the bad news. "To meet our aggressive schedule we're laying stone just in time," Palo said, "two days ahead of the emperor's procession."

"Just in time? This vexed province has no sense of time." Minem was tempted to stop and give Palo a good thrashing, but preferring to further distance himself from Vindex, sped up instead.

"Naturally, one breakthrough led to another," Palo continued, trotting alongside without breaking a pant. "To keep pace, the quarries had to abandon their wheelbarrows and donkey carts in favor of quicker, but more costly horse and chariot services."

Minem stopped to catch his breath while Palo suffocated him with a warm stream of increasingly expensive updates. Sucking air through his grit-laden teeth, Minem felt dumb, dizzy, and doomed for having ever set foot in Hispania. Running for his life in a race against Vindex, his only hope was to scratch out distance. "Don't tell me you're paying next day delivery rates for stones," he said between gasps. "Do you have any idea what that will do to our costs?"

Palo pulled a scroll out of his orange and blue tunic. "This is my *curriculum vitae*, sir. I'd be happy to discuss promotional opportunities with Imperial Associates at your earliest convenience."

Minem grabbed the scroll, threw it to the ground, and stomped on it. "How can you even think about promotions when you can't even move a few stones from point *alpha* to point *beta*?"

The approach of a stone-filled cart, bearing the painted slogan, "Don't Panic, Ship Trans-Hispanic!" gave Minem a chance to escape. He flagged a ride and looked back to see Vindex emerging from the tavern, nose glowing like a Spanish sunrise.

Minem hunched down into the footwell until the driver assured him that Vindex was no longer visible. After one hour on the wagon, the bouncing advisor felt like he had received a day-long beating. The bumpy ride bruised his thighs, rattled his bones, and risked shaking what little confidence he had left. At the sight of a newly built town along the road, Minem jumped off the cart.

The pristine village had been one of his own designs and with Vindex now far behind him, he took some time to inspect the work. He had commissioned a series of eye-pleasing facades to be populated with well-paid IA staffers in local dress who would wave and cheer as the royal procession passed. The philosophy behind this effort was simple: why bother the emperor with the raw grime of real life. Tasteful and well-controlled roadside towns would provide Hadrian with a good impression of the province and keep the riff-raff away from his royal person.

Minem explored the site, satisfied with the progress. At least something in Hispania was on schedule. The fresh whitewash needed only a few more hours to dry and the illusion would be complete.

The sound of approaching thunder reminded Minem that Vindex might be closing the gap. The sky turned gray and fecund clouds lumbered in from the coast. Minem shivered. In the absence of passing carts, he had no choice but to walk the remaining two miles to Tarraco and hope that the soles of his sandals would withstand the ragged road for just a little while longer.

Light rain soaked his tunic. A crow flew overhead and cawed mercilessly. Fearing the wrath of Vindex, Minem picked up his pace. If he could make it to Tarraco before the gladiator, he might have a chance of convincing the governor who the real threat was.

Minem pressed onward but each stride was a battle against tight muscles and grinding knees. With the hope of a warm bath before him, and the certainty of Vindex behind, Minem ran until his feet flattened. Stumbling towards town on wobbling legs, he was buoyed to see that the triumphant arch he had commissioned was largely in place.

Unfortunately, it was largely in the wrong place.

The construction crew, a dodgy group of petty thieves that normally would have been fodder for a small town arena, was milling about. A hazardous scaffold, nothing more than stout reeds and sticks lashed together with twine, swayed like a dizzy cobra. Seeing Minem approach, the crew began tossing bricks up to a man atop the structure who dropped more than he caught.

Minem was wet, sore, and tired of the gross incompetence that plagued the province. "Hey!" he yelled, trying to get the attention of the indifferent crew. "Who's in charge here?"

The man above hurled down a brick that burst into fragments at Minem's feet.

Minem jumped back to inspect the ragged arch from a safer distance. "There's a problem here," he yelled, waving his arms at the misplaced edifice. "The road is supposed to pass under the arch, not around it!"

Bricks and insults rained down from the dark sky, splashing mud onto Minem's tunic. He turned to run but, before he could flee, a balding felon, barely one hair taller than the tiny advisor, grabbed him by the back of the neck.

"Who are you to come around here and tell us what to do? How come a little guy like you talks so big?" The little criminal tossed Minem into the mud and stomped away to laugh with the gang.

Minem scrambled out of the mud just before another volley of bricks rained down at him. Fearing Vindex might be near and seeing no point in socializing with the larcenous work crew, he abandoned the men to their shoddy work. Once the bedeviled arch was far enough behind, Minem dropped to his dirty knees and trembled with exhaustion. He hated to admit it, but things were not going according to plan.

Cold, wet, and aching, he trudged towards a structure he recognized as one of IA's recently built Temples of Saturn. Unable to remember the exact location he had specified, he nevertheless knew that it should not be blocking the primary entrance into the city.

"Another blunder." he muttered through clenched teeth. "Mistakes may be the price of moving quickly, but at this rate, moving any faster will grind things to a halt."

He made a mental note to fire SlavePower and stumbled uphill to the Villa, propelled by rage alone. He stopped once to glance across the rooftops and confirm that the arena repairs had yet to start. Instead, a tenement block near the center of town lay in steaming ruins, inexplicably torched and demolished. In protest, the former residents had thrown together a tent city, a shantytown in the middle of the formerly upscale marketplace. Rain falling on the charred remains of the structure now filled the streets of Tarraco with soot.

"Vexation!" Minem reminded himself that wherever problems arose, opportunities abounded and, regardless of the outcome, IA was indemnified. The Roman Empire could fall before breakfast and Imperial Associates would still get paid by supper. The odds for having the provincial capital in shape for the emperor were sinking fast, but with whitewash and a little luck, the illusion of a tidy, well-heeled town might still be possible

Minem was relieved to sneak into the Villa unnoticed. He crept into a guest room, washed the mud off his face and donned a clean toga. Feeling safe until Vindex returned, he rallied his flagging spirit, flew down the corridor, and knocked a playful pattern on the governor's unlocked bedroom door.

"You wanted to see me, Excellency?"

"I want to kill you!" Rufius' normally round face was taut and bloodless. He grabbed Minem by the toga folds, pulled him inside, and slammed him against the wall.

"A quick update, Excellency?" Minem peeled himself off the wall, straightened his tan toga, and smiled. "I'm sure you'll be pleased with our progress."

"We have a change in plan." Rufius locked the door.

"A change?" Minem stiffened. "I think you're starting to show signs of strain, Governor. Perhaps another vacation—"

"You tried to send me on a permanent vacation." Rufius' head pounded from bad wine and accumulated frustration. He struggled to focus on Minem, but one eye twitched and the other veered off course. Minem appeared to split into two mouse-faced consultants, both radiating false innocence and expensive optimism.

"Quite a racket you've got going, no?" Rufius rubbed his eyes, hoping to make one Minem disappear so he could kill the other. When this failed, he squinted at the undersized consultants with the oversized fees and tried to guess which one was real. "You're either a simpleton or a scoundrel. Either way, I've figured out your role in this royal scam."

"It's natural to be a bit tense during times of rapid change." Minem moved towards the door, "but you didn't need to send that big villain to fetch me."

"Vindex is back on payroll. He's one of the few villains I can trust around here." Rufius grabbed an empty goblet and looked through the curved glass hoping to merge the two little men into one clear target. Hedging his shot, Rufius threw the goblet at a point in between, missing both.

"I can see you're a bit perturbed," Minem said.

"Perturbed? I'm going to perturb your thieving little spine if you have one."

"Perhaps a bath would—"

"My last bath nearly killed me." Rufius charged towards the two demons floating before him. "One of you has to be real, and both will be a joy to strangle!" he snarled, diving for the wrong Minem.

"If you truly feel a bit of exercise would help resolve your issues, Excellency, I—" Minem sidestepped the next attack and edged towards the door.

Unable to tell which Minem was real and which the reflection, Rufius lunged again and missed. Struggling to commit his eyes to the same orbits, he chased the Minems around the room, but they ran in opposite directions.

"Stand still you monstrous little mice!" Rufius reached for a vase to throw, but the Minems easily dodged his missile.

Rufius stopped to catch his breath. His head pounded so hard that, for a second, the two consultants became four. "The empire can crumble for all you care. Either way, IA's on the winning side. The only problem with killing you is that the pleasure would be so short," Rufius shouted."

Rufius collapsed into the sofa and cradled his spinning head.

Minem backed out the door. "Believe me, sir, I've seen many talented clients become emotional and, at times, even a bit belligerent. The good news is that your passion is a great asset: well-channeled rage is almost as powerful as rage run amuck."

Without a sound, Vindex entered the room, grabbed Minem by the shoulders, and tossed him so high that his head banged into the ceiling. Vindex then caught him by the ankles.

Dangling upside down, Minem flailed at his captor with one hand and clutched his toga tails with the other. "Put me down, you killer!"

"As you wish." Vindex dropped him onto the tile floor.

Rufius opened both eyes, thought the better of it, and closed one tightly. He crawled to the edge of the bed and spoke very slowly. "Listen, and listen carefully you Macedonian magpie: The emperor, may he show me mercy, will be here in a matter of days. If he takes me down, you're coming with me."

Thirty
XXX

Three nights after the siege in Southern Gaul, the Emperor's barge stopped to inspect the town recently laid waste by a "rogue cohort from Hispania." After a somber inspection of the destroyed village, the emperor deployed a handful of elite troops to seek out and punish the errant legionaries who had violated the empire's internal tranquility. He then withdrew to a local magistrate's villa in the Pyrenean foothills to hunt and relax.

Hadrian traveled more than he tarried, touring his lands to get a firsthand impression of their bounty. He was fascinated by the variety of cultures and peoples now amalgamated under his great crest and frustrated when each official visit turned into a dreary repetition of the last. The local authorities carefully orchestrated his every waking—and many of his sleeping—moments so that he only saw what they wanted him to. In their relentless attempts to curry favor, the governors and their minions consistently reduced the savory stew of Roman civilization into a bland and predictable porridge.

Feigning exhaustion, he went to sleep early with orders not to be disturbed. An hour after the oil lamps had dimmed, he shaved his thick beard, outfitted himself in a rough tunic, and left his royal trappings behind. The athletic emperor slipped out of a window and stole a horse from the stable. He rode quickly, relishing his temporary freedom and the communion between rider and steed. After an invigorating gallop, he arrived at a nearby town and looked for a place to encounter the real men of the realm. Seeing a tavern called "The Bottomless Amphora," he dismounted and stepped inside.

At the counter, Marcus Valerius was sniffing at his pungent stew. "I could eat a horse," he said, shoving the bowl aside, "but this is worse than donkey meat."

"I'll take it." Severus reached for the bowl. He was hungry for the first time since the siege and counterattack had turned his intestines inside out.

After leaving the remnants of *Scipio IV Hispania* near the border, the soldiers had exchanged their uniforms for drab winter tunics so as not to attract attention. After a day's trek, they stopped at "The Bottomless Amphora" to spend the night before returning to the Ponus Valley. In the morning, they planned to retrieve the governor's strongbox and continue their mission.

While Severus shoveled the local fare into his mouth, Valerius' tired gaze turned to the tall, recently shaved man entering the tavern. There was something both out-of-place and familiar about the stiff, muscular man that put Valerius on alert. If their paths had crossed before, this evening's chance reunion in a backwater tavern might not be a coincidence.

The arrival of the curious stranger forced Valerius to reconsider his secrecy. He needed to reveal more of the mission to Severus or risk condemning it to failure. "Listen," he said, "this is important."

"Count on me." Severus swallowed another mouthful of meat, and mopped the bowl with a scrap of flatbread.

"No matter what happens, one of us needs to recover that strongbox we hid in the mountains. The box needs to go to Londinium,"

"*Londinium?*" Severus pulled at a lock of his uneven hair. Londinium was as distant and unimaginable as the pyramids of Egypt. "The capital of Britannia?"

Valerius nodded with grave certainty. "Britannia: where women carry knives in their cleavage and men braid their beards to look like vipers. The further north you go, the more people resemble animals."

"I wonder what they say about us."

Valerius glanced around to make sure no one was listening. "The cargo needs to be delivered to the governor's brother, Consul

Rufius, in Londinium. That's our mission, and a soldier's mission is sacred. No matter what happens, one of us must see it through."

A stubble-faced drunkard fell asleep on an adjacent stool and slouched against Gaius Severus. Surprised, Severus stepped aside and the drunk fell to the floor without waking.

"Pay attention, Severus," Valerius said, though he was distracted by the curly-haired stranger now weaving through the crowd. He tried to place the man's familiar face and confident demeanor. "Don't ask me what's in the strongbox."

"Understood, sir. I'm not sure I could keep it secret anyway. If the enemy were to torture me, I might spill the chickpeas."

"Don't ask me what's in the vexed box, because I don't have the faintest idea what we're transporting."

"It wasn't heavy enough to be filled with gold, sir."

Valerius had already drawn the same worrisome conclusion. There were only a few treasures a politician might consider more valuable than gold, none of which would be safe to transport.

Valerius glanced discreetly at the approaching stranger. Compared to the ragged dress and furrowed faces of the local men, this tall, regal fellow was ripped from a different cloth. His pale jaw line had recently sported a beard. His teeth were clean to the point of glowing. Whoever he was, his presence did not bode well. "That fellow's not from around here. See how he's looking around? I'll bet he's secret police."

Hadrian caught Valerius' glance, studied the disguised soldier, and seemed to size him up quickly. Small, though muscular, Valerius also appeared out of place among the corpulent farmers and hunched tradesmen. He bore the bronze hues of a lifetime under the sun and the air of authority. The emperor saw that his escape had fooled no one; the honor guard had been vigilant enough to deploy a modicum of protection. The Praetorians were worth their salt, and they liked to rub it in. Hadrian surveyed the tavern's colorful patrons, relieved to see no more undercover security than necessary.

"Tough trek tomorrow." Valerius feigned a yawn and avoided Hadrian's gaze. "I'm going upstairs to find a bunk without bedbugs."

An old, three-fingered hooker who had been working the crowd followed Valerius up the stairs, but could not consummate a deal in spite of her willingness to negotiate. Rebuffed but not defeated, she fluffed her wavy gray hair and headed towards the *incognito* emperor warming his backside by the hearth.

She was prevented from reaching Hadrian when a plume of dust whipped across the floor and forced her to jump back. Her cursing was drowned out by the patrons cheering as a terrified cat with a sandal tied to its tail darted across the room, doing its best to evade an angry, shoeless drunk.

"Throw it in the pot," shouted a squat man to a chorus of general agreement that boiling a cat would provide some much needed, though short-lived entertainment.

Hadrian tried to get out of the way, but the impact of the shoeless drunk sent him sprawling into a bystander who responded with an angry shove. Before much of a brawl could start, the innkeeper's stocky wife pushed Hadrian aside, rescued the wet cat, and threw it out the doorway. She then caught the shoeless man and beat him with his own sandal.

"I didn't do it," he protested, but the mild violence was far too crowd-pleasing for the hardworking woman to stop thrashing him. After a few good swats, she threw his sandal into the road and went back to collecting empty plates from the red-stained tables.

The old hooker waited for the shouting and shoving to subside before taking a long drink from an abandoned pitcher to prop up her sagging spirits. Seeing her approaching, Hadrian retreated to the counter where Gaius Severus sat watching the colorful crowd.

Severus acknowledged the golden-haired newcomer with a nod, but not wanting his Spanish accent to betray him, said nothing.

"What are you drinking, bricklayer?" the innkeeper asked, eyeing Hadrian with the suspicion provincials everywhere reserve for outsiders.

Pleased to see that his disguise was working, Hadrian pointed to a rack of pitchers along the wall. The innkeeper grunted with indifference and filled a large jug with the lifeblood of the Roman Empire.

"Not from around here, are you?" Hadrian turned towards Severus and filled both of their cups with water and red wine.

"I'm a Spanish mason, heading north." Severus took a sip of wine to be polite and, to his surprise, found it to be drinkable. He took a deeper gulp and felt a sudden urge to smile at the fellow who had filled his cup. Valerius had misjudged the man. He was no spy. Severus even detected a glint of kindness in his dark brown eyes. "I'm going north to build Hadrian's Wall."

"We'll drink to the great wall." Hadrian raised his cup, drained it, and turned to men standing nearby. "Any of you lot like to follow this chap north to work on the wall?"

A rosy-cheeked man standing next to Severus laughed so hard he slumped against the counter and gasped for breath. "Hadrian's vexed wall!" he wheezed, before continuing his silent negotiation with the three-fingered prostitute signaling from across the room. Using sign language to settle on the price—two fingers and one thumb—he extracted himself from the crowd and followed her upstairs.

The first few cups of wine left Severus feeling friendly toward the tall fellow whose dark eyes seemed friendly enough. By the time they started the second pitcher, Severus felt like confiding his troubles to the generous stranger, but was distracted when the hooker reappeared a moment later, chasing her latest client down the stairs. Flushed and angry, she pursued the terrified man across the tavern.

"Tried to stiff her," the innkeeper mumbled.

To the crowd's delight, her undressed client ran out into the street, leaving his sandals, sash, and dignity on the floor behind. Strutting back into the room, she flashed Hadrian a suggestive pout.

"She's flirting like a horse in heat," Severus said, nudging Hadrian with a bony elbow and refilled both of their cups with undiluted wine. "I think she fancies you."

"Old hookers rub me the wrong way," Hadrian said.

Now more than a little tipsy, Severus raised his glass and fixed the emperor in his cloudy gaze. His previous familiarity with wine had been limited to an occasional Sabbath sacrament. The cozy feeling from the first pitcher faded and the wine now seemed to sprout horns and turn against him. Each additional gulp made him feel angry and acidic as if an inner spigot had opened a scalding torrent of rage. His very breath felt flammable enough to burn down the world.

"Here's to the end of everything." Severus drained his cup and smashed it down on the counter.

Noting Severus' sudden mood swing, Hadrian pulled back to a more comfortable distance. "What do you mean?" he asked.

"The empire is crumbling under its own weight," Severus tried to refill his cup, but instead spilled wine onto the counter. He reached for Hadrian's shoulder and looked him in the eyes. "It's every man for himself and the Gods against all."

"How so?" Hadrian suppressed a grimace at being touched by a plebe. This was, after all, exactly the sort of authentic intercourse he had been craving. He inhaled deeply, filling his lungs with the refreshing sting of raw sincerity never found at court. "Rome is hardly crumbling. The empire's at peace and the emperor is just—"

"Peace? Justice?" Feeling pigheaded and loose-lipped, Severus laughed with pity at the soft-cheeked simpleton beside him. The golden-haired patriot was good for a pitcher of wine, but not much else. Slipping off his stool, Severus steadied himself on wobbly legs and wandered away.

Hadrian watched Severus stumble away and marveled at the bloody-minded pluck of the common man. Unable to get another drop of wine from the busy bartender, he left his place at the counter to break up a nearby brawl over the cut-rate affections of the aging prostitute.

He pried her fist-swinging suitors apart and held them at arm's length until the innkeeper's wife arrived to chastise them all with her thick wooden ladle. The hapless hooker then slapped Hadrian for disrupting her commerce and kept swinging at him until he got control of her flaying hands, at which point she twisted brazenly into his arms.

"Y'er solid as a ship," she said, thrusting her full keel into his royal rudder. "Let's go upstairs and raise the sails." The aging Aphrodite tossed her graying curls backwards. Her lips quivered with the promise of reasonably priced rapture.

After Hadrian pried her away, the rejected old harlot found ready acceptance and a fair price with a three-chinned farmer on the far side of the room.

Relieved to be rid of her, Hadrian slipped back into the crowd, and resumed his quest to soak up the rich pageantry of the plebes. He set his sights on an unattended pitcher and drinking horn on a nearby table, but his path was blocked by a shrill musician wielding a lyre. The minstrel seized Hadrian's hard shoulder and used it to boost himself onto the table, the contents of which he cleared with his feet. Strumming his discordant strings, the troubadour led the crowd in a rude ballad about three soldiers and a mule.

Angry with alcohol and buoyed with rising belligerence, Gaius Severus joined in the stomping and shouted out the bawdy chorus. By the time the second verse finished, the crowd was thick with song and drink. Hadrian tried to move away from the eye of the storm, but two plastered masons dragged him into a wobbly jig that quickly sent him spinning into Severus.

"Watch it!" Severus shoved the emperor back in the other direction.

Half the tavern erupted into a popular song about a pig and a magistrate while the other half insisted on repeating the previous ballad at greater volume. For one glorious moment, the emperor soaked up the raucous ecstasy that often precedes a battle. Life at court seemed farther away than the stars. Caught up in the moment and unfettered cacophony, Hadrian shouted for joy.

"Long live Rome!"

The tavern fell silent except for the crackling hearth and rhythmic slobbering of a blind dog under a table. People looked at Hadrian in disbelief, but he was saved from a mass beating by the arrival of a brawny German ducking through the entrance with a screaming girl in tow.

Severus recognized her at once. It was Lena, the innkeeper's daughter, the most desirable creature he had ever seen. Seeing her captor jerk the leash and paw at her perfect shoulders was too much for Severus to bear. Fever rose in his veins as he stomped towards the muscle-bound giant.

The German kept Lena off-balance as she swung her bound fists at him. A few men cheered when she drove a heel into his knee and scraped her muddy boot down his shinbone. He pulled her hair and she stomped on his foot. As the two struggled, the crowd took sides, some cheering for him, others betting for her.

Severus tried to jump into the fray but Hadrian grabbed the back of his tunic. "You're no match for that bruiser."

"Let go, you coward!" Severus shouted, struggling against the emperor's grip.

"She's no stranger to trouble." Hadrian twisted Severus' tunic and held firm. "Just give it a second."

"Time's up!" Severus tore himself free. He shoved forward and wedged himself between Lena and the enormous demon. Drunk, furious, and more than a little love struck, Severus surprised everyone by planting a fistful of knuckles into the big man's face.

The crowd covered their bets as the German wiped blood from his nose and raised the stakes with a right hook that Severus managed to duck. Not waiting for encouragement, Lena delivered a solid kick below the German's sash and the big man doubled over. Emboldened by wine, woman, and song, Severus grabbed a ceramic jug and smashed it across the German's forehead. The innkeeper's wife contributed a similar blow to the back of his head and burly northerner stumbled and fell unconscious to the ground.

Severus untied Lena's wrists. "What are you doing here?" he asked, pulling her close. He wiped her tear-streaked cheeks with the back of his chapped hand.

Lena shook him away and she stormed out the doorway.

Severus followed her out into the narrow road where steady rain fell against the swollen planks of dark, sagging storefronts. Even in her darkest moment, Lena lit up his gloom like a harvest moon. Her return offered a seed of hope that the recent days of war, loss, and vengeance had eclipsed. The Fates had intervened on his behalf.

"It's going to be all right," Severus stuttered, awash in the aftershock of what had just happened.

"No, it isn't." Lena spun around, hunched her shoulders, and balled her fists. "You don't understand. That man in there—I belong to him."

"Belong?" Severus swallowed hard against what felt like a dry knife lodged lengthwise in his throat. Could it be true that she belonged to another? "You're promised to *him*?"

"Not promised," she said, dropping her gaze to the ground. "Sold."

Severus pondered her words, but they sunk through the depths of his exhaustion without making sense. *Sold?* He felt his heart spring from his chest and watched it splatter onto the mud. "Nobody can own you," he insisted.

"Wrong." Her face hardened and rain dripped from her long, tangled hair. It's a trick my father plays for money. There's usually nothing to it, but that gladiator managed to escape from my dumb, lazy brother. I need to buy my freedom or that pig will never stop dogging me. He'll—"

"Did you just say '*gladiator*?'" Severus felt something sear his insides. A volcano of purpose rose in his chest, its flames fanned by something joyous and completely improbable pulsing through his heart. "Listen," he said, almost choking from excitement. "Did you see the way we brought him down? You and I ... we're meant to be together."

Hadrian's horse whinnied and shook rainwater off its ears.

Severus took Lena's hand and nodded towards the tied horse. "If we can make it to Tarraco, we'll be safe."

A smile broke like sunrise across her bruised face. Needing no more prompting, she unhitched the horse.

"This is so crazy it must be right." Severus struggled onto the horse's wet back.

Hadrian appeared at the doorway a second before the German shoved him aside and burst into the street.

"Halt!" The German waved a fist at Lena. "You're my slave."

"Stop!" Hadrian shouted. "That's my horse!"

Lena scrambled up behind Severus and wrapped her arms around his waist. "I hope you know how to ride," she whispered into his cold ear.

The fine horse burst into motion with a splash of hooves.

Thirty-one
XXXI

Festus Rufius rolled out of bed later than ever, his eyes swollen like stagnant puddles. Settling into a pile of pillows, he tried in vain to get comfortable, but Winus Minem's arrival made it impossible.

"Count on me, Excellency," Minem chirped as he moved aside a wooden plank and entered through the jagged hole in the bedroom wall. His tone invoked certainties that could never be proven. "Believe me; the emperor will be very impressed."

"I need to be impressed with the emperor of great ideas right about now." The governor's hands lay hidden under the folds of his blanket. His lips barely moved as he spoke in a low, mean-spirited monotone. "Unless you want to consult with crocodiles, you'd better have a plan."

"Imperial Associates is always at your service!" Minem had just received notice from IA that all contracts needed amending to assure payment in the event that Festus Rufius failed to survive the emperor's visit. "Listen carefully. I know you're going to love this plan."

"Love isn't in the air ... even air is in short supply." Rufius rose, tried to pace, but instead dropped weak-kneed onto the sofa. To assuage his misery, he tried to remember happier times, but the contrast depressed him even more. He then tried to remember worse times, but none came to mind. When he returned to the present, Minem was in mid-sentence, talking fast and bouncing around the room like a cat on fire.

"...with our best boats. We need to fall back and focus on what really matters," Minem was saying. "All but the most essential construction projects must be stopped. The only roads we fix now are the ones running from the port to the Villa. No more arches, no more viaducts. The new theatre project has been cancelled, twice. This time we cancel it for good! Forget the arena; we concentrate on the port and—"

"Wait a second." Rufius tried to make sense of Minem's sudden flood of ideas. "The arena needs to be finished. You don't want to die in an unfinished arena, do you? And why the sudden concern over the port?"

"As I said a minute ago, Excellency, my new plan is to send a boat up the coast to intercept the emperor, may his wind never fail. We'll offer to transport him south to his father's homeland, bypassing Tarraco entirely. If he insists on coming here, we can distract him for a day and then ship him off faster than a rumor out of Rome."

Rufius considered the proposition and one half of his head stopped hurting. The plan was so simple, so brilliant that he failed to understand why the other half of his head now ached twice as much. "What about the senators, the honor guard, and the rest of those freeloaders?"

"I admire you, Excellency. Even in a time of crisis you have the presence of mind to think about others." Mincm opened the heavy drapes without noticing Rufius wincing at the sudden daylight. A cool breeze blew in through the hole in the wall. "If we can get a couple more boats, we'll offer to transport the essential members of the entourage: the senators, a few bodyguards, some food tasters …"

Once his mind caught up with the onslaught of ideas, the pressure in Rufius' head ebbed and drained. Something so good was falling into place that he could almost taste it. "And the honor legion? Do you have a boat big enough to send those hoodlums to the sea floor?"

"Don't worry, I've thought of everything. Hadrian's legion will march night and day to keep up with the boats. They'll be in such a hurry to pass through here that they probably won't even spend the night. If we can keep all the important people floating, the foot soldiers and low-ranking riff-raff will never notice that the province wasn't ready."

"You're as devious as you are dangerous." The governor smiled for the first time in days. Minem's plan dovetailed nicely with Rufius' desire to send Hadrian to Hades. He considered his good fortune until it hurt. Opportunity had landed in his lap like a pork chop falling on a sleeping dog, but the plan was too simple, too perfect. There had to be something Minem was overlooking. "Do you think Hadrian will accept our offer? What if he suspects something?"

"Hadrian always suspects something, that's why he's in charge. He just bypassed half of Gaul so I'm sure he'll be eternally grateful if you help him move faster."

Rufius stopped in front of the cracked window and stroked the woven curtain. In spite of the gray sky, he felt giddy, almost rejuvenated. For the first time in days, his world had stopped spinning backwards. He began to pace, slowly at first, then more regally, kicking aside a half-empty bowl of sea urchin dumplings that he could not remember having requested or eaten.

"Wait a second!" Rufius whirled around to face Minem. "I knew there was something missing. Where in Jove's name do I get boats? We can't put Hadrian in a galley and force the senators to row."

Minem nodded. "Anticipating your agreement, I've already ordered your fastest messengers to get the word out. With any luck, we'll have ships ready before Hadrian crosses the border."

"With any luck, we'll keep our heads." Rufius drew a slow, stiff breath through his teeth. "This has to work. Even the winds can't be left to chance."

"It won't come for free." Minem ran his hand over the bald spot that had recently taken root on the back of his head. "You'll have to absorb some expenses for canceling a few contracts and launching others."

Rufius daydreamed while Minem rambled about early termination clauses, and produced new documents for approval and old scrolls for revisions. Rufius suspected that it would take three generations to pay off the debts that he had already accumulated, but given his prospects for survival, another boatload of *sesterces* hardly mattered.

"We'll need to focus all our energies on the local improvements," Minem advised. "What little Hadrian sees of Tarraco will need to sparkle."

Rufius' head began to pound again "I knew your plan sounded too perfect. The emperor will never travel without security forces," he said, pounding a fist into his thigh. "More than a handful of Praetorians will confound everything."

"I've already figured that out. You'll provide security. Just dress up what's left of *Scipio IV Hispania* to look like an honor guard."

"Those bunglers, are you crazy?"

"I've been thinking about the *Scipio* boys, Excellency. Perhaps we're being too harsh with them." Seeing every dark cloud as an opportunity to irrigate, Minem reached into his tan toga for a fresh scroll.

"Too harsh?" Rufius scowled until it hurt. "Those idiots attacked a friendly village and lost half a cohort in the process."

"Perhaps it was a simple misunderstanding."

Minem unrolled a new document and Rufius rolled his tired eyes.

"I don't think those *Scipio* boys are such a bad bunch," Minem said. "Look at it from their point of view, Excellency. A few southern soldiers and a handful of doe-eyed conscripts travel into a northern region with unfamiliar customs and practices. They take offense at things that the local people intend as hospitality. Tempers escalate, words are exchanged, and pretty soon a friendly little town is under siege."

"Two words." Rufius pushed the contract back unsigned. "Hogwash."

"Honestly, Governor, we need to prepare our legions for the future," Minem insisted, but his smiling eyes revealed faint worry lines for the first time. "The old days were times of war. If someone was different, you simply killed him. Now? Now we're at peace—it's confusing for soldiers, disorienting."

Rufius turned his back. "Enough!"

"With all due respect, Excellency, every day our unprepared soldiers encounter strange people from distant provinces. We send our boys north to build walls alongside foreigners who don't look or act anything like them. If we don't arm the Roman Legion with proper training, that torched village in Southern Gaul will look like a neighborhood pig-roast in comparison to the disasters—"

"Stop! I'm not buying it anymore. Hispania is out of money and out of time."

"But the empire is so vast. What's normal in one province is offensive in another. Just think of your own experience here in Hispania."

"My experience here is about to end with a beheading." Rufius gestured for the exhausting little advisor to leave. "I can only hope my father has a little money stashed away somewhere."

"I'm sure he does, Excellency. A good father is always happy to pay for his son's education."

Rufius smiled at the hidden truth. If all went well, his father would have an emperor in the family and, once ascendant, Rufius would put Winus Minem and the jackals from Imperial Associates on a slow boat to Hades.

Thirty-two
XXXII

In the cold foothills of Southern Gaul, Valerius wrapped the bearskin cloak around his shoulders and increased his pace up the snow-covered road towards the Ponus Inn. He was alone after Gaius Severus had gone missing without leave. According to a witness in the tavern, Severus had fought with a German for beating a slave girl. Thrashing a woman was no crime, but assaulting a man and stealing his horse was. The story was sketchy but not entirely surprising. Severus, ever mysterious, had emerged from the shadow of a doubt into the full light of larceny.

Anticipating Lady Rivus' high prices, Valerius had stopped earlier in a mountain village and spent his last few coins to buy an old donkey and a rickety cart from an even older peasant. Unlike men, who become more stubborn with years, the weathered beast followed dutifully when Valerius tugged at the harness.

After a day of steady trekking, Valerius and the sullen donkey arrived at the border station just ahead of nightfall. They were stopped by a small, squinting, dog-faced man wearing an official, though oversized, tunic who had set up a makeshift roadblock near the border.

"Good evening, travelers." The fellow thumbed through his logbook and did not look up. "Carrying any meats, fruits, spirits, or leather goods, are we?"

"Nothing to declare." Darkness was coming and Valerius had no time to waste with borderline formalities. He intended to recover the strongbox and reach the Ponus Inn before the wildcats came out to stalk their supper. "I'm a soldier. Let me pass."

"Technically speaking, that donkey qualifies as meat."

The intransigent border guard thumbed through the tattered pages in his codex and haggled over the definition of "meat," until

Valerius was weary enough to agree to anything. "The donkey is also made of leather."

"A live donkey is neither meat nor leather."

"Wrong. It's both."

"I'm a Roman soldier." Valerius pulled out his *gladius* and ran his thumb across the edge. "You will let me pass or negotiate with this."

The border agent ran away, leaving Valerius free to knock down the flimsy barrier and continue towards the Ponus enclave. Moments later, at the edge of the field where he had stashed Rufius' cart, Lady Rivus appeared in a swirl of colorful scarves.

"Centurion!" She smiled and approached with excessive friendliness. "How lovely to see you again."

"And you, Lady." Valerius bowed curtly. He then scanned the snow-covered clearing, but the cart he had stashed under a canvas tarp had vanished. Vanished like Severus. Vanished like the promise of an early pension. The lot was strewn with the wreckage of other carts that had been left to her care. "I've returned for my cart."

"Your cart?" Lady Rivus looked at the centurion playfully. She pulled the scarf from her head, and wrapped it slowly around her neck as she shook her long black hair loose. "Surely you know where the cart is. After all, you're the commander, aren't you?"

"The cart was here. You agreed to store it for an immodest fee."

"Which I'm happy to say has been paid in full."

"What happened to the other carts?" Valerius nodded towards the piles of axles, wheels, and debris pock marking the snowbound field.

"I'm now in the spare parts business." She flicked a wayward tress from her face and forced a smile. "Far more profitable."

Valerius stared at her, but he had never been able to read a woman. This one, for example, was trying to conceal the evident fact that her carts had been ransacked. If she was concealing something, it wasn't her left shoulder, now visible under her falling cloak.

"Would you like to come inside … share a jug?"

Valerius ignored her flapping eyelashes and tried to imagine who might have ravaged her inventory. It was clear from the damage that more than one person had been involved. He noticed a thin ribbon of steam rising from the charred bed of a cart that had been too wet to torch. The damage was fresh. Whoever had snatched Rufius' cart and strongbox might still be nearby.

"Who took my cart?"

"A nice soldier with dishy eyes." Lady Rivus swiveled her ample hips and radiated enough heat to thaw the snow pack. "He passed through here yesterday."

"Soldier? What did he look like?"

"Why, a Roman soldier, of course. Really, Centurion, you surprise me," she said, pouting. "Now why don't we talk about something more interesting than donkey carts?"

Valerius had the dizzy feeling of having tripped at the finish line of a twenty-year marathon. His stomach churned with the certainty that he had failed his last official duty. Since entering Hispania, he had wandered under a bad star that had finally fallen on his head. "This reeks of fish," he said. "You promised that you would keep the cart for me."

"Don't be so dull." She twirled a long lock of black hair. "I'm sure that stupid cart is in better hands than yours."

Valerius considered her story. In the fading light, her face revealed no treachery, but if she was not lying, why was she acting so coy? Perhaps spies for the governor had been following him all along, setting him up for a failure that would cost him his pension. Was the governor behind this? Rufius was not a strategic thinker; born lucky perhaps, but not a clever man by any stretch of the imagination. Severus, on the other hand, he was clever.

"The conscript," Valerius demanded, "the skinny boy I was traveling with?"

"Skinny? No."

"How many were there?"

"Just one well-fed fellow," she said, bouncing her long hair to one side. "Much friendlier than you and he didn't have a thing for skinny boys." She covered her shoulder, tightened her scarf, and left in a huff.

Valerius considered following her, but he was too old-fashioned to beat a confession out of a woman. Perhaps there was a logical explanation for the broken carts. Perhaps her story held water and nothing was amiss. Perhaps fish were dancing in the desert. Valerius cursed himself for having been so easily duped

"I don't suppose you'll need that tired little donkey anymore," Lady Rivus said, looking back. She scanned the worn wheels on his old rig from a distance. "I'll buy the donkey, but you can keep that worthless cart."

Valerius glared at her. He had no desire to leave the sad old donkey with the hungry Ponus clan, but where he was going, the beast would be a burden. "I'll sell it to you under one condition."

"Only one? You're not much of a negotiator, are you, Centurion? You couldn't buy a book off a blind man."

"The donkey's yours if you keep it off the dinner table until after I'm gone."

She sashayed back and handed him a few coins less than he had spent on the dull beast. "Now you had better go and find my brother at the inn, but watch out!—he's been in a bad mood ever since his daughter …"

"The girl is missing?" Valerius decided not to reveal any of what he had heard in the tavern. It seemed incredible, but the swirling fragments of slave girls, Germans, and stolen horses began to gel. "What happened to Lena?"

"Girls will be girls." She winked. "Some more than others."

Valerius swallowed the taste of defeat. He had faced down armed men and angry beasts, but had never quite figured out women. It was surprising that no emperor had ever tried to conquer the world with an army of females. Valerius took careful leave and tramped across the icy path towards the Ponus Inn. Along the way, he heard a rustling in the underbrush, but did not draw a weapon. Better to be eaten by a mountain lion than suffer whatever new deceptions the trouser-clad Ponus clan had in store.

When the smoking chimney of the Ponus Inn finally appeared around a bend, he passed through the small, stone village and banged on the heavy door.

The old innkeeper pretended not to recognize him and kept Valerius in the cold for an exchange that ran the same crooked course as their first encounter. "The inn is full," the haggling started. "Soldiers are bad for business," it continued. And when, "Soldiers pay full price," didn't work, Ponus insisted on cash up front.

Worn thin with chill and frustration, Valerius eventually brought the negotiation to a point where he could enter the drafty, dirt-floored room. He took a moment to thaw by the granite hearth and inspect the tarnished elephant tusk hanging above the mantle. Had Hannibal really passed this way? What had first seemed preposterous now seemed possible. The rogue Carthaginian who had almost defeated Rome would have felt right at home in this den of outlaws.

"Has my young conscript been here?" Valerius asked, watching more for the old man's reaction than a truthful response.

The old man looked away. He hobbled over to the fire and poked it with a long, charred stick. "You pay full price. Good hearty dinner, free with full price bed!"

"Any other people tonight?" Valerius insisted. "Soldiers?"

"People yes, soldier no. You lose soldier?"

"I didn't lose anyone … but you did … a girl, no?"

The old man's enormous son now entered the room, slowly easing his bulk through the narrow doorway. His dripping nose had almost fused with his frozen moustache. The young giant wiped snow off his badger-like beard and looked at his father cautiously.

Valerius intercepted the glance and wondered what it meant. Had young Ponus stolen the strongbox, or was he just checking with his father as to the nature of tonight's scam?

"Donkey?" Ponus the Younger asked.

Valerius vowed to return with half a legion and teach these donkey poachers an unforgettable lesson. The old innkeeper, his bear-sized son, Lady Rivus—con artists, the lot of them. Was there any difference between the red-trimmed scoundrels fleecing the empire from above and the red-nosed scavengers fighting over the scraps below? Ponus the Elder and Festus Rufius could change places tomorrow and no one would be the wiser. Valerius finally applied the only leverage available besides his short sword. "I saw your daughter," he said.

Ponus and son exchanged another conspiratorial glance and Valerius saw that his ruse had worked. Though he had not seen her, it seemed likely that she was the girl fighting in the tavern and Severus was just the type to go missing over a doomed infatuation. The two young swindlers were in league, in love, or both. Whatever their story was, the pieces fit.

Ponus the Younger lumbered over to the hearth, pulled a boiling pot from the fire, and slammed it menacingly onto the tree-stump table. A sharp exchange of devious sounding dialect convinced Valerius that his talk of the girl had struck a nerve. Sensing the soured atmosphere, he positioned himself in the half-open doorway and raised the stakes. "The strongbox for the girl—"

For once, the Ponus men were in no mood to negotiate. Ponus the Younger grabbed the boiling pot and charged the doorway with a surprising burst of speed. Valerius leapt across the threshold and slammed the door before the steaming kettle and its pungent contents splashed and smashed against it.

Young Ponus wrenched the door open, but Valerius took advantage of his head start and outran the oath-shouting ogre who soon abandoned the chase. Once out of shouting range, Valerius descended quickly through the dark, nightmarish forest that seemed to be closing in around him. The border between night and day, the yawning moments when tormented spirits shifted in their sleep had arrived.

Valerius wondered how many hapless travelers old Ponus had duped into buying Lena, only to be ambushed by her outsized brother. If the Ponus men had been willing to kill him over a vague innuendo, they had no doubt robbed and killed other unsuspecting guests, disposing of their corpses in the forests nearby. A proper send-off for the victims was out of the question as Ponus the Elder was too cheap to pay the boatman. Valerius' earlier trepidations about the mountains now made perfect sense. The hills were inhabited by restless spirits.

It was enough to fret a crow.

Valerius was both thankful to leave the Ponus Valley and reticent about the road ahead. Leave he must, but where was he going? He had no good reason to return to Tarraco. Nothing but shame awaited him in the capital. Since a court martial would likely be his life's last chapter, why not forge south to Mauritania where he could avoid the Legion's harsh justice and live out his days in anonymity?

If he returned to Tarraco, he would be condemned. The case against him was simple. He had been unable to prevent an attack on an innocent village and lost half a cohort in the brutal aftermath. He had botched a final, simple mission to deliver a wooden box from one place to another. To top it off, his lone conscript had turned to crime. Valerius tried to swallow his shame without choking. He was honor bound to accept his fate. Marcus Valerius had never run from responsibility and would not start now.

A last burst of sunlight scratched the gray underbelly of the clouds just as the noise in the underbrush returned. Whatever had been tracking him was fast approaching. Valerius drew his sword and vowed to land one clean blow before being dragged into a dead man's crevasse.

"Yes!" came a small voice from behind him.

"You again!" Valerius sheathed his blade and turned to see the small, fur-clad mountain boy. "You're the little scarab who got me into this mess."

"Yes!" Remo flashed a wide, toothless grin.

"Any chance *you* know where my strongbox is?"

"Yes!" The boy bounced from one foot to the other.

"Thanks anyway, kid." Valerius recalled the boy's limited vocabulary and started walking. "Better get home before nightfall."

"Follow Remo!" The boy grabbed Valerius' hand and pulled him into the forest.

Having nothing left to lose, Valerius followed Remo through a break in the trees along a narrow, snow-packed trail. After fifty paces, the trail led to the edge of a steep ravine into which the boy pointed excitedly.

Once his eyes adjusted to the darkness, Valerius made out a familiar shape of Rufius' strongbox at the bottom of the ravine.

"Vesuvius!"

Valerius descended quickly but Remo beat him to the bottom.

"Who did this?"

Remo said nothing. He pointed to a sharp, heavy stone jutting out of the snow and indicated for Valerius to pick it up. Remo rocked the box back and forth to make Valerius aware of a faint scraping sound.

Valerius tipped the box over. Whoever had broken open and emptied the box from the top had missed the rustling beneath the bottom panels. The oak planks were thick and did not yield quickly, but Valerius' heavy blows eventually broke through, opening a narrow wound for his *gladius* to widen. Probing the hidden compartment, the tip of the short sword scratched against a scroll that he was able to extract in short order.

Valerius examined the hidden treasure, running his fingers over an elaborate wax seal that, along with a few block letters, indicated officialdom. Whatever else the strongbox may have contained, the scroll was its true prize, and returning it might just salvage his career from its icy slide. Perhaps he could even use it to bargain with Governor Rufius for clemency.

"Good work, little soldier." Valerius tucked the scroll into his tunic and gave Remo's shoulder a squeeze.

After climbing back to the dark junction between the hidden trail and the main path, Valerius mussed Remo's hair and pointed up the mountain. "Time for dinner," he said. "You better go now."

"Remo come?"

"With me?" Valerius warmed to lad's wide smile and feigned innocence. He knelt down and gave the boy a parting hug.

Thirty-three
XXXIII

For the first time since coming to Hispania, Festus Rufius sensed his bright future stretching out before him. He had a plan that was elegant and more deadly than his estranged wife back in Rome. He would no longer suffer the whispering of fools in the forum or the caprices of the haughty heiress his father had deemed marriage-worth. Rufius' frigid wife had recently frozen his credit, but before she could reach across the Mediterranean to seize his dwindling assets, he would seize the reins of the empire and saddle the howling winds of history.

Festus Rufius felt that his time had come; time to step up onto the pedestal and double down on destiny.

"Sub-centurion Habeas Novus is waiting to see you, Excellency." Carbo crawled through the hole in the bedroom wall and pulled the sheets off the bed before his daydreaming master could roll over. He helped Rufius into a freshly starched toga and escorted him through the confusing corridors to the atrium.

Novus stood rigid, his leather armor polished and firm as if carved from walnut. His black hair was freshly oiled, his short sword polished.

"Acting Centurion Novus." Rufius saluted, flattering the young officer with the hint of promotion. He filled a glass with wine, but offered none to his guest. "Did you bring back the oak barrels?"

"Mission accomplished, sir. The cohort performed brilliantly. They fought heroically in the face of barbarism."

Rufius draped himself authoritatively across an uncomfortable sofa while Novus stood at attention and lied at length. As the saga spun, Rufius' focus drifted to yet another tasteless new fresco where a naked Hadrian, cast as Ulysses, was strangling a three-headed Hydra. The monster's faces looked like Rufius, his father, and his dead brother.

"... then we were ambushed by a band of bloodthirsty rebels."

"Dreadful." Rufius turned his gaze away from the foreboding fresco, stood up, and gave Novus a playful wink. "I hope you taught them a permanent lesson."

"The rebels fled before we could respond in full." Novus curled his toes and avoided eye contact as Rufius hovered closer. "They took refuge among the local townspeople."

"Cowards!" Rufius paced a tight circle around the stiff soldier. "Imagine using civilians as a human shield. Who could place such little value on human life?"

Novus gave a shallow nod. "We had no choice but to go in after them."

"You're cleverer than Mercury." Rufius ran a hand over the young man's solid shoulder and gave his bicep a squeeze. "Hard as an apple."

The veins along Novus' neck tightened. "After liberating the village, the thankful townspeople fêted us with almost unbearable delicacies and offered us three barrels of wine to show their gratitude."

"I look forward to sampling it." Rufius settled back into his sofa without taking his eyes off Novus.

"Under the circumstances, sir, I let the troops have a bit to drink and, well, my orders were to bring you the empty barrels, so I thought ..."

"You did the right thing, young Novus. All men deserve their little pleasures, don't you think?"

Carbo emerged from a shadow to refill Rufius' goblet, pilfer another handful of almonds, and disappear like vapor.

Rufius drank slowly and listened to Novus contradict Winus Minem's recent intelligence report and two letters of protest from the Governor of Gaul. The ambitious young officer was clearly unaware that Hadrian himself had already toured the sacked village and was now seeking justice and reparations. By all accounts except Novus', the cohort had disgraced the very notion of warfare. They had run amuck and violated every common sense *modus* for covering their tracks. Hadrian's initial response to the shameful siege was just a foretaste of the punishment to come.

The more Rufius listened to Novus' twisted yarn, the more of himself he saw in the ambitious young officer. It was a pity that such a strapping specimen might need to be sacrificed for the greater good of saving the empire.

".... in summary, Excellency," Novus continued, "*Scipio IV Hispania* returns to your service in triumph. We await your further orders, sir."

"Novus, Novus, my dear, loyal Novus." Rufius let his words linger for a few intimidating seconds and the let his face sag into an avuncular smile. "You surely would have been destined for greatness under different circumstances."

"Would have been, sir?"

Rufius picked at a cluster of imported figs, and found none to his liking. "How could you have known that one of my rivals, the Governor of Gaul, has whispered some very poisonous allegations into the ear of our beloved emperor? May superior wisdom triumph over mendacity."

"May the Emperor never be swayed by your enemies, Excellency."

"*Our* enemies, Novus. *Rome's* enemies." Rufius stared at the enterprising soldier as if looking into a mirror that rendered people younger, slimmer, and less worldly. He thought it a shame to lose such a devious and deadly young man, but the empire suffered no shortage of scorpions. Rufius drew a troubled breath, tightened the folds of his face into earnest outrage, and rose from the sofa. "Alas, it appears that our confused emperor, may his wall never crumble, is under the illusion that your heroic peacekeeping efforts were actually an unforgivable act of war."

Novus stood rigid as wood and betrayed no emotion. "Is this the thanks we get?"

"My reaction exactly. It's surprising, really. One would expect a living God to be wise and infallible." Rufius whispered up into Novus' ear and reached down to squeeze the hilt of his sword. "Between ourselves, Novus, there's increasing concern at the very highest levels that Hadrian, may he not encounter any danger when he arrives here tomorrow, has been behaving, well, oddly."

"Oddly, sir?" Novus' gaze remained fixed. "It's disconcerting when a superior behaves oddly."

"Ruthless, restless, in constant motion for no good reason—Hadrian's all but abandoned Rome." Rufius stepped back and looked Novus up and down; the young warrior was like a Greek statue come to life. "One day he orders imaginary walls built across Britannia, next he doubles his poor citizens' taxes. He's unpredictable, more capricious with each passing moment. Think about it, Novus. To punish an entire cohort for a minor misunderstanding between neighbors; irrational, isn't it?"

"Now that you mention it—"

"Ever wondered why so many of our finest soldiers are being skewered against moldy trees in Germania? Why do you think our proudest, most able-bodied fighters have been reduced to building a slave's wall across Britannia? Disgraceful, isn't it?"

"Indeed, sir. As a soldier, of course, I never—"

"Of course, Novus, but as a promising officer, you need to look at the bigger picture. How many more capable young military leaders like you will be sacrificed on the altar of Hadrian's hubris? Oh, the price we pay to appease this imperial charade!"

Rufius dropped back down onto the cushions, picked at a white fig, and feigned exhaustion. "I'm so sorry it's come to this. Maybe someday someone will step up and deliver us from this menace." He waved a hand to dismiss the young officer. "You may go, Novus. Try to enjoy your last day among the living."

Novus remained fixed in place, barely batting an eye. "Excuse me, sir. Did you say, 'tomorrow?' Our beloved emperor, may his legions linger, will arrive here tomorrow?"

"I hear he's as crazy as Caligula, so confident of his divinity that he isn't even traveling with bodyguards." Rufius arched his stiff back over a rigid cushion but could not get a single vertebra to crack. "I shouldn't tell you this, and please don't mention it to your troops, but Hadrian wants to make a brutal example out of the surviving *Scipio* boys. His messengers keep asking if the arena will be ready. Such a waste."

A fly landed on Novus' nose, but he did not twitch. "It can't be allowed, sir."

"Alas, no, but what can we do? We're only human and, for the moment, he's immortal. I'm hoping that you and the lads can play a small, redeeming role in welcoming Lord Hadrian before you're all thrown to the lions."

"What kind of 'role,' sir?"

"In the absence of an imperial honor guard, I'm assigning you to welcome the Emperor, may his passage be peaceful. When his boat arrives, you're to make his descent down the gangplank quick and memorable."

"Memorable?"

"Indeed." Rufius peeled a fig and tried to read Novus' inscrutable posture. The young soldier seemed to be taking the bait, but one never knew with such schemers. Rufius tossed the fruit aside, stood up, and put a fat hand on Novus' hard shoulder. "Remember one thing, Novus. Never forget this ..."

"Sir?"

"Cursed are the meek, Novus. *Fortes fortuna iuvat.* Remember that, won't you? Fortune favors the brave."

Thirty-four
XXXIV

After weaving through a mountain valley where large, porous boulders appeared to have been strewn about by the gods, Marcus Valerius left the smell of pine, hemlock, and deception behind. He trekked across a seemingly endless expanse of muddy wheat fields and when he looked back at the dim, distant outline of the Pyrenees, he was relieved to see that no vultures, human or avian, had followed.

The dull winter light was fading and he was unsure of his bearing. Valerius had hoped to be in Tarraco instead of lost in the hinterlands. Convinced that the scroll with the official red seal and the unintelligible markings might be his ticket home, he would keep it close to his chest until he could speak to Governor Rufius. His plan was to exchange the governor's scroll for an honorable discharge, but the Fates who toyed with Hispania seemed to specialize in setbacks.

Twilight traced a vague gray line across the water-logged fields of winter wheat behind him. He had not seen another soul, living or dead, all day. The few shepherd shacks and meager dwellings he had encountered along the way had all been empty. Just before nightfall, a thin ribbon of smoke from a distant dwelling offered a wisp of hope for a hot meal and a hard bed.

As he drew near a weathered shack, he heard crying and sounds of shrill commotion. He rapped on the door and, when no one answered, stuck his head inside the room where a dozen dirty, wild children were chasing each other, laughing and shouting like demons. A few filthy toddlers crawled between tables while others mucked about in a wet patch of earthen floor, happy as piglets. None looked to be more than five years old; all of them needed baths and beatings.

Though Valerius had spent a lifetime conquering barbarians, he had no mind to tame this lot. Whoever had left them alone had done so for good reason. Before he could fully withdraw from the doorway, a mud ball hit him in the side of his head. The gaggle of wild, treacherous waifs did not correspond to any omen he knew; neither did they inspire much hope for the future.

Concerned that he might have imagined the shack full of demons, Valerius trudged into the coastal foothills. He wondered if the empire had somehow collapsed while he had been knocking about in Hispania. The possibility that he had been condemned to wander, starve, and die as punishment for losing a battle, a strongbox, two donkeys, and a conscript loomed large in his mind.

In apparent confirmation, the unpaved road grew worse with every winding mile. As the hours passed, the smell of mud gave way to the faint scent of the distant sea. Long past midnight, a full moon emerged, the clouds started to clear, and the temperature dropped. Chilled, he wrapped his wet bearskin tight and walked until he came across a donkey cart with one wheel stuck in a rut.

"Help me out here, will 'ya?" the driver said with evident irritation. "I've been stuck since sundown."

Valerius put his shoulder to the wheel and the driver urged his donkey forward, but the cart would not budge.

"What have you got here," Valerius asked, "a ton of bricks?"

"Not quite a ton," the driver said. "Get it rocking a bit, will 'ya?"

Valerius threw his weight into the wagon but the wheels refused to roll. "Let's unload her a bit."

"Can't … time is money."

"Since when?"

The driver was angry, the cart was heavy, and the donkey needed no further reason to be obstinate. When the man whacked the beast with a stick, it all but sat down in the road.

"Like I said," Valerius insisted, "lighten the load."

"Can't … I'm in a hurry."

"But you're stuck."

Valerius had seen it before: people so worked up over their problems that they made them worse. He foraged in the chaparral and used his *gladius* to uproot a thick shrub, which he stuffed under the entrenched wheel. The branches and bramble provided just enough bite to dislodge the cart once the donkey chose to cooperate. When the cart was free, Valerius asked for a ride over the hill, but the driver was reluctant to return the favor.

"I gotta get these stones to the coast before they go worthless," he said. "Prices are falling. Tomorrow or the next day these stones won't be worth a rat's tail."

Valerius tried to fathom the driver whose head seemed to be full of the same stones he was hauling. "Stones don't go bad."

"These will. They'll rot like old fruit."

"If you say—"

"I do! SlavePower is paying top coin for —"

"*SlavePower?*" Valerius reached back and pulled a stone from the cart. It hardly weighed anything. "This isn't road stone, it's porous. I could crush this with my bare hands."

"That's how I keep my costs down."

The donkey snorted, nodded its head, and stopped to examine the full moon reflected in a puddle. The driver whipped the donkey, but the beast was unmoved by the encouragement.

"Deep enough to break an axle," Valerius said after probing the pothole.

Reluctantly, the driver let Valerius fill the hole with a few precious road stones and guide the donkey over the obstacle. Once beyond the minor hazard, he insisted that Valerius recover the pavers.

Valerius tossed the better half of a broken stone back into the wagon.

"Careful with the merchandise!" the man warned. "Get in the cart before you break something else."

Valerius mounted and sat beside the flustered driver.

"The coast is just over the ridge." The man gestured towards a faint glow now seeping over the hillcrest. "We'll make up for lost time on the way down."

And so they did. Valerius held on to his seat as the cart chased the terrified donkey down the scalloped road. They careened around the tight curves and shot down the switchbacks. As they rounded a final escarpment, the first fingers of sunlight burned the fog off the coastline and revealed the blue-green Mediterranean beyond.

The donkey's pace and panic did not subside until the cart stopped just short of a pile of wagons littering the intersection with the *Via Augusta*. A night's worth of traffic had accumulated into a slag heap of iron, wood, and stone. The sea breeze set a wheel spinning on the broken axle of an overturned cart.

Valerius inspected the wrecked rigs. Some were from the eastern side of the province, a few bore markings from as far away as Northern Gaul. Mud, haste, and coastal fog had been a recipe for disaster.

Indifferent to the damage, teams of workers supervised by men wearing orange and blue 'SlavePower" tunics salvaged stones from the detritus. A supervisor whose nametag read "Palo" wagged his finger and approached Valerius with grave authority.

"Two bronze a day is what we're paying, Grandfather."

"Two bronze for what?" Valerius noticed a dead driver under the wreckage and remembered that the fallen soldiers of *Scipio IV Hispania* had not been properly ushered into the afterlife either. The province would soon be crawling with unsettled spirits. "You should—"

"You should get busy, or get moving," Palo interrupted. His sharp overbite and angled eyebrows hovered in a cuneiform of contempt. "I've no time for distractions."

Valerius grabbed the supervisor's boney shoulder and spun him around. "That body needs to be cremated before—"

"Later." Palo shook free of the centurion's grip. "The stones are more important."

"Why?"

"Because they're imported. Now make yourself useful or shove off!" Palo stormed away towards a reckless crew of freedmen tossing stones into a barrow.

Valerius went in the other direction. He approached the work line to get a better sense of what the commotion was all about. Hundreds of laborers were linked in a human chain, passing the salvaged stones southward like a bucket brigade fighting a distant fire.

"Who needs all these paving stones?" Valerius asked an old man hobbling along with an armful of paving stones.

"The emperor," the man said with breathless reverence. He dumped the stones on a pile and limped away to find more. "The emperor is coming."

The notion was too preposterous to pursue. "Where are these stones going?" Valerius asked a thin young woman near the end of the work line. Her tunic was nothing more than a patchwork of rags.

"Tarraco." An incoming stone hit the ground and splattered her with mud. "Uf!" she said, scowling back at Valerius.

"Hey, Grandpa!" Palo the supervisor returned with a vengeance. "Stop disturbing the workers or I'll have you arrested!"

Too tired to take offense, Valerius retreated south towards Tarraco, never far from the long line of people shuttling stones to the capital. The crowd kept their spirits high with a popular song about a pig and a magistrate, punctuated by an occasional shout when a stone dropped on somebody's exposed toe. Children darted underfoot carrying pitchers of water, doling out quick mouthfuls of bread, and picking up fallen stones to reinsert in gaps along the line. The snaking mob of slaves and underpaid freedmen was quick to adjust pace and fill the holes when workers collapsed from exhaustion.

The human chain's intensity increased as Valerius neared Tarraco. Stones flew by faster and faster until a joyful rumble descended from the far north. Like rolling thunder, the roar of excitement clamored towards the point where Valerius stood.

"Last stone!" The shouting buzzed towards him. "Here comes the last stone!"

As the flat piece of substandard pumice raced towards Tarraco, a human wave rippled behind it like a cracking whip. After passing the final stone down the line, people raised their arms in the air and joined in the raucous cheering and congratulations.

Valerius watched slack-jawed as the commoners moved with a sense of urgency he never thought possible in Hispania. To impress their emperor, the simple subjects of Hispania had just whipped themselves into a stone slinging chain that had stretched for miles across the province. Why did road repairs typically take months? A legion of Spaniards could pave the empire in a week.

After ten minutes of sending victory waves back and forth, the line unzipped and dispersed. The free workers collected a handful of bronze coins from the SlavePower supervisors and headed back to their feral children and faraway homes.

When Valerius reached Tarraco's main gate, he found paving stones piled into three distinct heaps before a half-finished temple. The main road split into three segments, one winding towards the port, the other two snaking towards the Villa and the arena. Workers with wheelbarrows shuttled stones down the three paths, frantic to finish the final details.

For the first time in days, the sun chased away the clouds. The sea and sky exchanged blue reflections as if sharing a poorly-kept secret.

"Hurry, people!" called a SlavePower supervisor. "Today's the day."

Valerius stood at the junction and watched the pavement fall into place like a porous puzzle. Dust rose as citizens and slaves chipped, butted, and stomped stones into submission. There was no time for mortar.

Once the last few stones went down, freshly painted facades were hoisted and braced into place. Valerius watched dumbfounded as Tarraco's sagging storefronts smiled like society wives at the theater. After the frenzy of last-minute masquerade, the grimy docklands almost looked tidy.

"Boats spotted!"

Cries from the harbor echoed through the streets. The great moment was nigh.

Propelled towards the docks by the chanting throng, Valerius noticed a clutch of poorly disguised men loitering by a nearby storefront. He recognized a few faces from the cohort he had entrusted to Habeas Novus. Another gang of dubious impersonators appeared on rooftops. Pulling himself from the human tide, Valerius hid behind a low-hanging banner and watched the legionaries assume strategic positions along the street that wound from the waterfront to the forum. Some were dressed as artisans, others like merchants; all had suspicious bulges along their waistlines. While citizens and slaves rushed to greet their emperor, the merciless men of *Scipio IV Hispania* fanned out across town on a darker mission.

Noise rose like steam. The dockside crowd began clapping in anticipation of the godlike emperor's visit to their long-forgotten town. Their cheers drifted out to sea, blew back on the breeze, and bounced off the high wall of the governor's mansion where Festus Rufius watched over Tarraco like a greedy uncle.

Valerius resisted the power and danger of the crowd's euphoria. He needed no omens to confirm that something was wrong. The crowd could shout and sing until nightfall. They could lose their collective heads to the thrill of an imperial visit, but until told otherwise, Marcus Valerius was still a centurion, and a centurion needed to keep his wits about him. Delivering the governor's scroll would have to wait. Something bigger was at stake.

The giddy menace of a mob gone wild was nothing compared to the armed men moving among them. Valerius stiffened as more undercover soldiers slipped by him, not bothering to conceal their weapons as they hurried towards the waterfront.

The crowd swept him down towards the docks. Caked with mud, shamed by his failures, and exasperated by every breath he had taken since arriving in Hispania, Marcus Valerius pulled out of the surging crowd. Squinting uphill at the Villa, he could just discern the plump outline of Festus Rufius watching over the proceedings.

The governor had his arm around a small, animated man in a light brown toga.

Thirty-five
XXXV

Flush with the governor's flattery, Habeas Novus pushed through the crowd, using his sharp knees and elbows to persuade anyone unimpressed with his parade armor. He was winding towards the wharf when Marcus Valerius appeared alongside him.

"Centurion." Novus halted in mid-stride, looked down at the compact commander, and swallowed his surprise. "What unexpected luck. The governor told me you retired."

"Retired?" Valerius looked up at the plumed helmet that outshone Novus' true rank.

"An honorable discharge with full pension ... it was supposed to be a secret." Novus smiled but kept his teeth hidden. He clapped Valerius' hard shoulder and a few dried mud flakes fell to the pavement. "Congratulations."

Valerius brushed the dirt off his other shoulder and pretended not to notice the loosely disguised legionaries heading towards the docks. Like the others scattered throughout the town, their ill-fitting tunics barely concealed the armor and intensity rippling underneath. "So, tell me, how goes the mission?"

"Everything is under control, Centurion. You can relax and enjoy your golden years."

"Before I leave the service, I'd like to see the emperor, may his days be long."

Novus nodded and snuck a quick glance towards the Villa to where Festus Rufius watched history unfold from a safe distance. Short of asking, there was no way to tell if the old centurion was in league with the governor or still loyal to Hadrian. Novus took leave of Valerius and ducked into the crowd.

Tarraco had swollen to twice its population. The rural outskirts had turned inward, forcing the elite to rub their perfumed elbows with the poor. Many of the erstwhile workers had followed their road stones south to the town. Along the parade route, children squirmed on their parents' shoulders and waved red-trimmed banners bearing crude facsimiles of the emperor's silver eagle. Snack vendors shouted out inflated prices and quietly haggled for less. The air smelled of seawater and sausage.

"Imperial ship sighted," a man cried from the harbor watchtower.

Anticipation rumbled thicker than thunder. Caught up in the commotion, Valerius strained to see above the heads of the crowd. He was too short to see the ship, but it took little effort to locate the red plume of Novus' helmet bobbing like a brass-footed rooster above the festivities.

"An auspicious day," Valerius said, sliding into a gap next to the young legionary.

Novus was not happy to see Valerius again. He removed the conspicuous helmet, and still stood a head higher than Valerius. "The governor asked me to head up the honor guard. Frankly, between us, I think something strange is going on."

"Strange?" Valerius waved away a baby-faced boy selling unfired and overpriced Hadrian figurines. "Strange compared to what?"

The crowd pulsed with excitement as a ship with square, red-trimmed sails rounded the jetty. A bearded figure in a white toga and a purple sash appeared on the bow and waved. The vessel's square sails dropped liked crimson petals and an array of oars splashed into the water to pull the ship forward. The first vessel in Hadrian's armada lurched into the harbor, raising a plume of white spray and a tide of goodwill.

"*Avé* Hadrian!"

The din bordered on delirium. Cheers and salutations, bravos and benedictions swelled from the lowest wharves to the farthest ramparts. The most powerful man in the world, the commander-in-chief of civilization itself, had returned to his homeland.

Marcus Valerius did his best to resist the euphoria and keep his feet on the ground as he followed Sub-centurion Novus towards the dock. Even to Valerius, the emperor's presence made all of the frustrations he had weathered seem worthwhile. He inhaled deeply and tried to savor the smell of history.

But something still stank in Hispania.

Valerius nudged Novus and pointed to the approaching boat. "A historic moment, no?"

"And history rewards the bold." Novus raised an eyebrow as he repeated the governor's code words.

When Valerius nodded but said nothing, Novus loosened a flagstone with his foot, and stooped to pick it up. "Look at this shoddy work," he said, turning the broken stone in his wide hand. "The entire province has been pulverized to get Tarraco ready to receive and, let's face it, deceive the emperor, may he show us mercy."

"The same mercy you showed those villagers?"

Novus pointed towards the Villa. "The governor is up there on his balcony, smiling down on this big, fat fantasy. Why isn't he down here to greet the emperor?"

"Maybe he sent you to do his bidding."

Novus leaned forward to whisper, cupping his left hand to the centurion's ear. "I smell sardines, sir, something isn't right—"

Novus slammed the stone into the side of his head and Valerius crumpled to the ground. He kicked Valerius to verify that he was unconscious, removed his concealed *gladius,* and left his former commander to be trampled by the surging crowd.

The original plan had been for Hadrian to be killed by an irate "shopkeeper" in the streets of Tarraco. But the original plan did not include Valerius and his possible reinforcements. Novus saw that he had to change course. By taking history into his own hands, the glory would be his alone.

Novus cut through the throng like a blade through cloth. Sunlight hit his armor as if Apollo himself was on his side. He adjusted his weapons, and embellished his alibi. *After assassinating the emperor with a well-thrown knife, rogue soldier Marcus Valerius died at the hands of the enraged crowd. Second-in-command Habeas Novus, now a decorated centurion, arrived on the scene, restored order, and handed imperial power over to Governor Festus Rufius.* Unlike the warped planks underfoot, the story pieces fit together perfectly. Novus suppressed a smile and squinted out to sea where the second ship held its position near the entrance to the harbor.

Hadrian continued waving from the deck of the first ship as his oarsmen maneuvered into the docks. Barely audible above the cheering, Novus ordered his loyal guards to secure the ship's ropes to the pylons. The crowd's adoration rose skyward, loud enough to wake the gods, smothering the crash of the gangplank hitting the pulsing dock.

A red carpet with purple trim unrolled as if kicked loose from the heavens.

Habeas Novus stood poised at the foot of the gangplank, ready to salute and slaughter his supreme commander. He scanned the docks for trouble, but the commotion and confusion only aided his plan. He glanced once again towards the Villa where Governor Rufius watched from the balcony, a bit too nearsighted to see the future arrive ahead of schedule.

Far below, Marcus Valerius struggled against a sea of sandals, one of which had just walked across his chest. His right eye was swollen shut and the sound of stomping feet laid siege to his head, but still he tried to stand. Being crushed by Spaniards was not a fate he could accept. He had blasphemed and doubted, botched his last mission, and lost innocent men, but he was still a loyal legionary. He had not served Rome for twenty years only to see her ravaged by jackals.

He crawled to his knees just as a chapped hand pulled him up by the back of the tunic.

"I never trusted Novus, sir, and I didn't like the way he hit you." Gaius Severus pulled Valerius upright.

"Neither did I." Valerius leaned against Severus and took a deep breath to steady himself and restore his wounded pride. After a moment, he remembered that Severus had gone missing. The kid had never proven trustworthy, but neither did he lack valor. "How did *you* get here?"

"On horseback." Severus smiled and rubbed the small of his back. "Not the most comfortable way to travel."

Valerius used a sleeve to wipe the blood from the broken skin around his swollen eye. "What about the girl?"

"Lena?" Severus turned towards the Villa to hide his blushing face. "She found work in the governor's kitchen. Free room and board, out of harm's way."

Valerius looked down at the blood on the pavement. He held on to Severus' arm and stooped to pick up the bloodstained stone that had brought him low. Returning upright, he squinted with his one good eye and located Habeas Novus standing rigid at the base of the gangplank.

"Something's wrong," Valerius warned, but his voice was lost to the fanfare.

Two long, straight trumpets blared from the deck and four fearsome Praetorians marched down to the bottom of the ramp. Gray haired men with crimson sashes descended next. Their white togas caught the breeze like sails. The men of distinction were followed by a standard-bearer proudly raising the silver eagle.

When the emperor emerged from the ship, the crowd grew still. The sun cast golden light onto his wavy brown hair. Alone at the top of the ramp, Hadrian waved to the slaves, citizens, and freedmen of Tarraco. Majestic and alone, he walked midway down the gangplank and stopped to survey the crowd and bask in their favor.

"*Avé Imperator!*" Jubilation swelled like water behind a dam. People threw red scarves into the air and the breeze spread them like ribbons across the sky. The ecstasy echoed off the walls of the Villa and flowed back over the crowd.

"The emperor." Valerius ignored his throbbing skull. He clutched the stone and squeezed it hard to draw down the pain as he pulled ahead of Severus. "Hadrian's in danger."

With his good eye Valerius could see the undercover *Scipio* men moving towards Hadrian's security guards. Valerius cursed himself for not having seen the threat earlier. Now he was too late and too far away to attract Hadrian's attention. Realizing that a shout would go unheard in the cacophony, he forged onward, powering through the pain and the people, damning the overwhelming odds. He reached for his *gladius*, but discovered it was missing.

"*Avé!*" the crowd around him shouted. "Hail Caesar!"

Valerius saw Novus raise one hand to salute and the other to strike. He drew a sharp breath and hurled the stone. Seen through his squinting eye, the broken piece of pavement seemed to fly forever, spinning along a slight arc until smashing squarely into the back of Novus' neck.

Novus lurched forward and dropped Valerius' blade. Dazed by the blow, he pulled off his helmet and turned to find the perpetrator.

"Stop him!" Valerius yelled, but his words hung listless in the air. He shoved spectators aside, but time itself seemed to hold him back.

Above it all, Hadrian appeared unaware of the danger. When he raised his arms skyward in a wide gesture of benediction, the folds of his toga unfurled like great white wings.

While Hadrian hovered like a seabird, Novus reared and charged up the ramp like an angry stallion. At the last possible instant, Hadrian sidestepped the threat and planted a sharp elbow in the back of Novus' neck.

The crowd cheered as the attacker fell and sprawled face forward on the gangplank.

"*Ave!* Hadrian the Warrior!" Tarraco cheered in unison at the unexpected spectacle of an emperor who moved like a gladiator. Fighting broke out between the soldiers and irregulars. The crowd surged to catch a glimpse of the action on the docks. Parents lifted their children above the sea of shoulders to watch the soldiers fight. The greedy sausage vendors quelled their commerce to watch the battle unfold. Only the pickpockets continued to ply their trade.

From his vantage point on the wharf, Gaius Severus had seen Novus rush the white-winged emperor. Feeling the weight of his terrible oath to kill Hadrian, Severus fumbled for his knife, clenched his teeth, and steeled his nerves. Though his palms were wet as clams, he was determined to fulfill the promise he had made to his brother. His ancient tribe longed to be free, and he had been chosen as their angel of deliverance.

"With praises of God and a two-edged sword in hand to execute vengeance upon the heathen ..." Severus remembered a passage from a psalm of

David. David, a poor nobody like Severus himself, had defeated a giant. Now that his moment had come, Gaius Severus could feel David's spirit surging through his veins. Today in Tarraco, another Goliath would fall.

Severus fixed his sights on the emperor. While Novus struggled to his feet, Hadrian smiled and waved from the gangplank as if floating on a white cloud of pure love. The emperor walked halfway down the ramp until a sudden clash of swords, shields, and soldiers below drew his attention. At that moment, the *Scipio* men smashed into Hadrian's outnumbered dockside security contingent.

Severus was pushing to reach the gangplank when a stout, pig-faced fellow shoved him from behind. Unable to pass in front of Gaius Severus or see over his head, the man shoved the young conscript out of the way, accidently pushing him off the edge of the wharf.

Severus fell ten feet into the dark water. Nearly paralyzed by the sudden cold, he struggled against the weight of his soaked tunic and the harbor surge.

The crowd filled the hole where Severus had been standing a second earlier, erasing any evidence of his presence.

"Help me!" Severus shouted from sea level. His throat burned with seawater and bile. "Drop me a rope!"

When no one responded, he wriggled out of his waterlogged sash and wrapped it around the pylon. He spat out a lung full of seawater and cursed the wet hands of death. Had the gods discovered his plan to kill one of their own? He looked up at the brushstroke of sky above him but there was no reason to expect help from his own God. After littering the centuries with prophets and miracles, Jehovah had long since gone missing.

If God and the Fates had abandoned him, he vowed to defy them both. He had not cheated death's many disguises to dissipate in the sea like gull waste. He hugged the pylon and used the sash to pull himself up towards the indifferent crowd.

Not far from where Severus struggled, Marcus Valerius shoved past the brawling guards and legionaries. He picked up his fallen *gladius* but it appeared no match for Novus' sword. Valerius ran past the emperor, hoping to close in before Novus recovered his footing.

The crowd wagered that youth, size, and hubris were a lethal combination and the odds makers gave Novus the advantage. When Novus lunged, Valerius sidestepped the sword and knocked it aside. Surprisingly agile in his parade armor, Novus responded with a kick that sent Valerius to his knees.

"It's time to make history, Hadrian," Novus snarled. His drawn dagger was pointed unequivocally at the emperor's heart.

Novus charged but Valerius grabbed his ankle. The onlookers erupted into feral cheers when he twisted, fell, and planted a knee into Valerius' chest.

The pig-faced man who had shoved Severus into the water began taking bets. "Two-to-one on the centurion," he shouted. "Easy money here!"

"Too low," said a sausage vendor, sizing up the contenders. "The old geezer doesn't stand a chance."

"Even odds on the emperor," another odds maker barked. "He's a fighter! Place your bets, friends!"

Up the ramp, Novus waved his sword and glowered over Valerius. "You'll die for this, you stagnant old piss pot!"

Valerius waited until the last possible second and narrowly twisted out from under the sword thrust. Infuriated, Novus cursed and slashed but Valerius rolled and sprang to his feet. The older man ducked, dodged, and then slapped Novus into a headlock from behind.

Novus bent a knee and flipped Valerius over his shoulder, but the centurion held fast. Armor clattering, both men rolled together down the gangplank.

"Attack!" Novus shouted, but no reinforcements arrived. He squirmed but could not break free of the headlock.

Seeing their leader struggle, Novus' dockside loyalists fled. They had overwhelmed the first few Praetorians but had no stomach for a possible shipload. The odds maker, pockets jingling with bets placed against Valerius, disappeared in the soldiers' wake.

Alone below the fray, Gaius Severus gasped for life. He wrapped his aching legs around the pylon and held his breath during the surges. He inched upward during the lulls by grappling with his knife and digging his fingernails into the wet timber. With every painstaking bit of progress he grew colder, weaker and more repentant. The dock did not appear to be getting closer until a familiar face appeared at its edge.

Lena extended her hand as far as she could without tumbling into the water. She shouted encouragement, but her words were lost in the churn.

Coughing up seawater, exhausted but determined, Severus struggled towards her. If he was fated to drown, he vowed that it would be in her embrace. When a lock of her long, loose brown hair dropped down and brushed his forehead, he felt Neptune's grip loosen.

She pulled the scruff of his wet tunic and helped him clamber onto the dock. Severus rolled onto his back and gasped for air. Lena fell upon him with a kiss as wet as the sea she had just pulled him from.

"Bad time for swimming." Lena pulled Severus to his feet and pointed towards the gangplank where Marcus Valerius and Habeas Novus were still locked in combat. Hadrian watched from above, apparently amused by the struggle.

Severus remembered his sworn duty to behead the imperial snake. He had taken an oath in the names of Abraham, Isaac, and Jacob but when he looked at Lena, the patriarchs seemed very far away.

They pushed towards the gangplank and Severus nearly tripped over a fallen *Scipio* irregular. Only a few seconds remained before the future of his tribe would slip out of reach, maybe forever. He grabbed the dead man's sword. Heart pounding, he blinked hard to clear his watery vision, and get a fix on Hadrian. Severus summoned his resolve, but could find no vengeance in his veins. He tried to believe himself an instrument of God's will, but came up lacking.

The emperor stood and smiled like a bearded statue. His tribe's mortal enemy was in reach but all Severus could see was that Marcus Valerius was in trouble. Severus tried to convince himself that the cause was just. *Justice, justice, shalt thou pursue*—were these not God's very words? But what kind of vexed God couldn't see the difference between justice and vengeance? A lifetime of doubt welled in his stomach. How would killing Hadrian make things better? Had swords ever resolved anything?

Severus looked back at Lena and something stronger than vengeance surged through him. He turned away from her green-eyed gaze and leapt onto the gangplank. Ignoring Hadrian, Severus joined the fray on the off-chance his unsubstantial weight might tip the scales against Habeas Novus.

The crowd cheered at the prospect of a renewed battle and booed when Praetorian Guardsmen ran down the ramp to end the fighting. Most of the elite soldiers surrounded Hadrian while others rushed to where Severus and Valerius had just subdued Habeas Novus.

Bloodied but not defeated, Valerius stood above Novus, his sword wedged against the assailant's jugular.

"Traitor!" Novus shouted. "Son of a jackal!"

"I never knew my father," Valerius said, "but I know myself and I'm no traitor." He resisted the crowd shouting for him to kill Novus on the spot. Justice was the emperor's prerogative, though Valerius was ready to deliver the sentence if Hadrian willed it.

Four guardsmen bound Novus' wrists and ankles and, after lodging a few solid kicks, dragged him aside.

As the emperor approached, Valerius stole a quick glimpse at what he feared might be blinding divinity. Hadrian looked familiar, almost common, nothing like the bearded face on the gold coin. His brown hair did not glow like the sun; his eyes were not those of an eagle. If Hadrian was a god he did not flaunt it. There was something provisional, all too human about him.

Marcus Valerius bowed before the emperor he had almost failed. Trembling from exhaustion, he felt more shame than awe. He could never explain his negligence, filth, and incompetence to the most powerful man on earth.

"Ho, Valerius," a familiar voice whispered. "Close call, no?"

Valerius looked up in surprise to see his old comrade, Fidelis Magnus disguised as Hadrian. The snail scoffing security guard grinned from behind a false beard.

"Magnus?" Valerius stuttered. "I thought you were … I mean … the last time I saw you, you were eating snails."

Magnus waved away the honor guard. He winked his lazy eye and turned out the purple collar of his toga just enough to reveal a small patch bearing the emperor's insignia. "Imperial Security Forces," he said. "I've been working this corridor for a year in advance of the royal visit."

"ISF?" Valerius was incredulous. "You cockeyed bastard! You're with ISF?"

"You don't need to shout, old crow," Magnus looked up and stiffened like a champion before the adoring crowd. "These brutes will tear us limb-from-limb if they find out I'm a fraud."

Magnus pointed down the ramp to where Novus lay bound and defeated. "Slap him into leg irons," he ordered. "When we get out to sea, throw him in the drink."

The guards dragged Novus up the gangplank and Magnus raised a small dust cloud by slapping Valerius on the back. "Come on, old friend. Let's get you cleaned up."

Fidelis Magnus turned and waved goodbye to the cheering crowd. Tarraco returned the gesture, waving like a thousand birds taking flight.

Pointing towards the Villa, Magnus spoke to one of the remaining Praetorians. "Get up there and arrest Winus Minem, the governor's little advisor. Charge him with the murder of Governor Biberious, but be careful. Don't let his tiny size and big words fool you. He's a viper."

"A viper killed Biberious?" Severus asked.

"Maybe not, but I'll wager two-to-one he leads us down the right hole." Magnus looked Severus up and down and then turned to Valerius. "I need to leave a clever person behind to keep an eye on this rat house. Know any smart lads who can keep a secret or two?"

"Severus fits the bill." Valerius nodded in the conscript's direction and offered the closest thing to approval left in his depleted arsenal. He noticed that Lena had squeezed through the throng to take his former conscript's hand in hers. There was no denying how right they looked together, even if the innkeeper's daughter was a half-head taller and half again as sneaky. "A bit too smart for his own good, but he can keep a secret."

"Sorry I was such a lousy soldier," Severus said

"Lousy?" Valerius laughed, and clasped his former conscript's shoulder with what bordered on affection. "You saved my life three times in two weeks," he said. "Gods be with you, Gaius Severus, whoever you are."

"May the Lord bless you and keep you, too, Centurion."

Valerius considered the odd benediction until the crowd's shouting drew his attention towards the Villa.

Vindex now loomed large on the balcony, towering behind Festus Rufius and the visibly agitated Winus Minem. To the townspeople's delight, Vindex grabbed Minem and dangled him by the ankles over the edge of the balcony. A shower of scrolls fell from Minem's toga and floated like loose feathers above the delighted crowd.

While the crowd was distracted by the spectacle on high, Valerius noticed the second vessel hesitating at the entrance to the harbor.

"Hadrian's on the other ship?"

"Of course." Magnus gave a regal salute to the assembled people of Tarraco and led Valerius up the ramp. "I could quite get used to this." He smiled and turning once more to wave at the crowd. "Nobility suits me, don't you think?"

A distinguished old man, a gray eminence in a senator's toga emerged at the top of the gangplank. Senator Rufius was the flaccid, spitting image of his son. "Excellent work! You ISF boys really rake up the riff-raff." The senator looked along the dock. "Speaking of which, where's my idiot son, Festus?"

Magnus pointed towards the balcony to where Vindex still dangled Minem like a fishwife's laundry and Festus Rufius waved sheepishly to his father.

"Keeping above the fray, I see." The senator scowled up at his son and then looked directly at Marcus Valerius. "Are you the bumbler who lost my son's strongbox?"

Valerius lowered his head and produced the sealed scroll from inside his tunic. "With all due respect, Senator—"

"Good work, soldier." Senator Rufius took the scroll and rolled it between his short thumb and stubby fingers. After verifying that the document had not been opened, he looked up at his son and brandished the scroll accusingly. "If this forgery were a stick, I'd beat him with it."

With exaggeration worthy of a Greek drama, he tore the papyrus to pieces, and threw them in the water. Turning to Magnus, the tired patrician said, "The emperor, may he not learn of any irregularities here, is in a hurry to reach Cadiz."

Magnus took the cue. "I'm sure your son will understand the change in plan." He turned to a nearby soldier who had just rolled up the carpet. "Signal the main ship to change course. We're heading south immediately."

Before the senator disappeared into the boat, Magnus reached out and tapped his soft shoulder. "Centurion Marcus Valerius did a bit more today than just save the emperor, may he favor Rome's unsung heroes."

The senator turned to Valerius and nodded in grim approval. "I had hoped my son would avoid trouble out here in the provinces, but I'm afraid he'd cause a panic in paradise. How can I thank you for keeping his name, and mine, out of the dirt?"

Valerius glanced down at his filthy boots and then looked directly into the politician's face. "Senator, I've served Rome faithfully for twenty years. I've seen triumph and I've seen tragedy, but I've never wavered in my loyalty." Valerius hesitated and then forged onward. "I ask you, sir, does Rome still honor those who have honored the empire?"

"She does."

Marcus Valerius stiffened and held the senator's gaze. "Then all that this loyal centurion requests is the pension I've earned, sir, nothing more."

"Granted, General."

"Centurion, sir."

The senator's smile set his wrinkles rolling. "It's General, now, General Marcus Valerius. You'll find that generals have much better pensions than centurions, including use of the ship's bathing facilities, which you're in sorry need of, son."

The senator looked over the tarted-up town of Tarraco. Shading his eyes with a fat hand, he glanced towards the Villa's now empty balconies. "Looks like Festus did a reasonable job getting this dump into shape," he said. "But you can't keep a toga on a tomcat. I'm sure I'll see the bill soon enough."

Dockhands untied the ropes, soldiers raised the gangplank, and the ship cast off. After clearing the jetty, the main sail unfurled and the eagle crest caught the wind.

Tarraco waved farewell to the emperor.

Moments later, Fidelis Magnus, now wearing a simple brown toga, came out on deck. He stood beside his old comrade, drew a deep breath, and exhaled with evident satisfaction.

"A document?" Valerius asked. "Is that all I was defending?"

"And a few shiny stones to keep it from blowing away," Magnus said. "That scroll the senator just shredded was a fake will. Falsified evidence in Trajan's forged hand. It 'proved' that Hadrian, may he never hear of this, usurped the throne. Festus Rufius and his brother hoped it would pave their path to power."

General Marcus Valerius drew a deep, satisfied breath knowing that soon the lawless province and its conniving inhabitants would be half a world away. He stood in silence and watched the coastline recede. The next rain would restore Tarraco to its original squalor, but already the town's false facades were sagging like a pig in a toga.

Acknowledgements

My deep thanks and apologies to the many friends, agents, publishers, and loved ones who slogged through early drafts of this opus and offered helpful critiques, encouragement, and well-deserved whacks upside my head.

Milles mercies, endless love and gratitude to my wife, Ouided, for encouraging this project and to my sons Neil and Ryan for becoming such fine young men.

Breinigsville, PA USA
11 May 2010

237793BV00001B/1/P